MALORY

THE ROUND TABLE AND THE HOLY GRAIL

MS. Bibl. Nat. Fr. 116

MALORY

BY

EUGÈNE VINAVER

OXFORD
AT THE CLARENDON PRESS

Oxford University Press, Ely House, London W. 1

GLASGOW NEW YORK TORONTO MELBOURNE WELLINGTON

CAPE TOWN SALISBURY IBADAN NAIROBI DAR ES SALAAM LUSAKA ADDIS ABABA

BOMBAY CALCUTTA MADRAS KARACHI LAHORE DACCA

KUALA LUMPUR SINGAPORE HONG KONG TOKYO

12/1982

FIRST PUBLISHED 1929
REPRINTED LITHOGRAPHICALLY IN GREAT BRITAIN
(WITH A NEW PREFACE)
AT THE UNIVERSITY PRESS, OXFORD
BY VIVIAN RIDLER
PRINTER TO THE UNIVERSITY
1970

TO
THE MEMORY OF
MY FATHER

PREFACE TO THE
1970 IMPRESSION

I HAVE long been reluctant to let this book be reprinted in the form in which it first appeared; partly
because it was based upon a text of Malory's works—
Caxton's edition of 1485—which has now lost the stamp
of authority it once had, and partly because the principal
aim I then pursued in studying Malory no longer seems
to me to be significant or even valid. But the interest in
Malory and in the Arthurian tradition generally has grown
so much in recent years at all levels of specialization that
there now seems to be a case for making even a book published forty years ago available once more. This is what
the Delegates of the Oxford University Press have asked
me to do, and the only way to do it short of rewriting
most of the book is to refrain from altering any of the
things with which I no longer agree. Presented in this
way, with a bibliography of critical writings on Malory
numbering less than twenty items, the work will, it is
hoped, illustrate the nature and scope of Malory studies
in the year 1929 and the radical change in their orienta-
tion which has taken place since then.[1]

The change came in the wake of two separate events.
The first was the discovery in 1934 by W. F. Oakeshott
of a manuscript of Malory's romances in the Fellows'
Library at Winchester College; the second, the realization
that literary history had other—and possibly better—things
to do than try to reach the author through his work. But
for the second event the significance of the first might well
have eluded us; and it is indeed fortunate that Oakeshott's

---

[1] The corresponding list in my second edition of *The Works of Sir
Thomas Malory* (Oxford, 1967) contains 177 items. The Introduction and
the Commentary which accompany the text in that edition (pp. xix–xcix
and 1261–1664) express more fully than anything else I have so far written
my present views on Malory and some of the related problems of medieval
literary history.

epoch-making encounter with a fifteenth-century Arthurian manuscript at Winchester College occurred just then—
at a time when some of us were ready to understand the
message and benefit by the implications of the discovery.

We used to think that what the critic had to do was to
discover the thoughts, the attitudes, and the character of
the man behind his writings. In the medieval field the
illusion that such a thing was both possible and fundamental to the interpretation of the work was fostered partly by
our inadequate knowledge of the material and partly by
our misunderstanding of the complexities of the creative
process itself. Hence the confident description of Malory
the man and the writer, of his outlook and his attitude of
mind, given in the three central chapters of this book,
those entitled *Narrative Technique*, *Romance and Reality*,
and *Camelot and Corbenic*: a description based upon the
notion that anything borrowed from a source is expend-
able and should in fact be subtracted from the work in any
attempt to assess its originality and discover its meaning.
Caxton says in his Preface to *Le Morte Darthur* that
Malory borrowed his material from 'certain books of
French', and we knew what these French books were:
they were mostly thirteenth-century French Arthurian
prose romances, the most voluminous and forbidding-
looking ever written. All our training had convinced us
that these romances were simply a collection of disjointed
tales, interesting because of the themes they contained,
but artistically non-existent. Montaigne in a famous passage of his essay on education went so far as to describe
them—the translation is Florio's—as 'time-consuming
and wit-besotting trash'. And it followed logically from
this view that if Malory succeeded as he did in prolonging
the life of the Arthurian legend, it was because he made
this vast body of incongruous tales into one artistic whole,
a single unified epic, the 'noble and joyous book entitled
Le Morte Darthur'.

Like everybody else I firmly believed this to be the case
and looked upon Malory as an author who made a great
book out of a worthless conglomeration of stories. Since

the discovery of the Winchester manuscript, however, we have all had to get used to the disturbing notion that this was not what he really did. We have had to accept the fact that instead of making a variety of heterogeneous tales into one tale, he broke up whatever source material he had into smaller units, divided them from one another and inserted endings to mark off each one. The obvious inference from this was that there must have been something in his models that invited this kind of treatment—some structure to break up, some themes to split, some threads to cut. Any indication of a deliberate loosening of narrative texture could only mean that the texture was there, firm and closely knit. And so a new perspective opened, revealing the entire development of medieval fiction, and with it a new field of inquiry. It became clear that whatever Malory had found in his 'French books' was not 'chaos' as we once believed, but a design of great complexity, characterized at one and the same time by a vast proliferation of themes and a complete cohesion of parts. And it was also clear that this design was not something extraneous to Malory's endeavour as an artist; that what was needed for an understanding of his work was an appreciation of what happened to it within the framework of a developing and changing literary form—a process as fascinating to watch as the growth of any living thing. Malory the man, as my earlier investigation seemed to show, may have 'disliked' certain things about his models—their structural intricacies, their frequent insistence on the supernatural, their strictly doctrinal treatment of the Grail theme; but Malory the author of the only living Arthurian romances could not have been entirely unreceptive to those things—to echoes of earlier and anticipations of later events, so characteristic of the French 'cyclic' technique, to a certain measure of the marvellous, to a sense of the divine mysteries breaking in upon the worldly life of Arthur's knights; and whatever still survives of all this in the English adaptation has to be accepted not as something separable from Malory's own design, but as part of a new structure which he built out of the old.

An intuitive apprehension of this essential fact seems to lie behind C. S. Lewis's remark that Malory's book is like a cathedral, but that 'here, as you could not do in a real cathedral, you can always strip [your] favourite work of later accretions without pulling the whole thing down. [. . .] The whole might have been designed by one man [. . .]. But that is not what happened. Though every part of it was made by a man, the whole has rather grown than been made. Such things have a kind of existence that is almost midway between the works of art and those of nature.' I would still maintain that what we have in Malory is a work of art, not of nature, simply because, as C. S. Lewis himself said in another connection, it is in art and in art alone that dry bones can live again. The 'dry bones' of Arthurian romance do not live today in any other work in spite of many attempts by writers of all nations and all ages to revive them. And the reason is surely to be found in the unique impact of one type of imagination upon another, in the kind of re-creation that, of all Arthurian writers of the modern age, Malory alone was able to accomplish— a re-creation that to all intents and purposes is synonymous with creation.

An exact reproduction of my 1929 *Malory* might well in these circumstances serve as a useful reminder of the distance we have travelled in less than half a century, and it would have defeated the purpose of such a reproduction if I had tried to revise the text beyond correcting a few factual errors and clarifying the wording of some passages. Nor would it be fair to suggest that it all needed revision to the same extent. Some sections of the book call for no disclaimer on my part, least of all perhaps the chapters entitled *The Genius of Chivalry* and *Translation and Style*. And because there are certain things there which I do not disown even at this distance of time, I cannot let them appear again without acknowledging a debt of gratitude which I was unable to mention in the original Preface. Mr. Kenneth Sisam was at that time one of the officials of the Clarendon Press and in that capacity disallowed all expression of thanks for his help. The fact is, however,

that but for the constant encouragement and truly expert advice freely given to a very immature author this monograph such as it is, with all that it meant to me at the time and still means today, would never have materialized. Of those who guided my first steps in this field he was the one who taught me most, and whatever is valid in the following pages I owe in large part to his unfailing generosity in helping his fellow scholars to write better books.

E. V.

University of Wisconsin,
November 1969

PREFACE

*S*IR THOMAS MALORY'S Morte Darthur *is
famous without being well known, and Malory himself is to many a legend rather than a real person.
Imperceptibly but none the less surely he has come to be
identified with the spirit and the matter of his writings,
and has been held responsible for the entire body of the
old romantic tradition contained in his book. The
Malory with whom the present study is concerned is not
this legendary figure, but the great translator who
attempted to remodel the French Arthurian romances
of the Middle Ages in accordance with his own taste
and genius. Only with the help of his sources is it
possible to study his art and to reveal his real literary
character. I began this inquiry in my* Roman de
Tristan et Iseut dans l'œuvre de Thomas Malory
(1925) *and have now extended it to the other parts of
the* Morte Darthur *so as to introduce new problems and
widen the scope of my former conclusions. I know how
far my work falls short of completeness; I have but
endeavoured to suggest a method which may yet yield
better results.*

E. V.

*Oxford,
  April, 1929.*

CONTENTS

LIST OF ILLUSTRATIONS

Chapter One

SIR THOMAS MALORY AND HIS PRINTER

I

The 'Life and Acts' of Sir Thomas Malory

OUR knowledge of Sir Thomas Malory's authorship rests upon the modest statement at the end of his book: 'this book was ended the IX yere of the reygne of Kyng Edward the fourth by syr Thomas Maleore,[1] knyght, as Jhesu help hym for hys grete myght, as he is the servaunt of Jhesu bothe day and nyght.' These lines warrant the conclusion that he was a knight, and that he completed his work in the ninth year of Edward IV, i.e. between 4 March 1469 and 3 March 1470.

The only Sir Thomas Malory (or Malorey), knight, known to have been alive at that date is a Warwickshire gentleman of Newbold Revel (or Fenny Newbold). A consensus of opinion identifies him with the author of the *Morte Darthur*,[2] and I shall here attempt to summarize what is known about his life.[3]

The fundamental ideas underlying the *Morte Darthur* suggest that the author was of noble blood. Its tone is aristocratic throughout. The story of the 'rich blood of the Round Table' is largely based upon the distinction between noble and churl. Malory's favourite motive is that of a kitchen knave or cowherd's son who proves his noble descent by feats of prowess. Arthur, the foster-child of Ector; Gareth, the kitchen boy; and Brunor, of the 'evil shapen coat', are all examples of the same type

---

[1] On the spelling of Malory's name in the extant records, *v. infra*, pp. 115–16. It appears in the eleventh century as *Maloret*, later *Malore*, *Maleore*, *Malory*, &c. It is not unlikely that the name has its origin in the Old French verb *orer* (= to frame, to surround) and that *Maloret* was a nickname meaning 'ill framed' or 'ill set'. Cf. *Romania*, xxvii. 322.

[2] *V. infra*, pp. 115–16.

[3] The documents I have used are cited and discussed in Appendix I.

of hero representing nobility in disguise. If he succeeds
in his knightly adventures, it is not because he is indi-
vidually brave and strong, but because he is in reality a
noble. It is not he, but his lineage, which carries away the
victory. Before engaging in knightly quests, Perceval and
Agloval tell their mother that they may not dwell at home,
'for we be come of kynges blood of both partyes, and
therfor, moder, it is our kynde to haunte [1] armes and
noble dedes'.

This was also Malory's 'kind'. He belonged to an old
Warwickshire family of which the pedigree may be traced
with tolerable certainty as far back as the thirteenth century. As early as 1277 his ancestor, Simon Malory, was
lord of Draughton and Northampton.[2] In the fourteenth
century, Sir Thomas's great-grandfather, Sir Stephen
Malory, married into the family of Revels of Newbold
Revel, and acquired, in the right of his wife Margaret, the
family estate.[3] His son, Sir John Malory, was in his
county a person of consequence.[4] He had a son John,
Sir Thomas's father, who made the name of Malory still
more illustrious. This John Malory was on two occasions
Commissioner for the peace, and in 1413 was member of
Parliament for Warwickshire. He held the office of sheriff
in 1417 and in 1429; in 1420 he was 'by speciall Commission, with others, assigned to treat with the people
about a loan of money to the King'. He died old and left
a son Sir Thomas who in 1433 or 1434 succeeded to the
ancestral estate.

By that time Sir Thomas was already an accomplished
knight. Some twelve years before he succeeded his father,
he served 'with one lance and two Archers'[5] in the retinue of Richard Beauchamp, Earl of Warwick, at Calais,
'receiving for his lance and one archer 20 pounds per
annum and their diet, and for the other archer ten marks
and no diet'.[5] His association with Beauchamp is particularly significant in view of the well-known character of the
earl, whom all his contemporaries regarded as the em-

---

[1] = practise.   [2] *V*. Appendix I, part 2, sections A and D.
[3] Ibid., 2, D.   [4] Ibid., 2, E.   [5] Ibid., 3, B.

bodiment of the chivalric ideal of the age. The Emperor
Sigismound is reported to have said to Henry V that 'no
prince Cristen for wisdom, norture and manhood, had
suche another knight, as he had of the Earl of Warwick,
adding thereto that if all courtesy were lost, yet might it
be found again in him'.[1] Richard no doubt deserved to
be called the 'Father of Courtesy', but he was not merely
a knight in manners: he was much admired for his sense
of adventure and his feats of bravery. One of his exploits
strangely recalls the habits of medieval tournaments and
might almost have been told in the *Morte Darthur*. On
hearing of a great gathering near Calais, he 'cast in his
mynde to do sume newe poynt of chevalry', and styling
himself now as the Green Knight, then as a 'Chevalier
Attendant', he sent three challenges to the French court,
and three French knights accepted them. Richard unhorsed the first. Appearing the next day in another armour he smote down the second; and on the third day he
'performed his owne persone', and defeated the last of his
opponents.[2]

Not only does this episode recall the atmosphere of
romantic chivalry, but it has a close parallel in the seventh
book of the *Morte Darthur*. The sources of this book
are still unknown, but some parts of it are in all
probability of Malory's own invention.[3] The hero—
Beaumains—is Malory's own hero, and his name, impossible in any French romance, strangely resembles that of
Malory's patron. His successive battles with the Black,
Green, and Red Knights, and particularly his behaviour
at the tournament held at the castle of Lady Lioness, at
once call to mind the romantic adventure of Richard
Beauchamp. At that tournament the King of Ireland
wondered who Beaumains might be, 'that one tyme semed
grene, and another tyme at his ageyne comyng he semed
blewe. And thus at every cours that he rode to and fro
he chaunged his colour so that ther myghte neyther kynge

---

[1] John Rous, *Life of Richard, Earl of Warwick*, printed from MS. Cotton
Julius E. IV by Strutt, *Horda Angel Cynnan*, 1775–6; ii. 126.
[2] Ibid., ii. 124–5.   [3] *V. infra*, p. 138.

nor knyghte have redy congnyssaunce of hym'.[1] The parallel is so close as to lead me to believe that some parts of the book of Beaumains were written in remembrance of Beauchamp's gallant deeds. Malory spent his youth 'in the atmosphere of national unity and military enterprise',[2] and the noble character of the great knight who so brilliantly revived the traditions of medieval chivalry may well have suggested the topic and given him the inspiration for his life work.

In 1445, thirty-two years after his father had occupied the same seat, we find Malory a member of Parliament for his shire.[3] This was the culminating point of a career in which, as the next recorded fact leads us to believe, there was a sudden falling off. About the year 1451 he became involved in a local dispute about the priory of Monks Kirby. This priory had been transferred by Henry V to Epworth, and Malory, it seems, had done some injury to the prior and convent of the Carthusian house of Epworth, in the isle of Axholme, Lincolnshire. Richard Neville, the future 'king maker', and the Duke of Buckingham were directed to arrest Thomas Malory and his servant John Appelby, and to cause them 'to find mainpernors who will mainprise for them under a sufficient penalty that they will do no hurt to the prior and convent of the Carthusian house of Axiholme' (13 July 1451).[4]

In all probability the 'hurt' done to the priory of Monks Kirby was an attack on monastic property. It has been conjectured that 'the acts of extortion alleged against Sir Thomas Malory were made by him to recover possession of property taken on behalf of the Priory',[5] and that the source of discord was his claim for payment of tithe. But although Malory's 'extortion' was probably only a form of reprisal, it caused his imprisonment on 25 July 1451. A month later, on 23 August 1451, we find him accused of several other misdeeds at an Inquisition held at Nun-

[1] pp. 259–60.
[2] Cf. E. K. Chambers, Sir Thomas Malory (English Association, Pamphlet No. 51), p. 12.   [3] V. App. I, 3, B.   [4] Ibid., 3, D.
[5] E. Hicks, Sir Thomas Malory, His Turbulent Career, p. 50.

eaton and presided over by Humphrey, Duke of Buckingham.[1] The accusation was that Sir Thomas Malory, after
being committed to the sheriff's custody on Sunday,
25 July 1451, broke out of prison on the night of Tuesday
next following and swam across the moat, *sicque a custodia
dicti vicecomitis evasit*; that he and his servant John Appelby
with a number of yeomen, husbandmen, and others broke
in by night into the Abbey of Blessed Mary of Coombe,[2]
opened two of the abbot's chests, and carried away two
bags with money [3] as well as various other *jocalia et orna-
menta* to the value of £40; that on 4 January 1450, Malory
lay in ambush to attack the Duke of Buckingham; that
on Thursday, 29 July 1451, he and a number of other
malefactors broke eighteen doors of Coombe Abbey, in-
sulted the abbot, and stole £40 4s. 4d. from his chests; [4]
that on 31 August 1450 Malory and Appelby had extorted
by threats 20s. from John Mylner at Monks Kirby, 'and
in the same manner 100s. from Margaret Kyng and William
Hales on May 31, 1450'; and finally that Malory twice
broke into the house of Hugh Smyth of Monks Kirby and
raped his wife Joan, his goods, and chattels.[5]

It cannot be ascertained that Malory actually committed any of these crimes. It is not improbable that, as
in his attack on Monks Kirby, he merely attempted to
take by violence what he claimed by right. The charge of
'feloniously raping Joan, the wife of Hugh Smyth', is
most likely a legal fiction, and G. L. Kittredge reconstructs
the case thus:

'Malory and his servants had searched Smyth's house in vain.
Smyth's wife, who objected to the search, may have been roughly
treated; perhaps she was forcibly removed from the dwelling while

[1] *V*. App. I, 3, E.
[2] A Cistercian monastery situated between Newbold Revel and Coventry.
[3] *Unam bagam et viginti una libras auri in eadem contentas et unam aliam
bagam et viginti quinque marcas auri et argenti in eadem baga contentas.*
[4] Hicks (op. cit., p. 43) rightly conjectures that the two alleged attacks
were probably one and the same affair.
[5] Another accusation—that of stealing cattle from William Rowe and
William Dowde of Shawell—was raised at the same Inquisition before a
different panel of jurors.

it was ransacked. That would have been *raptus*. Then, on the first of August, the search was repeated with similar violence and with complete success. . . . On neither occasion is there any likelihood that Goodwife Smyth was actually ravished. The duplication of this particular charge is reason enough for rejecting such an idea: it is ridiculous to suppose that Malory actually ravished the woman twice.' [1]

Be that as it may, we know from another record [2] that when 'on the 15th day of St. Hilary's Term' Malory was brought before the king at Westminster he pleaded 'in no wise guilty' (*dicit quod ipse in nullo est inde culpabilis*), and 'thereupon the said Thomas Malory was handed back to the Sheriffs for safe custody', and the affair was ended.[3]

About this time, or a little before his first arrest and trial, Sir Thomas married Elizabeth. The known records have preserved neither her surname nor any mention of the family to which she belonged. It is perhaps as a tribute to his wife that Malory, instead of calling the Queen of Lyoness *Isabel*, as does the French version,[4] calls her Elizabeth. She bore him one son who, it seems, died quite young, sometime between 1466 and 1471, and while Sir Thomas was still living.[5] In Malory's eleventh book the description of the departure of Perceval and Agloval from their home may be a distant echo of this

[1] Quoted by Hicks, op. cit., pp. 52–3.
[2] Coram Rege Roll 763, Crown Side, Membrane 3.
[3] The *Calendar of Patent Rolls*, Hen. VI, vi. 51, contains a commission of Henry VI, dated 26 March 1452, which directs the Duke of Buckingham, Sir Edward Grey of Groby, and the Sheriff of Warwick and Leicester to arrest and bring before the King and Council 'Thomas Malorre, Knight, to answer certain charges'. The cause of this third arrest is unknown. *V.* App. I, 3, D.
[4] Cf. my *Roman de Tristan et Iseut dans l'Œuvre de Thomas Malory*, Paris, 1925, p. 229 (quoted later as *Rom. de Trist.*).
[5] We owe this information to Dugdale and Bridges, *v.* App. I, 2, D; 3, A; 3, B. G. L. Kittredge (*Sir Thomas Malory*, Barnstable, 1925, p. 11) questions its accuracy on the ground that an Inquisition held at Northampton records the death of a Thomas Malory and gives his heir as Robert Malory aged 23. But it is by no means certain that this Thomas Malory is identical with Sir Thomas Malory of Newbold, while there is no plausible reason to disbelieve Dugdale and Bridges, whose information on Malory is otherwise entirely correct.

tragedy: it contains the touching lament of Perceval's mother, which is not in the French source: 'A my dere sones', she says, 'whanne your fader was slayne, he lefte me IIII sones of the whiche now be tweyn slayne. And for the dethe of my noble sone syre Lamorak shall my herte never be gladde.' She kneels before her two sons and beseeches them 'to abyde at home with her', but they refuse. Then she resumes her 'pyteous complaynte' for the death of Lamorak 'that of knyghthode had but fewe felawes'. 'Thenne ther was but wepynge and sobbynge ... and she felle in swounynge in myddes of the Courte.'[1]

After the trial of 1451 Malory, though he was 'handed back to the Sheriffs for safe custody', was probably soon released. But his freedom was only temporary, for not only was he arrested again in 1452,[2] but we again find him in prison in 1468, and this time on a charge of sedition rather than because of local disputes.[3] He appears to have taken part in a Lancastrian uprising, but he is excluded from the general pardon granted to the Lancastrians by Edward IV on 24 August 1468. On 1 December 1468 he is again excluded from a pardon, and we have no definite evidence that he was ever set free. It was during his seclusion that he wrote the larger part, if not the whole, of his book. Not 'in the window-seat of some country manor',[4] nor 'in his estates in Warwickshire'[5] as certain critics have imagined, but in the lonely cell of a prison. Of the hardships he endured during his last imprisonment he himself tells us in a few stirring lines of the ninth book of the *Morte Darthur*:

'So sire Tristram endured there (in the prison of Darras) grete payne, for sekenesse had undertake[6] hym, and that is the grettest

---

[1] Cf. *Rom. de Trist.*, p. 213.   [2] See *supra*, p. 6, footnote 3.
[3] Sir Edmund Chambers thinks (op. cit., pp. 13, 16) that Malory was not a Lancastrian and that his imprisonment in 1468 was due to some renewal of the local dispute. He adduces no evidence, and the fact that Malory was twice excluded from a general pardon rather suggests that he was involved in politics.   [4] Chambers, op. cit., p. 3.
[5] V. D. Scudder, *Le Morte Darthur of Sir Thomas Malory, A Study of the Book and its Sources*, London and New York, 1921, p. 179.
[6] = seized.

payne a prysoner maye have. For alle the whyle a prysoner may
have his helthe of body, he maye endure under the mercy of God
and in hope of good delyveraunce. But whanne sekenes toucheth
a prysoners *body* thenne may a prysoner say, al welthe is hym berefte,
and thenne he hath cause to wayle and to wepe. Ryght so dyd syre
Tristram whanne sekenes had undertake hym, for thenne he took
such sorou that he had almost slayne hym self.'

This again is one of the passages which Malory did not
find in his source,[1] and its intensely personal note can
hardly escape the reader's ear. He, too, lived 'in the hope
of good deliverance'; and in concluding his book he again
adverted to his own misfortune:

'I praye you all jentyl men and jentyl wymmen that redeth this
book of Arthur and his knyghtes from the begynnyng to the endyng,
praye for me whyle I am on lyve that God sende me good delyveraunce, and whan I am deed, I praye you all, praye for my soule.'

In the silence of his cell his thoughts naturally turned
toward the tragic events of his time and the causes which
had led to them. Nothing could more inspire him with
such meditations than the book he was writing, the story
of the rise and fall of the great kingdom of Arthur. To
him Arthur was the perfect English king, and his reign
the very embodiment of the past glories of England. Unlike his French predecessors Malory was not a mere
observer, a passionless narrator of a fairy tale; but one
who used his material as a commentary on the glory of
English chivalry, so that 'noble men' might see 'the jentyl
and vertuous dedes that somme knyghtes used in tho
dayes',[2] and learn 'love, trouthe and feythfulness'.[3] The
contrast of this ideal world with the fickleness of that of
his contemporaries suggested itself to his mind; and long
before the tragic climax of his story, in the account of
Dynas's revolt against King Mark, he made the latter
appeal to the rebels in the name of reason and justice.
Mark declares that he himself will go to the Pope 'to

---

[1] Cf. *Rom. de Trist.*, p. 183.
[2] Caxton's *Preface*, p. 3 in Sommer's edition (see Bibliography). This
edition is a faithful reprint of Caxton's text, and I have used it here for all
my quotations from, and references to, Malory's text.
[3] p. 771, ll. 34–5.

warre upon the miscreauntes. And this is a fayrer werre than thus to areyse [1] the peple ageynst your kynge.' [2] But it is in the final scenes of Arthur's tragedy that Malory's reflections on the decay of his country are most clearly expressed. Instead of describing the details of Mordred's preparations for the treacherous attack upon the king, he gives vent to his own feelings and appeals to English patriotism: 'Lo ye al Englissh men, see ye not what a myschyef here was for he that was the moost kyng and knyght of the world. . . . Now myght not this englyssh men holde them contente with hym. . . . Alas! thys is a grete defaulte of us englysshe men, for there may no thynge plese us noo terme.' [3] After taking an active part in the civil strife he remained loyal to his cause and urged in his book that no man should 'take battles in a wrongful quarrel for no law, ne for no worlds good'. There is, in this defence of the royal authority, a note of warning and reproach.

Whether death found Malory in prison, or whether he was set free soon after 1468, is a matter of doubt. It has been supposed that he either benefited by the general amnesty of 1469 [4] or was released some time between October 1470 and March 1471, i.e. after Henry VI had emerged to power. [5] He died on 14 March 1471, and was buried in the chapel of St. Francis at Greyfriars, London. On his tomb were written these words: 'dominus Thomas Mallere, valens miles, ob. 14 Mar. 1470, [6] de parochia Monkenkyrkby in comitatu Warwici.' [7] His wife Elizabeth outlived him by eight years, and died on 30 September 1479, leaving as her only heir her grandson Nicholas, son of Robert. Nicholas Malory died in 1513 leaving no male heirs, and with him Malory's name disappears from public records.

---

[1] = arouse. [2] p. 497. Cf. *infra*, p. 91. [3] p. 840.
[4] Cf. G. L. Kittredge, *Who was Sir Thomas Malory?* Boston, 1897.
[5] Cf. Chambers, op. cit., p. 13.
[6] This represents 1471 in our reckoning (cf. Chambers, op. cit., p. 16).
[7] *V*. App. I, 3, I. Miss Alice D. Greenwood in her article on 'English Prose in the Fifteenth Century' (*Cambridge History of English Literature*, ii. 335–6) says, not without reason, that Malory's 'burial in the Grey Friars may, possibly, suggest that he died a prisoner in Newgate'.

II

William Caxton

The two remaining copies of William Caxton's black-letter edition of 1485 are the earliest form in which we have the *Morte Darthur*. Malory's manuscript has not been preserved and we must perforce regard as our sole authorities[1] these two survivals from Caxton's press. One of the copies is perfect;[2] the other[3] lacks eleven leaves which have been replaced by facsimiles from the complete copy. Neither copy has a title, and the traditional title of the book seems to be the result of a misunderstanding. Caxton says in the colophon:[4] *Thus endeth thys noble and ioyous book entytled le Morte Darthur.* To ascribe such a title to Malory seems impossible, not only because it does not occur in his own colophon, but because when earlier on he uses the phrase *Morte Arthur* (Book I, ch. 7) it clearly refers to the final portion of the work—the portion that corresponds to the French thirteenth-century *Mort Artu* and the English stanzaic *Le Morte Arthur*. While extending this title to the whole work, Caxton realized its inaccuracy, and to the colophon quoted above added an apology:

'*Notwythstondyng it treateth of the byrth, lyf, and actes of the sayd Kyng Arthur, of his noble knyghtes of the rounde table, theyr mervayllous enquestes and adventures, th'achyeuyng of the Sangreal, & in th' ende the dolorous deth & departyng out of thys world of them al.*'

Caxton's edition was 'enprynted and fynysshed' at Westminster on 31 July 1485, i.e. a little more than fifteen years after the book was concluded by Malory. It is impossible to say exactly how much in the course of

---

1 Of a third copy the second leaf of the table of contents is alone extant. Cf. Sommer, op. cit., vol. ii, p. 2; *infra*, p. 190.

2 Now in the Pierpont Morgan Library, New York. See Bibliography, No. 1.

3 Now in the John Rylands Library, Manchester. See Bibl., ibid.

4 p. 861.

5 It is probable that Caxton, not Malory, is responsible for the spelling '*la* cheualer du charyot' which occurs in line 13 of p. 796. Only a few lines above he gives the correct form (796$_5$).

book of kynge Arthur ₢ of his nobce knyghtes of the rounde
table/that whan they were hole togyders there was euer an C
and yl/and₂ here is the ende of the deth of Arthur ;J praye
you all Jentyl men and Jentyl wymmen that redeth this book
of Arthur and₂ his knyghtes from the begynnyng to the en ⁊
dynge / praye for me whyle J am on lyue that god₂ sende me
good₂ delyueraunce/₢ whan J am deed₂ J praye you all praye
for my soule/for this book was ended₂ the ix yere of the regne
of kynge edlbard₂ the fourth/by syr Thomas Malcore knyght
as Jhesu helpe hym for hys grete myght/as he is the seruaunt
of Jhesu bothe day and₂ nyght /

¶ Thus endeth thys nobce and Joyous book entytled le morte
Darthur/Notwythstondyng it treateth of the byrth/lyf/and₂
actes of the sayd₂ kynge Arthur/of his nobce knyghtes of the
rounde table/theyr meruayllous enquestes and₂ aduentures /
thachyeuyng₂ of the sangreal/ ₢ in thende the dolorous deth ₢
departyng out of thys world₂ of them al/Which book was re
duced₂ in to englysshe by syr Thomas Mabry knyght as afore
is sayd₂ /and₂ by me deuyded₂ in to xxi bookes chapytred₂ and₂
enprynted₂ /and₂ fynysshed₂ in thabbey westmestre the last day
of Juyl the yere of our lord₂ /M/CCCC/lxxxv /

¶ Caxton me fieri fecit

THE LAST PAGE OF THE *MORTE DARTHUR* WITH CAXTON'S
COLOPHON (Pierpont Morgan Library Copy)

its printing Caxton altered his original. He himself admits having divided it into books and chapters.[1] Malory's manuscript had no such divisions. The author occasionally noted the end of a story or reproduced the divisions he found in his source. Caxton utilized these indications in the seven passages [2] with which he links his books. The work thus fell into eight unequal parts. Caxton of his own accord then split it in thirteen other places and inserted *explicits* and *incipits* in English or in Latin. As a result the *Morte Darthur* was divided into twenty-one books of unequal length, most of the divisions being mechanical.

More arbitrary still is the division of books into chapters. These were introduced to help the reader 'to understand briefly the content of this volume'. In the text itself the chapters have no titles, but at the beginning of his edition Caxton inserted a 'Table or rubrysshe of the contente of chapytres shortly' of all the books of the *Morte Darthur*. All this, however, is of very little service to the reader. To give but one example out of many: the twenty-first chapter of Book IV, entitled 'How a knyght & a dwarf stroof for a lady', relates really the story of Sir Pelleas, the 'dolorous knight', and of Lady Ettard. The dolorous knight overcomes ten knights, but lets himself be 'bound hande and foote and tayed . . . under the hors bely'.[3] When he is led away the knights discuss the 'dooleful fyghte'.[4] Then a knight and a dwarf come upon the stage and occupy our attention for some fifteen lines. They do in fact 'stryve for the lady', but their quarrel remains unsettled and they depart. There follows a short fight between Gawain and two other knights. This ends

---

[1] Preface, p. 4: 'And for to understonde bryefly the contente of thys volume, I have devyded it into XXI bookes and every book chapytred as here after shal by Goddes grace folowe.' Cf. also p. 861: 'And by me devyded in to XXI bookes, chapytred and enprynted.'

[2] At the beginning of the romance of Tristan (Book VIII), of the story of 'La Cote Mal Tayle' (Book IX), of the 'second book' of *Tristan* Book X), of the *Quest of the Holy Grail* (Book XIII), of *Perceval* (Book XIV), of the adventures of Gawain, Hector, and Bors (Book XVI), and at the end of the *Quest*.   [3] p. 145.   [4] p. 146.

in a reconciliation, whereupon one of them tells Gawain
the whole story of the dolorous knight. In the middle of
his speech the chapter ends. The episode of the dwarf
and the knight 'striving for a lady' is thus only a brief
interpolation, and by no means justifies the title of the
whole chapter. It should have been entitled 'Of Sir Pelleas and Lady Ettard', and should at least extend beyond
the twenty lines which follow. This is no isolated instance. It may be an exaggeration to say that in Caxton's
print 'new chapters are sometimes made to begin in the
middle of a sentence',[1] but it would be tedious to enumerate the chapters which begin in the middle of a
conversation.

Caxton was in no sense a scrupulously accurate printer
and in several places his inattention made the text unintelligible.[2] But careless though he was he published his
volume with his customary 'enthusiasm in the cause of
good literature'.[3] For he fully sympathized with, and
appreciated, the matter and manner of this 'noble and
joyous book'. His *Preface* is a spirited tribute to the moral
and sentimental teaching of the *Morte Darthur*. He
relates that he undertook its publication at the request of
'many noble and divers gentlemen of this realm of England' who said that he 'ought rather t'enprynte his
(Arthur's) actes and noble feates than of Godefroye of
Boloyne or ony of the other eyght,[4] consyderyng that he
was a man borne wythin this royame and kyng and Emperour of the same'. Caxton at first objected to this on
the ground that there was 'no suche Arthur', 'wherto they
answerd, and one in specyal sayd, that in hym that shold

[1] A. W. Pollard, Bibliographical Note to Macmillan's edition of the *Morte
Darthur*, p. vii.
[2] But for the help of the French sources Ch. XX—XXI of Book VIII
would still remain obscure. He may have obscured other passages to which
we have no clue. Dr. Sommer's list of 'Errors, omissions, and ortho-
graphical irregularities in Caxton's impression' (op. cit., ii. 21—5) contains
over 400 misprints and other mistakes. Cf. also *Rom. de Trist.*, pp. 221—5.
[3] A. W. Pollard, loc. cit.
[4] i.e. Hector of Troy, Alexander the Great, Julius Caesar, Joshua, David,
Judas Maccabeus, Charlemagne, and Arthur.

say or thynke that there was never such a kynge callyd Arthur myght wel be aretted (= reckoned) grete folye and blyndenesse. For he sayd that there were many evidences of the contrarye'. Among these evidences, the noble gentleman mentioned the tomb at Glastonbury, the stories of Arthur in Boccaccio's *De casibus virorum illustrium*[1] and in Geoffrey of Monmouth, and various relics 'in divers places of England', in Westminster, Dover, and Winchester.

In face of these arguments Caxton 'coude not wel denye but that there was suche a noble kyng named Arthur'; and 'enprysed [2] to enprynte a book of the noble hystoryes of the sayd kynge Arthur and of certeyn of his knyghtes, after a copye unto me delivered, whyche copye Syr Thomas Malorye dyd take oute of certeyne bookes of Frensshe, and reduced it in to Englysshe'.

Caxton clearly states the object of his publication: it was 'set in enprynte to the entente that noble men . . . take the good and honest actes in their remembraunce and folowe the same'. 'Doo after the good and leve the evyl, and it shal brynge you to good fame and renommee.'

There is more in these words than the reading of an ordinary Arthurian romance would suggest. It would have been preposterous to have written such a *Preface* for one of the French Arthurian romances of the Middle Ages, which were not intended either as historical records or as works of moral edification. It is therefore not of the French romances that Caxton speaks, but of the English *Morte Darthur*. His words reflect some characteristic aspects of Malory's philosophy. Malory died long before his work was 'sette in enprynte' by Caxton, and it is not likely that they ever saw each other. Yet Caxton's *Preface* contains some of the best and soundest criticisms of the book. It stands nearest to Malory's initial inspiration, and shows a close bond of sympathy between Malory 'the noble knight' and Caxton the 'simple person'.

---

[1] Caxton describes it as 'thystorye of bochas in his book de casu principum'.
[2] = undertook.

Chapter Two
THE GENESIS OF ARTHURIAN ROMANCE
I
The Awakening

Ueber der Art wie es zugegangen liegt der Schleier des
Geheimnisses, an das man glauben soll.
J. GRIMM, *Ueber den altdeutschen Meistergesang*, p. 16.

THE plot of the Arthurian romances has its origin in
the *Historia Regum Britanniae* written by Geoffrey of
Monmouth between the years 1136 and 1138.[1] Geoffrey's
story of Arthur presents a mixture of pseudo-history and
romance, typical of medieval 'histories'. The Arthur section proper[2] is but a long account of wars with two intervals of peace. Arthur subdues nearly every nation in
Europe: the Saxons, the Picts, the Scots, Iceland, Goth-
land, the Orkneys, Norway, Gaul, and finally Rome. Between the Scottish and the Irish campaigns he marries
Guinevere (*Guanhumara*). During the Roman campaign
he leaves Britain in the charge of the queen and Mordred,
and finds on his return that Mordred has started a rebellion. He overcomes the traitor at Richborough and at
Winchester, but Mordred strikes again at Cambula
(= Camel), and there both he and Arthur find their deaths.
Arthur is borne thence for the healing of his wounds to
the island of Avalon, and this happens, in Geoffrey's
reckoning, in the year of Our Lord 542.

This fantastic story was, according to Geoffrey, borrowed from a *Brittanici sermonis liber vetustissimus*, which
he received from his friend and patron Walter, Archdeacon of Oxford. Much labour has been lost in the
attempt to discover this *liber*, but even the extreme Celti-

[1] Cf. E. Faral, *Geoffroy de Monmouth, les faits et les dates de sa biographie*
(*Romania*, liii), pp. 18–22. On the question of dating see also E. K.
Chambers, *Arthur of Britain*, pp. 40–52; and A. Griscom in *Specu-
lum*, i. 129.　　　　　　　　　　　　　　　　　　[2] Books IX—XI. 2.

cists have at length admitted that 'no document, either in Welsh or in Breton, has yet been found even remotely resembling that which Walter, the archdeacon, is said to have brought over from Brittany'.[1] Recent scholars regard Geoffrey's reference to the *liber* as 'a jest, or a literary convention, or a fraud'.[2] It is hardly a jest, but it is beyond doubt a literary convention and a fraud at the same time. In disclaiming responsibility for his inventions and sheltering them under the wing of an old authority (*vetustissimus*), Geoffrey follows the fashion of his age. His 'fraud' is not unlike Thomas's allusions to Breri, or Wolfram von Eschenbach's reference to a Provençal source, and may equally well be discounted. His originality, in spite of his efforts to conceal it, is clearly apparent. Having collected a few vague references to Arthur in the old chronicles,[3] he forges the whole story, models Arthur's personality, court, and conquests upon those of Charlemagne,[4] and adorns his account with rhetorical embroidery drawn from Latin authors. It has been suggested that he had political reasons for forming Arthur in the image of Charlemagne[5] and giving the Norman kings a predecessor as exalted as the venerable white-bearded Emperor of the *Song of Roland*. However this may be, the work is essentially a product of imagination, not of historical study or of popular mythology.[6] Under the cloak of an historical account it contains one of the least historical

[1] *King Arthur in History and Legend*, by W. Lewis Jones. Cambridge, 1914, p. 63.   [2] E. K. Chambers, op. cit., p. 55.
[3] On the sources of Geoffrey see H. Brandenburg, *G. v. M. und die frühmittelenglischen Chronisten*; H. Matter, *Englische Gründungssagen*; and Chambers, op. cit., pp. 53–99.
[4] Cf. ibid., pp. 38 and 57. One of the most typical instances of this is the mention of the twelve peers of Gaul who attend Arthur's festival at Caerleon.
[5] Cf. Gerould, 'King Arthur and Politics' (*Speculum*, ii), pp. 48–9; Dr. Sebastian Evans's epilogue to his translation of Geoffrey (Temple Classics, 1903); and W. Lewis Jones, op. cit., pp. 66–7.
[6] M. Faral aptly describes this as 'une sorte de mystification littéraire, par laquelle Gaufrei a "lancé" la poésie bretonne, un peu comme, six siècles après, Macpherson devait lancer l'ossianisme' (J. Bédier et P. Hazard, *Histoire de la littérature française illustrée*, Paris, 1923, i. 19).

romances, even less historical than the eleventh- and twelfth-
century French *chansons de geste*.[1] It cannot be conceived
apart from its twelfth-century Norman environment, and
whatever may be said of the historical Celtic Arthur, the
Arthur of Geoffrey of Monmouth and of Arthurian romance in general is a twelfth-century personage, well
suited to the setting of a Norman court and entirely independent of the legendary British chieftain of the late
fifth and early sixth century. The Arthur of Nennius, of
the *Annales Cambriae*, and of William of Malmesbury, was
a grim and ferocious warrior who 'made head single-
handed against nine hundred of the enemy and routed
them with incredible slaughter'.[2] In Geoffrey, not only
are the episodes of the story newly invented, but its spirit
and atmosphere are different. He is a deliberate romancer, and during the period of peace between the two great
campaigns he makes Arthur's court into a model for the
chevaliers of all Europe; the knights of Arthur's court
perform feats of bravery and are rewarded by the love of
their ladies. This part of Geoffrey's work, connecting as
it does Arthur 'the most renowned king' with the traditions of courtly chivalry, is more important for the history
of romance than all the descriptions of battles and conquests in the Carolingian style: it is the beginning of
the 'romantic' Arthuriad.

In 1155 a Norman poet, Maistre Wace, produced a
free rendering of Geoffrey's *History* in octosyllabic French
verse.[3] He pretended to have taken pains to verify

[1] The belief in Arthur's resurrection emerges, like the rest of the story,
some centuries after Arthur had ceased to be, and Sir Edmund Chambers
rightly remarks that 'perhaps the nearest analogy is once more to be found
in Charlemagne, the rumour of whose resurrection from the dead is reported by the chronicle of Ekkehard on the eve of the first Crusade' (op.
cit., p. 231).

[2] '. . . nongentos hostium solus adorsus incredibili caede profligarit', *De
Rebus Gestis Regum Anglorum* (William of Malmesbury, ed. Stubbs, i. 11).
It is interesting to observe that these lines were written only eleven years
before Geoffrey's *Historia*.

[3] He called the poem *La Geste des Bretons*, but it is generally known as *Le
Roman de Brut*, a title introduced by the scribes because of the references
to Brutus as the founder of the British race.

Geoffrey's account and to have explored the fabled Arthur-land, but all in vain: 'I sought marvels, he said in another poem, but found none. I returned as wise as I went; I went in search of folly, and esteem myself a fool.' [1] In reality, however, Wace was little concerned with the search for 'marvels' in fairyland. He merely romanticized Geoffrey's account of King Arthur's reign, and vividly set forth the splendour of the Round Table, 'of which the Bretons tell many stories', and which he was the first to introduce into Arthurian fiction. Arthur in Wace is not only a magnificent king, but a king with a courtly temperament, 'a lover of glory, whose famous deeds are right fit to be kept in remembrance: he ordained the courtesies of courts, and observed high state in a very splendid fashion'.[2] The best occasion for this was Arthur's own coronation with its endless festivities, games, and tournaments. Wace notes that on that day even the noblest knights could not win the favour of their ladies unless they were 'proved by chivalry'.[3] Arthur and his companions become 'Love's lovers', and although Wace is still a chronicler, not a romancer; although he is concerned with narrative rather than with psychology, the court of Arthur as he sees it is already fit to become a brilliant court of love.

The earliest courtly romances in the true sense of the word were the poems of Chrestien de Troyes written between the years 1165 and 1180.[4] Chrestien was the first to introduce into the narrative poetry of northern France the teaching and the psychology of the Provençal courtly

---

[1] *Roman de Rou*, ii, l. 284. [2] *Roman de Brut*, ll. 9258–60.
[3] Ibid., ll. 10791–6:

> Ne ja chevalier n'i eust,
> De quel parage que il fust,
> Ja peust, en tote sa vie,
> Avoir bele dame en amie,
> Se il n'eust avant esté
> De cevalerie prové.

[4] The term 'courtly' is generally used in a much wider sense. Here I only apply it to the romances which show a definite acquaintance with the southern theory of the 'service of love'.

C

school. His works inaugurated a new stage in the development of the Arthuriad, a stage marked by the coalescence of the Arthurian plot with the tradition of courtly love.

The distinctive feature of the Provençal *gai sçavoir* was that it placed woman on the pinnacle of a social and spiritual hierarchy, and made love a sacred cult. It was an attempt to exalt passion and at the same time to confine it within the close walls of a refined and sophisticated legislation. Woman, no longer viewed as the source of evil, was for the first time in the history of medieval thought regarded as the superior of man. 'Love was knighthood's service; it was loyalty and devotion; it was the noblest human giving. It was also the spring of excellence, the inspiration of high deeds.'[1] Yet it was a worship open only to those who were initiated into the new *sçavoir*, a religion designed for the chosen few. Ovid's *Art of Love* had already suggested the idea of subordinating the conduct of lovers to a doctrine. The Christian ideals of love and sacrifice, preserving their essential characteristics, were secularized by poets and formed the basis of the actual theory of service: the devotion of a Provençal lover to his lady had an intensely religious character and most probably an ecclesiastical origin.[2] Thus the new creed was supported by a rigid teaching. The knight, conforming to the prescribed rules of the service of love, could achieve his aim only by degrees, and passed from trial to trial before reaching the ultimate stage of perfection.

The new philosophy of love caused the growing of a new literature: this was the lyrical poetry of Provence where, in short songs of unmatched formal perfection, the troubadours glorified the god of love and his servants, lovers. This type of poetry spread widely; on one side of the Rhine it awakened the lyrical genius of the German

[1] H. O. Taylor, *The Mediaeval Mind* (4th edition), vol. i, p. 589.
[2] I am here unable to do more than summarize in this very brief statement an interpretation of the Provençal teaching to which I hope some time to devote a more detailed study. Hennig Brinkmann in his *Entstehungsgeschichte des Minnesangs*, Halle, 1926, suggests a similar theory.

Minnesinger, and on the other, of the northern French *trouvères*, while beyond the Alps it inspired the 'stil nuovo' of Petrarch:

> Sì come eterna vita è veder Dio,
> Nè più si brama, nè bramar più lice;
> Così me, donna, il voi veder, felice
> Fa in questo breve e fràile viver mio.

A French imitator of the troubadours, Conon de Béthune, goes still farther and challenges any human pursuit which can divert man from the service of love: 'Alas', he says when he goes on a crusade, 'how cruel a leave I must take from one who was never better beloved and served. May the good God bring me back to her as surely as I suffer when I leave her. Lo! what have I said? I do not leave her; *if my body goes to the service of our Lord, my whole heart remains in hers. I go to Syria sighing for her.*' [1] Obviously enough, the old semi-liturgical, semi-patriotic narratives, inspired as they were by religious and national sentiment, were incompatible with such thoughts. For the framing of the philosophy of refined love it was necessary to have a new form of narrative, a form unrestrained by historical and hagiographical conventions and free from any suggestion of reality.

The search for the unreal led to the discovery of the exotic, which left the poet free to lay his scenes in a realm of imagination only nominally and artificially connected with some known country. In the romantic literature of France this resulted in the acceptance of the Arthurian theme, which lent itself readily enough to the purposes of the new school of poetry. In the hands of Chrestien de Troyes, the Arthur story underwent a considerable change. Arthur, only vaguely described by Wace as 'one of Love's lovers', suddenly mounted the most dignified of all thrones to preside over the most brilliant assembly of lovers and adventurers. The adventures of the Arthurian characters formed the canvas which poets were to embellish with designs conceived in the spirit of courtly idealism. There,

---

[1] *Chansons de Conon de Béthune*, ed. Axel Wallensköld, Helsingfors, 1891, pp. 224–5.

in the mingling of the medieval service of love with the
wonders of fancy, lay the secret of the fascination of the
romances of medieval France for men of all generations.
And, indeed, there could be no better setting for the
stories conceived in the spirit of courtly idealism than the
matter of Britain, with its 'exotic names, its distant and
fabulous Arthur, its atmosphere of transformations and
cities caught in magic'; [1] and if Chrestien became the
founder of the new tradition, it was because he possessed
in the highest degree the art of interweaving love and
adventure, and combining the exalted theories of courtly
service with the stories of strange quests and magic lands.
The adventure of the fountain of Broceliande in *Yvain*
seems naturally attached to the love-story of the hero: both
are unreal, and attractive in their remoteness from the
actual circumstances of daily life. They lead us into a
world which is theirs, a world which is not that of idealized
and heroic reality, but of elaborate convention placed in a
supernatural frame:

> De rien nule ne li sovient
> Fors d'une sole, et por celi
> A mis les autres en obli.[2]

There may be outbursts of true romantic passion in
Yvain [3] and in *La Charrete*, there may be touches of
genuine lyricism in the concluding scenes in *Erec*, but the
mainspring of Chrestien's psychology is not the passion
which a modern reader is tempted to look for; it is what
Chrestien describes as *fins cuers et bone volantez*,[4] the anti-
nomian courtly love. Framed in the narrow setting of the
Provençal philosophy, love ceases to be tragic and real;
but what it loses in genuine pathos, it gains in intellectual

---

[1] E. K. Chambers, *Arthur of Britain*, p. 143.
[2] 'Naught save one only thing could he call to mind, and for its sake he had
forgotten all' (*La Charrete*, ed. W. Förster, ll. 724–6).
[3] Cf. *Yvain*, ed. Förster, ll. 2025–32.
[4]
> Onques del bevrage ne bui
> don Tristans fu anpoisonez,
> mes plus me fet amer que lui
> fins cuers et bone volantez.

(Chrestien de Troyes, Lai ii, ll. 28–31; ed. Förster, *Wörterbuch*, p. 208).

refinement; it naturally furnishes material for discussions and monologues where abstract psychology is given free play. The author, not content to tell adventures, intersperses them with his own comments. The personages appear as instruments in a subtle harmony of general ideas and conventional feelings: they lack individual complexity and variety, and their being is determined not by their own characters, but by the author's theory of characters. Love-stories are but illustrations of his theory of love, which is made to do duty for the lovers themselves. Chrestien's favourite hero is Lancelot, the finest warrior and knight the world has ever known. But Lancelot is by no means an individual character; he is the type of a perfect lover, who acts his conventional part with admirable precision. His love for the fair Guinevere dominates all his thoughts and deeds. It is a love which is fascination, idolatry, and learning in one. When he enters Guinevere's room he bows as though he were in a sanctuary:

> Si l'aore et si li ancline,
> Car en nul cors saint ne croit tant.[1]

The very sight of his beloved must make him faint: such is the rule of the order to which he belongs; and when he sees her passing by his window he is minded to throw himself out and break his body on the stones below. And he would have let himself fall out had not Gawain seen him and drawn him back.[2] Finding a comb in which are some strands of his lady's hair he bows his head over his saddle-bow: 'he might as well have swooned', the poet adds, 'so near was he to doing so; for in his heart he felt such grief that for a long time he lost his colour and his power of speech'.[3]

Lancelot entered a tournament and was the superior of twenty knights, fighting so doughtily that he held every eye. But the queen sent word to him, asking him to be defeated. 'And he replied,[4] like one who was altogether

---

[1] 'He worships her and kneels to her, for in no holy relic had he such belief' (*La Charrete*, ll. 4670–1). [2] Ibid., ll. 564–71.
[3] Ibid., ll. 1447–8. [4] Ibid., ll. 5675 ff.

hers: "Very willingly", and, till evening fell, he fought as badly as possible.' He was not averse from appearing guilty of cowardice, for he knew well that the duties of a lover were more important than those of a fighting-man; that his love, though subordinate to conventional rules, was yet stronger than honour and dignity; that it was at once a religion, an art, and a science.[1]

Next to this victim of romantic psychology there are in Chrestien a number of knights whose ambition is merely to undertake adventures. They have little to do with romantic sentiment, but provide a suitable background to the lover-knights. First in importance among the 'adventurous' knights is Gawain. It has often been remarked that in Geoffrey's account Gawain was next in importance to Arthur: there he takes the leading part, his prowess surpassing that of Arthur himself. He has behind him the traditions of Celtic folk-lore and a realm of enchanted forests and castles. As distinct from the sentimental, he embodies the adventurous aspect of life, and his combats and quests have no other than episodic interest. He is a figure of a tapestry, not a hero of a love romance: here is a pleasant landscape, full of running waters, moated castles, and green lawns, amongst which move bright figures in blue and white and red armour, and among them, the bravest of all, Gawain. Every now and then they stop to lay lance in rest and overthrow one another, and then swear eternal friendship and ride away.[2] Gawain embodies all the narrative tradition which, varied though it is, has but one underlying motive: the interest in adventure and episode for its own sake. His world is different in origin and character from the Provençal courts of love. Chrestien succeeded in combining them, but they remained fundamentally different from one another, and their antagonism underlies all the later growth of the Arthuriad.

The struggle between adventure and sentiment ended, here as elsewhere, in the victory of adventure. Ideas

---

[1] Cf. G. Paris, *Romania*, xii, pp. 516–17.
[2] Cf. E. K. Chambers, *Sir Thomas Malory*, p. 6.

LANCELOT AND GUINEVERE

MS. Bibl. Nat. Fr. 118

great intensity. It is different, of course, from Chrestien's in that the Provençal worship of the lady is replaced by a more human type of passion. The precious, gallant, and mundane attitudes of Chrestien's Lancelot are translated into a more spontaneous and natural language. The knight is no longer inferior to the lady, and the service of love calls for no humiliation on his part. The Provençal theory of the superiority of the lady did not strike root in the French romances, and except for Chrestien's poems it remained foreign to the majority of the northern works of fiction. The Lancelot of the prose romance is, therefore, a more representative figure than the Lancelot of Chrestien. In thirteenth-century poems such as *La Chastelaine de Vergy* and *Le Roman du Chastelain de Coucy*, the spirit of courtly idealism is still very acutely felt, but the lovers are equal before passion: 'égaux devant la passion, ils ne sont l'un et l'autre que les fidèles du même seigneur, du même dieu, qui seul commande'.[1] In spite of his courtly presentation of love, the prose writer divests his Lancelot story of its Provençal trappings and refrains from exhibiting the 'pagan' worship of the lady. Lancelot no longer kneels before Guinevere as before a holy relic. His love is still an art, a virtue, and a religion even as in Chrestien, but the object of his cult is not the lady; it is Love itself, a love which has preserved the essential characteristics of the courtly Amour, which requires initiation and obedience, but which has rid itself of an excess of sophistication. With this only difference, we may safely regard the prose romances as a continuation of the courtly tradition. In thirteenth-century romances Guinevere remains the prototype of the lady, and Lancelot is still the model of the lover. The characters live in the same fantastic world:

'dans un monde à part, qui a ses lois, son langage, ses mystères, au verger secret qu'ont si souvent décrit les poètes: si un profane, disent-ils, entendait les chants que l'on y chante, aussitôt on y verrait les arbres se dessécher et les sources tarir; mais nul vilain n'en

[1] *La Châtelaine de Vergy*, conte du xiiie siècle, publié et traduit par Joseph Bédier, p. xii.

trouverait l'entrée, car une invisible muraille l'enclôt de toutes
parts, une muraille d'air, résistante comme l'acier.' [1]

The unrestrained accumulation of adventures often obscured this aspect of late Arthurian romances, but for all
their obvious deformities they possess a strange and un-
definable beauty. Their attraction lies not only in the
'eloquence of the old French prose, with its languor and
its melancholy',[2] but in the hidden eloquence of the stories
themselves. Endless motives are interwoven, and each
new paragraph is a cross-roads whence the story may lead
us in any direction; but wherever it may lead it will never
take us out of the 'secret orchard' of medieval romance.
And in the wandering through this enchanted realm there
is a strange sense of delight not unlike the fascination of
following a half-forgotten, half-remembered melody.

[1] Ibid., p. xiv.   [2] W. P. Ker, *Epic and Romance*, p. 335.

Chapter Three

NARRATIVE TECHNIQUE

MALORY refers to his source as a 'Frensshe boke', and Caxton adds, probably on the authority of Malory's own references, that the book was taken 'oute of certeyn bookes of frensshe' [1] and 'reduced in to englysshe'.[2] We can well believe them both. To a student of French medieval romance Malory's work appears as a world-old story. It is a slightly modified and condensed translation of the French Arthurian novels. Not only are the stories themselves imitated from the French, but the order in which they are placed is wellnigh the same as that of the French prose cycle, from which there are only three important departures: Malory adds a romance of Gareth, or Beaumains, untraceable to any known French source; places the story of Arthur's Roman expedition immediately after the *Merlin*,[3] and instead of giving a continuous account of the *Lancelot* proper, reproduces two odd sections of the French romance (Books VI and XIX); the *Tristan* is interpolated between the *Gareth* and the *Quest of the Holy Grail*. Otherwise the stories follow in their traditional sequence.[4]

It is easy, therefore, to trace Malory's work to a definite cycle of romances. A much more arduous task is that of identifying the exact version he used in each part. The difficulty is that the French Arthurian romances exist for us to-day in innumerable manuscripts, each of which contains a slightly different redaction. In order to discover

---

[1] Preface, p. 3.
[2] Ibid.; cf. also p. 861. On the meaning of the word 'reduced', cf. *infra*, p. 31 note 3.
[3] In the French cyclic MSS. it forms part of the last branch (*Mort Artu*).
[4] No less than eight extant French manuscripts combine the *Merlin*, the *Lancelot* proper, the *Queste*, and the *Mort Artu* (MSS. Bibl. Nat. fr. 98, 110, 113–16, 117–20, 344; Arsenal 3479–80; Br. Mus. Add. 10292; Phillipps 1046). MSS. Bibl. Nat. fr. 112, 116, and 758 connect these romances with the *Tristan*.

Malory's source for each story it is necessary to compare his text with all the existing French manuscripts in succession and to choose the versions which are nearest his own. I have given an account of these investigations in Appendix II.[1] Here it must suffice to state briefly the conclusions to which they have led.

Malory had at his disposal a fairly late cyclic version of the French Arthurian romances: it contained the *Merlin*, parts of the *Lancelot* proper, possibly the *Gareth* and the *Tristan*, the *Quest of the Holy Grail*, and the *Death of Arthur*. Whether the *Gareth* and the *Tristan* were already combined with the rest, or whether Malory himself added them from another source, cannot be fully ascertained.

But in addition to his French source he certainly used for his fifth book the English alliterative poem entitled *Morte Arthure*.[2] All the rest, i.e. the remaining twenty books of the *Morte Darthur*, was actually 'taken out of certain books of French', and it is not unlikely that these books formed one manuscript divided into three or four large volumes.

The difference in size between these 'French books' and Malory's compilation is a striking one. The volume of his French original may be estimated at something like one thousand folios.[3] Malory abridged it considerably, reducing it to one-fourth its size in the *Merlin* section (Books I—V), to one-sixth in the *Tristan* (Books VIII—XII),[4] and to one-eighth in the *Lancelot* proper (Books VI and XIX).[5] The *Queste* and the *Mort Artu* were the two least voluminous sections of the cycle and

---

[1] See *infra*, pp. 128–54.   [2] *v. infra*, pp. 134 ff.

[3] I allow about 200 folios for the *Merlin*, 500 for the *Tristan*, 160 for the *Lancelot*, 75 for the *Queste*, and 65 for the *Mort Artu*. All these figures are only approximate.

[4] In measuring the rate of condensation for the *Tristan* I have not taken into account the 'third book' of the French *Tristan* which Malory entirely excluded. On the method of calculation for this section see *Rom. de Trist.*, p. 110 note 3.

[5] Sommer and after him Miss Scudder (op. cit., p. 178) contend that Malory 'reduced his materials to one-tenth their original bulk'. This only applies to some parts of the *Lancelot*.

required much less condensation. Malory, however, reduced them by over one-half their original size. The *Mort Artu*, containing as it did what Malory doubtless considered the most vital part of his epic, was condensed slightly less than the *Queste*.[1] Malory's actual treatment of the sources varied very little, and the general effect of his work [2] is due not so much to his dramatic power as to his skilful condensation of the sources and to the rejection of some of those portions of the story which had so unpleasingly obscured the structure of the French prose cycle.[3] The indiscriminate exaltation of adventure so typical of the French cyclic romances is foreign to him. He does not delight in lingering over episodic details, and slowly cuts a road through a jungle of interwoven digressions.

The rate of abbreviation for the *Merlin* and *Tristan* is, however, chosen very arbitrarily. Malory at first apparently miscalculated the size of his project, and for the early part of his book, which shows no signs of haste, condensed very little. The romance of Gareth, since it has no connexion with either the preceding or the following events, could have been omitted. Its inclusion tells

[1] The rate of condensation is : 1 : 2·5 for the *Queste* (Books XIII—XVII), and 1 : 2·2 for the *Mort Artu* (Books XVIII, XX, and XXI).
[2] Cf. *infra*, pp. 94 ff.
[3] In a recent article in the *Zeitschrift für französische Sprache und Literatur*, vol. 51, 1–3, pp. 133–69 (review of *Rom. de Trist.*), Professor E. Brugger suggests a new interpretation of Malory's 'reduction'. He contends that Caxton's words 'reduced it into Englysshe' have so far been wrongly taken in the modern sense, and that here the real meaning of 'reduce' is 'to bring into another language'. In support of this theory he quotes (p. 148) the *Oxf Engl. Dict.* ('reduce', 12a), Berners, and Caxton, and rightly remarks that the phrase 'to shorten in French' ('in eine andere Sprache kürzen') is illogical. He further says that since Malory always refers to the 'Frensshe Booke' in the singular (Caxton's reference to 'certeyn bookes' is not to be trusted because Caxton knew little about Malory's originals), his source must have been not only a single work ('ein einziges Werk'), but a single volume ('ein einziger Band'); and because a complete version of the cycle could not be held in one volume, Professor Brugger concludes that the abridgement is due not to Malory, but to the author of his source. Professor Brugger may be right in his interpretation of the word 'reduce'; yet the theory which he questions, namely that Malory himself

us that Malory was short neither of time nor of space. In the *Tristan* section he must have felt the necessity for more consistent abridgement, and he condensed it slightly more than the *Merlin*. The change of scale was, however, not sufficiently radical, for when he came to the end of the second book of *Tristan*, he had already covered a space equal to 577 pages in Caxton's print, and he had not yet written the three main parts of the Arthuriad: the *Lancelot*, the *Queste*, and the *Mort Artu*. At that moment he could not have helped realizing how vital it was to dispense with all unnecessary details. He then opened the third French book of Tristan and found in it a remodelling of the *Quest of the Holy Grail*. Hastily, he put it aside and turned to the real *Queste*. 'Here endeth', he said in his colophon, 'the second book of syr Tristram that was drawen out of Frensshe into English. But here is no rehersal of the third book.' No doubt Malory had that third book, but he never came back to it, and gave in a later part of the *Morte Darthur* a very brief report of Tristan's death. His object was to hurry to the end, and in this manner he succeeded, in the course of 250 pages, in carrying the story to its traditional conclusion.

Unfortunately in all these 'painful rejections' his critical faculty seldom served him well. He sometimes neglected important incidents while reproducing subsidiary matter. Lack of discrimination accounts for his omission of some of the essential threads of the story, so that he makes it at times more obscure than it has ever been. For instance where Merlin refers to Excalibur: 'Loo yonder is that swerd that I spak of',[1] his words are meaningless because

shortened his original, is based not on Caxton's statements (which are in any case of small critical value) but on the study of the French manuscript tradition. No extant French version can reveal anything approaching Malory's method of abridgement. It is obvious besides that a MS. divided into four volumes for purely mechanical reasons could well be styled by Malory as by any one else a 'Frensshe Booke' in the singular. I therefore maintain, with Schofield, Sommer, and Vettermann, that whatever Caxton may have meant by the term 'reduced', Malory's source filled more than one volume, and that he himself is responsible for the shortening of the romances they contained.   [1] p. 73.

Malory has in two previous passages [1] omitted Merlin's conversations with Arthur. 'Wit you well', says Merlin in the French source,[2] 'I know but one good sword in this land, and that sword is in a lake where the fairies dwell.' The story of Arthur's rescue from Accolon has also been obscured. Arriving while the knights are engaged in battle the 'Damosel of the Lake' not only recognizes Arthur but even understands the 'false treason wrought for him':

'But syre Arthur pressed unto Accolon with his sheld and gaf hym with the pomel in his hand suche a buffet that he went thre strydes abak. Whan the damoisel of the lake beheld Arthur, how ful of prowesse his body was and the fals treson that was wrought for hym. . . . And at the next stroke syr Accolon stroke hym suche a stroke that by the damoysels enchauntment the swerd Excalibur felle oute of Accolons hande to the erthe.' [3]

Without the help of the French original this is unintelligible. The French explains that Merlin, warning Niviene (*Nimue* in Malory) of the danger that threatened Arthur, had foretold all the details of the fight.[4] Niviene can therefore identify Arthur in his moment of gravest peril, and save him: 'she knew well the king, . . . for Merlin himself had told her what arms he (the king) would wear in this combat.' [5] By omitting Merlin's warning Malory makes Niviene's conduct at best inconsistent.

His work contains many more examples of needless obscurity.[6] Appalled by the complications of his episodic

---

[1] pp. 70 and 71; cf. Huth MS. ff. 89ᵛ and 93ʳ.
[2] f. 93ʳ col. 2: 'Et sacés que je ne sai en che païs c'une boine espee, et cele est en un lach ou fees habitent.' [3] p. 131.
[4] Huth MS. f. 188ʳ col. 2: 'Et il se doit demain combatre encontre un autre chevaliers cors a cors; si est en ceste maniere en peril de mort, car s'espee li faurra au besoing, et chis sera garnis de la millour espee que chevaliers porte orendroit et d'un tel fuerre que ja hom ki le (*sic*) port sour li ne perdera goute de sanc. "Par foi," dist la damoisele, "moult est chis meschiés grans et perilleus. Or vaurroie je que nous fuissons entre moi et vous la ou la bataille doit estre." '
[5] Ibid., ff. 210ᵛ col. 2–211ʳ col. 1: 'elle connut bien le roi par chou que . . . Merlins meismes li ot bien devisé quels armes il porteroit en la bataille.'
[6] Cf. ibid., pp. 61–6 and 160 (Malory's version of the Tramtrist story). See also E. Vettermann, *Die Balen-Dichtungen und ihre Quellen*, Halle a.S., 1918, pp. 78–82.

matter, he dashed through it, and overlooking a number of obstacles, stumbled and 'broke his spear'. Though his instinct was sound, his method was at fault. When he worked on a smaller scale he was much better inspired. Whenever he limited himself to the reforming of a few short scenes he generally attained simplicity. He has a favourite device of making one scene out of two.[1] The French romance, in relating Tristan's departure from Cornwall, makes him deliver two speeches: one in which he bids farewell to the Cornish barons, and another in which he addresses his crew. Malory combines the two as follows: 'whanne sire Tristram was in the see he said: "Grete wel Kyng Marke and all myn enemyes, and say hem, I wille come ageyne whan I maye. And wel am I rewarded for the fyghtynge with sire Marhaus, and delyverd all this countrey from servage; and wel am I rewarded" ', &c.[2] In Malory's version the speech gains impressively in dramatic power, and in the recurrence of Tristan's ironical phrase there is a distinct sense of dignified simplicity.[3]

The French writers had a characteristic method of complicating the plots of their stories: the characters, leaving each other for short intervals, soon met again.[4] The story teller could by means of this, and without the slightest effort on his part, easily split one adventure into two or more. Here again Malory attempts to simplify. By preventing the knights from parting company he avoids a whole series of unnecessary re-encounters. There is an instance of this in the story of Balin. In the French *Merlin*, Balin parts with his damsel, meets a hermit, and then rejoins the damsel. In Malory they do not part until the adventure is over.[5] In the description of Mark's adventures in Logres, Malory does not permit King Mark's

[1] Cf. *Rom. de Trist.*, pp. 113–14.　　　　　　　　　[2] p. 372.
[3] A similar instance is Arthur's words on p. 553: ' "Loo," said Kynge Arthur, "yonder Palomydes begynneth to play his pageant. Soo God me help," said Arthur, "he is a passynge good knyght".' The French version (MS. Bibl. Nat. fr. 99, f. 490ᵛ col. 1) attributes only the second sentence to Arthur. The first is ascribed to 'ceux qui voient comment il commence cete journee'.　　　[4] Cf. *Rom. de Trist.*, pp. 114–15.　　　[5] pp. 89 ff.

departure from Lamorak,[1] and Dinadan finds them together. In the French source,[2] on the contrary, Mark
leaves Lamorak twice, and Dinadan meets them separately.
Another feature of the French adventure romances is
an abundance of minor characters whose casual appearance causes the story to wander from the main point and
fall into a series of digressions. Malory resists this, but
on a large scale lacks the power to carry out his design.
He never goes so far as to leave out a knight of the Round
Table or any person of consequence, but confines himself
to reducing slightly the number of less conspicuous personages, who are mostly anonymous: the knights and
damsels who act as messengers or as guardians of castles
and towers, or again as hosts offering hospitality to knights-
errant. In the story of Balin (*Balaain*), according to the
Huth MS., after the tragic death of the daughter of the
Duke of Harniel and her lover, Balin meets a squire to
whom he tells all that has happened, *pour che que je voel
que elle* (i.e. the adventure) *soit mise en escrit*.[3] Malory
omits this: Balin simply rides away from the scene.[4] In
another passage [5] Malory, relating how King Pellinore
went in quest of a knight [6] who led off a damsel, leaves
out the 'varlet riding a thin and weary horse' who, according to the French version,[7] has heard the damsel cry and
has seen the knight riding 'straight towards Braait'.
Another anonymous knight accompanying a lady is
omitted from Book X, ch. 17. In the French source they
are introduced for the purpose of explaining the customs
of Morgan's Castle. In Malory it is Dinadan who says to
Palomides that 'therein duelleth Quene Morgan le fay
Kynge Arthurs syster. And Kynge Arthur gafe her this
Castel, the whiche he hath repented hym sythen a thousand
tymes', for she has since used it as a prison for Arthur's
knights.[8] Leaving as it does no loose end the omis-

---

[1] pp. 426–8.
[2] MS. Bibl. Nat. fr. 334, ff. 305^v, col. 2–306^v, col. 1.
[3] Huth MS. f. 143^v, col. 1.   [4] p. 96.   [5] pp. 113–14.
[6] Hontzlake of Wentland.   [7] Huth MS. f. 173^v, col. 1.
[8] p. 440.

sion of *un chevalier et une damoisele* [1] distinctly improves
upon the French version.

One of Malory's most successful methods is the making
of one character out of two. His *Bloyas de la Flaundres* [2]
is, in reality, a combining of *Belias* and *Flandrens*.[3] A
more familiar character, *Gwynas de Bloy*, probably identical with *Gwymyart de Bloy*,[4] replaces the French *Flandrens*.
In the French source Sir Sadok, setting out to find Tristan
whom Mark has put in prison, is joined in his quest by
the seneschal of the castle of *Arbraye*.[5] Malory, instead of
introducing this new personage, identifies him with Sir
Dinas, whom the reader already knows to be a faithful
partisan of Tristan and an enemy of King Mark.[6] Some
of the anonymous 'messengers' are treated in a similar
manner. The messenger whom Iseult sends to Tristan is,
according to the French version, a hitherto unknown lady.[7]
Malory unhesitatingly identifies her with Brangwain.[8]
Most characteristic of all is, perhaps, the case of the two
'Yvains'. In the French manuscripts there were two distinct characters: *Yvayns li granz* and *Yvayns aus blanches
meins*, who both took part in the quest of Tristan.[9] Malory
makes one knight of the two, and describes him as 'sir
Uwayne le fyse le roy Vieyne, and somme callid him
Uwayne le blaunche maynys'.[10]

In the romances of adventure one of the means of in-
creasing the *personnel* and complicating the plots was to
leave for a time certain knights unidentified, thus increas-
ing the suspense of the story.[11] When Malory was faced

[1] MS. B.N. fr. 334, f. 331.   [2] p. 55.
[3] MS. B.M. Add. 10292, f. 110ʳ, col. 1.   [4] Cf. pp. 54₂₄, 55₃₅.
[5] MS. B.N. fr. 99, f. 388.   [6] p. 495.
[7] MS. B.N. fr. 334, f. 222ʳ, col. 2.   [8] p. 380.
[9] MS. B.N. fr. 334, f. 255.
[10] p. 401. The epithet 'le fyse le roy Vieyne' refers to *Yvayns li granz*.
[11] This was one of the favourite methods of Chrestien de Troyes. Cf.
W. Förster, *Kristian von Troyes, Wörterbuch zu seinen sämtlichen Werken*
(Halle, 1914), p. 157: 'Er (= Chrestien) hat die Manie (das Wort sagt
hier nicht zuviel), um seine Leser in Spannung zu halten, die Geschichte
in mediis rebus anzufangen, ohne das zum Verständnis Nötige vorher
mitzuteilen; er liebt es, die Hauptpersonen namenlos zu lassen und deren
Namen erst im Laufe der Erzählung, oft sogar am Schluss mitzuteilen.'

with a case of this kind he almost always disclosed the
mystery as quickly as he could. In the *Morte Darthur*,
indeed, the names of most of the knights are given when
they first appear. The French source (Huth MS.) relates
Balin's adventure with the sword on f. 100 and calls him
'uns povres chevaliers qui estoit nés de Norhomberlande'.
His name is not disclosed until f. 104. But Malory gives
his name from the first: 'Thenne fell it so that tyme', he
says, 'ther was a poor knyghte with Kynge Arthur that
hadde ben prysoner with hym half a yere and mo for
slayng of a knyghte the whiche was cousin unto Kynge
Arthur. *The name of this knyghte was called Balyn.*'[1] In the
same way Malory deviates from the French, revealing early
the identity of Garlon,[2] the invisible knight; of Sorlouse
of the Forest; of Bryan of the Forest;[3] and of Belangere
the Constable.[4] In the French *Lancelot*, Morgan, Sibylla,
and the Queen of Sorestan, finding Lancelot asleep under
a tree, marvel at his great beauty and take him for a *chose
fee*, but evidently fail to recognize him.[5] In Malory, on
the contrary, as soon as 'these quenes loked on his face
they knewe it was Syre Launcelot'.[6] Such premature reve-
lations may detract from the magic of adventure,[7] but the
stories are simplified and the reading of them much facili-
tated. Once, perhaps, Malory carries his simplification
too far. After the tournament at the Castle of Maidens,
the knights of King Arthur go on a quest for the 'knight
with the black shield', who has performed feats of bravery
and whose name they are anxious to know. Before the
quest begins, Malory discloses that the name of the knight
is Tristan; and Lancelot solemnly declares that 'Syr Tristram hathe won the field';[8] when the tournament is over
the knights swear 'never to reste one nyght . . . untyl that
wee fynd Syr Trystram'. Yet, the object of the quest
is not to find Tristan, but to discover his name, and it

---

[1] p. 77.   [2] p. 90.   [3] p. 106.
[4] p. 467. In the French source Belangere is named on his second appearance. Cf. MS. B.N. fr. 99, f. 377^v, col. 1.
[5] *Agravain*, ed. Sommer (*The Vulgate Versions of Arthurian Romances*,
vol. v), p. 91.   [6] p. 186.
[7] *V. infra*, pp. 51 ff.   [8] p. 397.

never occurred to Malory that in the circumstances the mystery was much too obvious.[1] Malory's good intentions are, however, above suspicion. He tried hard to simplify his narrative.[2] As a last instance we may refer to his method of anticipating the coming events of the story. Merlin says to Arthur as early as p. 103: 'This poure man Aryes the cowherd is not his (i.e. Tor's) fader, he is no thyng syb[3] to hym, for Kynge Pellinore is his fader.' This is anticipated from a much later passage in the French source in order to remove an unnecessary complication.[4] The painful interweavings of half-hidden motives which give the early romance its characteristic suspense are not to his taste, and so, in another passage, as soon as he can he foretells the manner of Merlin's death,[5] which the French source[6] does not disclose until the very end of the romance.[7]

[1] Cf. *Rom. de Trist.*, pp. 111–12. Another such case occurs on p. 434. According to the French version, when Mark first sees Palomides he is told that the knight's name is *le chevalier a la beste glatissant*, which conveys nothing to Mark, for 'de cestui seurnon ne savoit il nule riens'. In Malory he at once recognizes Palomides, having learnt his name from a 'varlet'. Here, then, contrary to his usual procedure, Malory in order to disclose Palomides' name introduces an additional personage. Further examples may be found in Appendix I to *Rom. de Trist.*, under the following reference-numbers: 563_{32}, 4171_{7-36}, 514_{20}, 528_{38}, 549_{34}, 558_{16-27}, and 563_{32}.

[2] Perhaps the most efficient method would have been to substitute direct speech for indirect quotation. Malory seldom has recourse to this device. He renders 'et il dit que Diex la beneïe' by 'and he said: "Damoysel, God the blysse"' (*La Queste del Saint Graal*, ed. Pauphilet, p. 1_8; Malory, p. 612_8), and turns the French 'il lor conte coment une damoisele l'a laienz amené' into 'As God me help, said syr Launcelot, a gentylwoman brought me hyther' (*La Queste*, p. 2_{18-19}; Malory, p. 613_{4-5}), but rarely attempts greater modifications.   [3] = related.

[4] Huth MS. f. 173^r, col. 1.   [5] pp. 119–20.   [6] Huth MS. f. 207^r.

[7] These small changes are merely indications of the author's general tendencies and hardly affect the entire structure of the *Morte Darthur*. The endless quests of the knights-errant, the numberless fights and encounters, and the lack of architectural unity, are perhaps as typical of Malory as of his models. His achievement falls short of his intention, and he only succeeds in showing his essentially 'unadventurous' mind. Striving to compose a congruous narrative, he proves himself incapable of transforming the labyrinthine French Arthuriad into a well-proportioned edifice.

THE QUEST OF AN UNKNOWN KNIGHT

MS. Bibl. Nat. Fr. 116

Malory was not always content to follow the French Romances. His book contains several episodes which are not directly traceable. But he himself invented little. He usually either reproduced episodes previously related, or anticipated them from a later section of his source. An instance of this is found in the romance of Gareth, which fills the Seventh Book of the *Morte Darthur*. How much of this book is Malory's own work cannot as yet be definitely ascertained, but some parts of it must be credited to him.[1] Of these the most important is the story of a nobleman brought up in the kitchen who by feats of arms proves his noble descent. Until then, he is mocked by every one and suffers many rebukes from knights and ladies. Beaumains, who shows himself a good knight, is reproved by his 'damsel', Lady Linet, who cannot bear the humiliation of being attended by a kitchen knave. He nevertheless follows her on her dangerous errand, and finally marries her sister, Lady Lioness. For Beaumains is no churl, but a noble knight and a brother to Sir Gawain. A similar plot is found in the story of Brunor of 'the evil shapen coat' (*La Cotte Mal Taillée*)[2] which Malory draws from a French source, with considerable alterations.[3] Brunor, like Gareth, is a knight in disguise, and the lady whom he is trying to help rebukes him 'in the foulest maner'. Malory describes these 'rebukes' more elaborately than does the French source, but it is easy to see that his additions are modelled on the story of Gareth.[4]

---

[1] See *infra*, p. 138.   [2] pp. 338 ff.   [3] Cf. *Rom. de Trist.*, pp. 170–3.
[4] The story of Brunor has in its turn influenced Malory's version of the episode of Alixander li Orphelin (pp. 465 ff.). Contrary to his source, Malory states that Alixander 'revenged his faders dethe for the fals Kynge Marke slewe bothe syre Tristram and Alysander falsly and felonsly' (p. 478). It was obviously impossible for Alixander to revenge his father's death and then be killed by Mark, the slayer of his father. Had he really taken his revenge, Mark would have been dead. This inconsistency is due to Malory's imitation of his own story of Brunor, who also 'avenged his faders dethe' (p. 353). Like Brunor, Alixander marries the lady who has shared his adventures: 'Breune le noyre wedded that damoysell Male-dysaunt' (ibid.), just as Alixander 'departed with his lady Alys la beale pylgrym . . . and lyved there in grete joye' (pp. 477–8). Cf. *Rom. de Trist.*, p. 192, note 6.

Another instance of this method is found in Malory's use of the episode of Tristan's fight with the dragon. This episode exists only in that version of the prose romance which Malory used for his compilation.[1] Malory, however, does not reproduce it. He relates Tristan's journey to Ireland without mentioning the dragon-fight. But he reverts to it in a later section of the story. After Tristan has been exiled from Cornwall, he goes mad with grief and 'wold go in to the wildernesse and brast doune the trees and bowes'. At last king Mark finds him asleep by a well, but failing to recognize him orders 'his knyghtes to take that naked man with fayrenes' and bring him to the castle. When the queen hears of this she goes to see the 'sick man' and finds him in the garden. Her 'brachet'[2] at once recognizes his master; then Iseult understands that it is her 'own lord syr Tristram'.[3] This episode has some curious points of resemblance with the dragon-fight: in both cases Tristan is a 'seke man', in both Iseult finds him outside the castle and fails to recognize him.[4] It is, therefore, most likely that in writing this episode Malory remembered the fight with the dragon. But it is still more striking that he utilized his own version of the garden scene some two hundred pages further on, in the description of Lancelot's recognition by Elaine. Lancelot, rebuked by Guinevere, goes mad with grief, runs into the wilderness, and for a long time wanders in the forest.[5] When he appears at the court of Pelles in the guise of a fool, 'fewe wold brynge hym mete to his handes'. One day he goes 'in to the gardyn, and there . . . leid hym doune by a welle and slepte'. 'One of dame Elyans maidens' tells her about it, Elaine goes to find him, and 'whan that she beheld hym, anone she felle in remembraunce of hym'.[6] Although Elaine recognizes Lancelot without the help of a 'brachet'[7] the similarities between the two inci-

[1] MS. B.N. fr. 103.   [2] = a small scenting dog.   [3] p. 370.
[4] MS. B.N. fr. 103, f. 43ᵛ, col. 1.
[5] Two years, according to Malory; one month, according to the French source.   [6] p. 598.
[7] She is helped, however, by 'one of her maidens', i.e. Brisen, a trait

dents are clear. The process of 'invention' is simple: the dragon episode suggested to Malory the details of Tristan's recognition by Iseult in the garden of Tintagel, and this was utilized for the description of Lancelot's recognition by Elaine in the garden of Corbenic.

This process of self-imitation frequently occurs in late medieval romance. It is, perhaps, a degenerate form of the epic 'repetition with variation'—degenerate because, instead of permitting a free play of the imagination, it only helps the writer to find a ready-made plot. It demonstrates a lack, or at the least a very low degree, of imaginative power. This is apparent not only from the few episodes which Malory adds to his story, but also from some of the casual remarks which he inserts here and there. In a description of a single combat he will almost certainly say, and with a phrase entirely his own, that the knights fought 'foining, tracing and traversing like two wild boars', but having once used these words he will repeat them on other occasions and any number of times. In relating the arrival of Pertolepe, Malory says that 'he dyde to syr Gareth homage and feauté and alle tho knyghtes to hold of hym for evermore'.[1] This sentence is Malory's own, but in the course of a single page he repeats it five times. Examples of repetition are frequent. Malory has a small stock of episodic details, and he resorts to it perhaps too often. The great story-teller was seemingly incapable of creating a story; and even though a certain portion of the *Morte Darthur* has not yet been traced to any definite source, it is hard to believe that he himself invented any of its episodes.

His real originality lies elsewhere: not in the elaboration of narrative, but in the treatment of the old stock stories, which, though he often cut them short, he interpreted in his own fashion. He gave or at least attempted to give them a new direction, a new colour, and a new meaning.

peculiar to Malory, and untraceable to his source. Cf. *Rom. de Trist.*, pp. 215–16.
[1] p. 270.

Perhaps the fundamental reason why, in spite of all his good intentions, he failed in narrative technique is that his mind was reflective rather than creative. And it may be profitable to attempt a recovery of at least some traces of his general outlook and leading thoughts.

Chapter Four
ROMANCE AND REALISM

I

AN interest in the psychological elements of a story is frequently accompanied in medieval romance by a neglect of its adventurous aspect; and Malory's disregard of the latter, the chief motive of the *roman d'aventure*, is largely due to his concentration on the former.[1]

A most cursory glance at his alterations and additions will prove this. His original traces the love of Tristan and Iseult to a purely 'adventurous' cause: it is only because he sees Palomides in love with Iseult that Tristan decides to supplant his friend.[2] Malory rejects this version. In the *Morte Darthur* Tristan's passion has a spontaneous origin, and his envy of Palomides is not the cause but the effect of his love. He 'cast grete love to la beale Isoud' because 'she was the fairest mayde and lady of the worlde'. Tristan teaches her to play the harp, and she begins 'to have grete fantasye unto hym'.[3] While in the French source their parting is not even mentioned,[4] in Malory Iseult makes 'grete dole and lamentacion', and says: ' "O

[1] He differs in this respect from most of his English predecessors. The Middle-English Arthurian poets concerned themselves with the narrative itself rather than with its courtly interpretation. The romantic spirit of the French Arthurian poems was tolerated—sometimes respected, but seldom understood. The author of the English version of Chrestien's *Yvain* (*Ywain and Gawain*) not only omits the discourses on courtly love which are the very essence of Chrestien's art, but almost divests his heroes of their emotions. For its effect the story depends on sequence of incident rather than on delineation of feeling. The same applies to *Sir Gawayne and the Green Knight*: it is a masterpiece of narrative, but it shows little interest in the real aims and virtues of the French romance.

[2] MS. B.N. fr. 103, f. 39ʳ, col. 2: 'Tant regarde Palamedes Yseult que Tristan s'en aperchoit a son semblant qu'il l'ayme de tout son coeur. . . . Et puis qu'il vist que Palamedes la regardoit si merveilleusement, il dit qu'il l'avra ou il mourra.'

[3] p. 285.   [4] Cf. MS. B.N. fr. 103, f. 43ᵛ, col. 2.

gentyl knight, ful wo am I of thy departynge, for I sawe
never man that I oughte [1] so good wille to", and there-
withall she wepte hertely.' They swear eternal faith to
each other, Tristan gives her a ring 'and she gaf hym
another'.[2]

There is another parting, no less affectionate, but perhaps more tragic, later in the book. For now Tristan,
whose alternative is to be put to death by King Mark, has
to forsake his beloved for ever: 'And thereupon Isoud
felle doune in a swoune and soo laye a grete whyle. And
whan she myght speke she said: "My lord sir Tristram,
blessid be God ye have your lyf. And now I am sure . . .
as soone as my lord Kynge Mark doo knowe you, he wil
bannysh you oute of the countrey of Cornewaile, or els he
will destroy you. For Goddes sake, myn owne lord, . . .
drawe you unto the Courte of Kyng Arthur, for there are
ye byloved. And ever whan I maye I shalle sende unto
you, and whan ye lyst ye may come to me, and at alle
tymes erly and late I wille be at your commaundment to
lyve as poure a lyf as ever did quene or lady." ' [3]

This scene has a counterpart in the description (also
due to Malory) of the discovery of Lancelot in the garden.
Elaine finds him asleep and 'felle on wepyng soo hertely
that she sanke even to the erthe, and whanne she had thus
wepte a grete whyle thenne she aroos and called her may-
dens, and said she was seke'.[4] When Tristan has been
exiled and perhaps for ever separated from his beloved, he
goes mad with grief. He unlaces his armour and 'wold go
in to the wildernesse and brast doune the trees and bowes,
and otherwhyle, whan he fond the harp that the lady
sente hym, thenne wold he harpe and playe therupon and
wepe togyders'. He avoids the messenger whom Iseult
has sent to console him, and runs into the forest; 'and
somtyme whan sire Tristram was in the woode that the
lady wyst not where he was, thenne wold she sytte her
doune and playe upon that harp. Thenne wold sire Tristram come to that harp and herken ther to.' [5]

[1] had.   [2] p. 292.   [3] p. 371.   [4] p. 598.
[5] p. 366. Cf. *Rom. de Trist.*, pp. 124–5.

I have given these extracts at possibly needless length because here we no doubt have Malory's own words and behind them his own voice. He alone is responsible for the laments added to the Tristan story and for its strong sentimental colouring. In the midst of chivalrous combats and intrigues he pauses to listen to the beating of a human heart, to the music of human love. But it is only a pause, and the ultimate effect is, therefore, insignificant. As in the struggle against adventure, so in the glorification of sentiment he succeeds in little more than the showing of his intention, and lacks the power of achieving it. Here, as elsewhere, he seems to work on too small a scale. His 'psychological' additions, it is true, give some scenes a new meaning. But these are mere isolated passages, so scattered as to have little bearing on the work as a whole. Hidden in an episodic tangle 'copyed oute of Frensshe', they are important only in so far as they enable us to appreciate Malory's literary personality.

II

'Ancor vaut miauz, ce m'est avis,
Uns cortois morz qu'uns vilains vis.'
CHRESTIEN DE TROYES, *Yvain*, 31-2.

If we have cause to regret Malory's shortcomings in the treatment of adventure, his failure in psychology may be viewed as a virtue. For his 'psychology', robustly different from the courtly idealism of French Romance, was least appropriate to the subject of his tale. The passages quoted above, for all their human appeal and touching *naïveté*, argue a peculiar misconception of the theme and atmosphere of Romance: they tend to transform the world's greatest love story into a *comédie larmoyante*, drowning the tragedy of Tristan and Iseult in a flood of pitiful tears. Had Malory applied his method on a larger scale, the story of the lovers of Cornwall would have become a series of pathetic laments and no less pathetic swoons.[1] His immediate predecessors in France had taken a safer

[1] Cf. *Rom. de Trist.*, pp. 128-9.

course, simply neglecting the sentimental side of their stories and concentrating on adventure. Malory wanted to outdo them. He deliberately set out to emphasize sentiment and to give his stories a psychological meaning. But of all Arthurian writers he was perhaps the least qualified to surround his romances with an aura they had once had in the past. He was not, as Sir Edmund Chambers thinks, 'as deliberate an archaist as the writer of *The Faerie Queene* or the writer of *The Defence of Guinevere*'.[1] The courtly philosophy of medieval France was to him a closed book. His 'psychology', therefore, is strangely out of keeping with its venerable medieval environment and repeats the experiment of pouring new wine into old bottles.

Some of his additions to the text yield what might be called his profession of faith. His source contained stories of romantic love—love treated with the characteristic freedom of courtly romance. To Malory nothing could be less attractive. His most cherished ideal is that of fidelity in marriage, even though he knows what his favourite hero, Lancelot, understands by 'fidelity'. He adds a curious passage to his text. A 'damsel' reproaches Lancelot with being unmarried: 'But one thyng, syre knyghte, methynketh ye lacke, ye that are a knyghte wiveles.' She further regrets that Lancelot loves Guinevere 'and that she hath ordeyned by enchauntement' that he 'shal never love none other but her, ne none other damoysel ne lady shall rejoyse' him; 'wherfor many in this land, of hyghe estate and lowe, make grete sorowe'. Lancelot bluntly rejects the idea, because he has other things to do. 'For thenne,' he says, 'I must couche with her, and leve armes and tournementys, batayls and adventures.' There remain the 'paramours', but Lancelot refuses them as well, 'in pryncypal for drede of God, *for knyghtes that ben aventurous or lecherous shal not be happy ne fortunate unto the werrys*, for outher they shalle be overcome with a symplyer knyghte than they be hem self, outher else they shal by unhap and her cursydnes slee better men than they ben hem self. And soo who that useth paramours shalle be unhappy, and

[1] *Sir Thomas Malory*, p. 3.

all thyng is unhappy that is aboute hem.' This is slightly
incoherent, but leaves us in no doubt as to Malory's attitude towards love. Lancelot, busy as he is with tournaments and adventures, refuses to marry; he cannot spare
the time. But extra-marital love is also condemned, and
Lancelot, the very embodiment of adulterous passion, is
here made to preach morality and fulminate against 'paramours'.[1] Malory even acquits his hero of the charge of
being in love with Guinevere,[2] although the rest of the
story makes the fact sufficiently apparent. The English
author, had it rested with him, would have gone further
and would have made Queen Guinevere's lover a champion of pure life, only temporarily engaged in knightly
service, but eventually hoping to end his glorious days in
a cosy home and by the side of a loving spouse.[3]

A similar though much more confused discussion of
the same question is found in the last chapter of Book
XVIII, which, with the passage just quoted, shares the
distinction of being Malory's own. Caxton attractively
entitled it 'How true love is likened unto summer'. In
reality, Malory does not here make an attempt at romantic
symbolism. He begins by stating that in May 'every
lusty herte begynneth to blosomme and to bring forth
fruyte, for lyke as herbes and trees bryngen forth fruyte
and florysshen in May, in lyke wyse every lusty herte that
is in ony maner a lover spryngeth and floryssheth in lusty
dedes'. This, according to Malory, happens 'for dyverse
causes', the main cause being that 'thenne alle herbes and
trees renewen a man and woman, and lyke wyse lovers'.
Such a discourse on the effects of spring, had it come
from the mouth of a fifteenth-century naturalist, would
have been perfectly appropriate. But, coming from a ro-

[1] pp. 197–8.   [2] *Ibid.*
[3] pp. 197–8. Cf. also the following characteristic passage which is again
Malory's own (p. 797$_{1-7}$): 'In May when every lust herte floryssheth and
burgeneth, for as the season is lusty to beholde and comfortable, soo man
and woman rejoycen and gladen of somer comynge with hys fresshe
floures. For wynter with his rough wyndes and blastes causeth a lusty man
and woman to coure and sytte fast by the fyre.' This seems to subordinate
human 'morality' to the revolutions of the seasons.

mance writer who, after many days of almost mechanical copying, finally condescends to give us his own views on love, it is nothing if not unbecoming. He further affirms that, in May, lovers 'callen ageyne to their mynde old gentilnes and old servyse, and many kynde dedes were forgeten by neclygence; for, lyke as wynter rasure [1] doth alway arase and deface grene somer, soo fareth it by unstable love in man and woman'. In other words: with the awakening of nature even unstable love resumes its rights. This astounding fact makes Malory think of the disadvantages of such love: 'For in many persons there is no stabylyte. For we may see al day for a lytel blast of wynters rasure [1] anone we shalle deface and lay a parte true love, for lytel or noughte *that cost moch thynge*. This is no wysedome nor stabylyte.' But 'stability' in Malory's sense has little to do with the mystical medieval conception of fidelity. Stability is the virtue of the common man; it implies no sacrifice and no faith; it is, as Malory himself suggests, the denial of an over-dose of pleasure, not the belief in a predestined, transcendental union of two souls. It is an obvious anachronism to say, as Malory does, that 'in lyke wyse was used love in Kynge Arthurs dayes'. If by 'King Arthur's days' we are to understand the realm of medieval romance, it is abundantly clear that nothing was farther from it than Malory's philosophy of life and happiness.

One of the most striking examples of this contrast is his treatment of the story of Iseult of the White Hands. In the French romance, Tristan, when he marries the Second Iseult, does not forget Iseult of Cornwall. He sighs after her and says: 'A, fair Iseult, thou hast killed me!' And, as the story goes, 'he fell from his horse in a swoon'.[2] Kahedin, the brother of Iseult of the White Hands, overhears Tristan's complaint, and thinking that it is his sister whom Tristan loves, volunteers to help

---

[1] = cutting wind.

[2] MS. B.N. fr. 99, f. 79ᵛ, col. 2: 'Tant pensa qu'il jecta ung grant souspir et puis dit: "Ha, belle Yseult, tu m'as mort!" Lors chiet de dessus son cheval a terre tout pasmé.'

Tristan. Tristan gladly accepts the offer. It is only on his wedding-day that he becomes conscious of the mis-understanding and realizes that Kahedin wants to give him 'that Iseult of whom he never thinks', but, unwilling to confess his true love, he accepts her. Malory completely alters the story. Tristan easily forgets his beloved, *'for by cause Sir Tristram had suche chere and rychesse and alle other plesaunce that he hadde forsaken la beale Isoud'*. And with no comment whatsoever Malory goes on to say that 'soo upon a tyme sir Trystram agreed to wedde Isoud la blaunche maynys'.[1] Then, of course, he finds himself in difficulty, since he is unable to explain why 'whanne they were abedde bothe, sire Tristram remembryd hym of his old lady la beale Isoud, and thenne he toke suche a thought sodenly that he was alle desmayed, and other chere maade he none'.

Malory's Tristan not only accepts 'rychesse and other pleasaunce' in exchange for his 'stability', but throughout his career regards it as an important consideration. When he reproaches Iseult of Cornwall with infidelity, he makes it plain that he has for her sake given up 'many landes and rychesse'.[2] He in this way justifies his claim to her love. However far medieval and modern poets have wandered from the original theme of the Tristan story, they have certainly never stooped to treat it in the light of Tristan's financial sacrifices. But Malory's mind is essentially realistic. He is always conscious of the practical side of his heroes' lives. Thus, while adding nothing substantial to the story of Lancelot, he is responsible for the notion that to discover his whereabouts Guinevere sent to Bors, Hector, and Lionel *'tresour ynough for theyr expencys'*.[3] Apparently he sees no incongruity in having the expenses of the quest provided for.[4]

Malory is also fond of specifying the economic and

---

[1] p. 328.   [2] p. 364.   [3] p. 585.
[4] A similar instance is found on p. 199, where Malory adds on his own account that the 'thre score ladyes and damoysels' who have been prisoners at the castle for seven years had to do 'al maner of sylke werkes' to earn their living.

legal aspects of feudal contracts. In the story of Accolon's treason it does not content him to say that Arthur inflicted due punishment on the people, but he must relate how Arthur made Damas yield to Ontzelake 'alle the hole manoir with the appertenaunce, under thys forme, that sir Ontzelake hold the manoir of yow and yerely to gyve yow a palfrey to ryde upon, for that wylle become yow better to ryde on than upon a courser'.[1]

This realistic point of view does not always lead to incongruity. It sometimes causes the author to give particular attention to details of scenery and to descriptions of the splendour and brilliance of his heroes' garments. Thus, Malory gives us an exact account of the enchanted mantle worn by the damsel of Morgan le Fay: 'She brought with her the rychest mantel that ever was sene in that Courte, for it was sette as ful of precious stones as one myght stand by another, and there were the rychest stones that ever the kynge sawe.'[2] And a few pages further on [3] we find a carefully drawn picture of the three damsels who met the knights at the fountain: 'and the eldest had a garland of gold aboute her hede, and she was thre score wynter of age or more, and her here was whyte under the garland'. The second damoysel was 'of thyrtty wynter of age, with a serkelet of gold aboute her hede'; and the third, who was only fifteen, had 'a garland of floures aboute her hede'.

In his account of Arthur's hunt [4] Malory adds several lines to his source and describes the ship Arthur found floating on the river. The interior of the ship was 'rychely behanged with clothe of sylke', and a hundred torches were 'sette upon alle the sydes of the shyp bordes and it gaf grete lyghte'.[5] In most cases, however, it satisfies Malory when by adding a word or two to his French

---

[1] p. 134.   [2] p. 139.   [3] p. 144.   [4] p. 125.
[5] In the French source (Huth MS. f. 198r) Arthur enters the ship in darkness, and the torches are brought in later by the twelve damsels: 'Lors commenchent a aporter chierges et tortis et a metre par mi la nef a mont et a val, si qu'il vous samblast, se vous fussiés laiens, que toute la nef fust esprise, si avoit il grant clarté en la nef' (f. 198v, col. 1).

original he makes it more precise. The inscription which
Lancelot finds on the tomb in Corbenic [1] is 'of gold'. When
Tristan, Iseult, and Palomides start for the fourth day of
the tournament of Lonazep, the author adds that they are
'clothed al in reed bothe Isoud and alle they'.[2] Red and
gold are Malory's favourite colours, though we sometimes
see 'white mules under the canopy of green silk' and
knights in blue and white armour. And perhaps the best
way to appreciate Malory's picturesque qualities is to regard his work 'as a tapestry'[3] with bright figures moving
in pleasant though slightly artificial landscapes.

A realistic setting may well serve romance and would
not, in itself, detract from Malory's merit as a romancer.
But his realism is different from that of the author of
Flamenca, and indeed from any kind of romantic realism
either medieval or modern. It is fundamentally prosaic
and practical, and gives the romantic imagination no free
play. It may be unfair, perhaps, to expect a fifteenth-
century English author to understand the elaborate me-
chanics of the French medieval system of courtly love.
But he is indifferent to such obvious and universal aspects
of romance as magic and the use of the supernatural. Of
this there are abundant examples. Instead of following his
source and putting Tristan in a rudderless boat, *tout seul,
sans compagnie*,[4] Malory introduces a 'ryght wyse lady'
who tells Tristan 'playnly' where to go.[5] Tristan's journey
thus ceases to be a *navigation à l'aventure*; the hero leaving
nothing to chance sails straight to Ireland. In another
passage Malory discards the idea that the Lady of the
Lake could, walking across an invisible bridge, reach the
centre of the lake ('so that neither her feet nor anything
she wore was wet'[6]) and return with a sword for Arthur.
Nor does he admit Merlin's story of the magic lake under
whose surface lies hidden an enchanted palace, *clos d'en-
cantement*, that no one may see who is not of the castle.

[1] p. 572.   [2] p. 553.   [3] Cf. Chambers, *op. cit.*, p. 6.
[4] MS. B.N. fr. 103, f. 36ʳ, col. 2.   [5] p. 284.
[6] MS. Huth, f. 94ʳ, col. 1: '. . . a piet sec, en tel maniere que ses piés
ne autre chose de li ne fu mouillet'.

12198²

The lady, says Merlin, walks over a wooden bridge that few can see, but all those who belong to the enchanted castle can, though the bridge is invisible, walk over it.[1] In Malory the damsel simply advises Arthur and Merlin to take a barge and fetch the sword. Arthur and Merlin row over the lake, and 'whanne they came to the swerd that the hand held, syre Arthur toke it up by the handels and toke it with hym'. The description of the enchanted lake is omitted. 'Improbable' incidents had no appeal for Malory.[2]

It has been remarked [3] that Malory's failure to understand the basic significance of the story of Balin (Book II) shows itself in his omission of the references to Fate, such as: 'He says that he is the most miserable and vile of all knights . . . for now he clearly understands that Fortune is against him, and that she dislikes him more than any other man.' [4] The French text says that when Balaain came to a castle he saw a cross with an inscription which read: 'Dost thou hear, knight, who seekest adventures? I forbid thee to go from here toward the Castle. And wit thou well that its adventure is not easy for a knight.' [5] Balaain neglects the warning because he thinks it beneath his dignity to turn back 'for a written word'. But then appears an old 'vavassour', who tells him that since he has passed *les bornes* his doom is sealed. In this account there is a sense of fatality about Balaain's progress towards the enchanted castle, a relentless fatality which has an unmistakable appeal. For no sooner has the old man uttered those sinister words than Balaain hears a horn 'as if some

[1] Ibid., f. 95ʳ, col. 1.
[2] Near the end of the *Merlin* section Malory makes another such change in the text. In the French, the 'damoisele del lac' comes to Arthur in the semblance of an old woman: 'et se fu si atornee par enchantement que li rois ne la coneust ja mais en cele semblanche, car il vous samblast bien, se vous la veissiés, que elle eust passé soisante ans et plus' (MS. Huth, f. 228ᵛ, col. 2). In Malory nothing is said about her appearance, and the 'enchantement' is not even mentioned. (p. 139: 'Wyth that came the demoysel of the lake unto the Kyng and said: "Syr I must speke with yow in pryvyté." ')
[3] Cf. E. Vetterman, *op. cit.*, pp. 82–3.   [4] MS. Huth, f. 129ʳ, col. 1.
[5] MS. Huth, f. 144ʳ, col. 2: 'Os tu, chevaliers errans qui vas querant aventures? Je te deffenc que tu n'ailles de chi prés dou chastiel. Et sache que elles ne sont mie legieres a un chevalier.'

one was hunting a hart or a wild boar' [1]; and then there come out of the castle over a hundred maidens, *karolant et dansant et chantant*, who tell him with alluring and mysterious voices: 'Welcome to the good knight who by his fighting shall now delight all the ladies and damsels of this Castle!' [2] And they go around him *dansant et ballant*. But in Malory the magic atmosphere which surrounds this page of the French original will be sought for in vain. He reduces the story to a few lines relating in an unpleasantly abrupt manner that the inscription on the cross read: 'it is not for no knyght alone to ryde toward this Castel', and that Balin saw 'an old hore gentylman' who said: 'thow passyst thy bandes to come this waye, therfor torne ageyne and it availle the'.[3] The old man vanishes; Balin hears 'an horne blowe as it had ben the dethe of a best',[4] and 'anone with all he sawe an hondred ladyes and many knyghtes that welcomed hym with fayre semblaunt and made hym passing good chere'. Malory specifies, with his usual partiality to luxurious surroundings, that the letters of the inscription were of gold, but he goes no further. He discards the most important traits of the story, and 'reduces' it to a mere skeleton—in this case a most unwelcome alteration. It shows an utter inability to grasp the profoundly poetic meaning of the scene,[5] and a complete lack of sympathy with the grace and mystery which are the very essence of romantic magic.

[1] 'aussi comme ce fust de prise de cierf ou de porc sauvage.'

[2] 'Bien viegne li bons chevaliers qui de son jouster fera hui renvoisier toutes les dames et les damoiseles de cest chastiel.'

[3] This is supposed to render the French *il n'a mais riens del retorner.*

[4] p. 96. Compare also Balin's words in the French text: 'Qu'es che? Me tiennent il a pris, qui cornent de prise?' with the weak humour of the English: 'That blast is blowen for me, for I am the pryse and yet am I not dede.'

[5] In a recent essay on Malory's Book of Balin (*Mediaeval Studies in Memory of G. Schoepperle Loomis*, Paris and New York, 1927, p. 181) Miss L. A. Hibbard has attempted to justify Malory's version of this episode. 'The inscription on the cross', she says, 'is the only thing in the whole scene described by the French author which is essential to the dramatic situation. Malory emphasizes it by saying that its letters are of gold.' It will suffice to note that, if Malory really meant to emphasize the inscrip-

This statement may seem surprising to those who are accustomed to regard Malory's work as a perfect embodiment of romantic beauty. But whatever magic the *Morte Darthur* contains is not Malory's own. And if we are to study his methods and ideas at all, distinguishing them from those used by his French predecessors, we can only base our judgement on his treatment of their works, and not on the *Morte Darthur* as it stands. The magic of the book is French, not English, and whenever our English author interferes with it, the supernatural loses something of its original power.

He was a well-intentioned, honest, and righteous man, and probably a true gentleman. He had a very strong sense of the realities of life, and well knew that to every human pursuit there was a practical side. Yet, for all his sound common sense and his noble purpose, he was incapable of appreciating the fundamental *motif* of his 'Frensshe Bookes'. His sense of colour and his love of adornment hardly atone for his failure to understand and sympathize with the real medieval romance. And if there are readers who are ignorant of this antagonism between the author and his book, readers to whom the *Morte Darthur* still remains the apotheosis of chivalrous romance, it is because the work has preserved some remnants of the old and powerful stories which, stronger than Malory, have survived and conquered his prosaic realism.

tion on the cross, the obvious thing for him to have done would not have been to mangle it. I fail to see that by saying that the letters were of gold Malory emphasized the 'dramatic situation'.

Chapter Five

THE GENIUS OF CHIVALRY

IT is of paramount importance for the study of Malory's work to remember one point of his hypothetical biography. He was an active participant in the gallant doings of Richard of Warwick, the 'Father of Courtesy', under whose patronage he served.[1] In the early years of his life he was initiated into the art of war and chivalry, and, like Perceval in the *Morte Darthur*, learned 'to haunte armes and noble dedes'. His book witnesses that none of the elements of medieval romance had a more direct appeal to him than the traditions of knight-errantry. He may have despised the old methods of story-telling, he may have misunderstood the psychology of romantic love, but with the ideals of perfect knighthood he never lacked sympathy. And he was not content to reproduce the French fairy tales about King Arthur's knights. He deliberately set out to extol their 'kynde', to give them greater importance, and to make them a living 'ensample' to his own generation.

His attitude towards the legacy of the Middle Ages was essentially that of a moralist. He had none of the romantic enthusiasm for the marvellous. He did not take his theme because 'the savage pomp and the capricious heroism of the baronial manners were replete with incident, adventure, and enterprise and framed rich material to the minstrel muse'.[2] Visions, miracles, and legends did not appeal to him by reason of their distinct poetic quality, but because they helped him to express his own moral doctrine. He used his 'French books' to show his readers how virtuous knights had come 'to honour, and how they that were vycious were punysshed and ofte put to shame and rebuke'. And he wished 'al noble lordes and ladyes . . . that shal see and rede in this sayd book and werke' to

[1] Cf. *supra*, pp. 2–4.
[2] Warton, *History of English Poetry*, vol. iv, p. 21.

'take the good and honest actes in their remembraunce
and to folowe the same'.[1]

This attempt to restore to the world the moral teaching
of medieval chivalry was by no means original. Similar
efforts had been made both before and during Malory's
own time. The founders of the Orders of Knighthood
were prompted by the same desire and had a like admiration for 'jentyl and vertuous dedes'. Edward III in his
earlier years was presumably one of the best representatives
of this spirit, and his object in establishing the 'most
noble' Order of the Garter was to exalt the dignity of
knighthood and, by encouraging knightly service, to create
'a Bond or Tye of Fellowship'. According to Ashmole,[2]
the knights 'deemed it (the Order) would prove a very
great advancement to Piety, Nobility and Virtue'. The
idea that chivalry could be used as a means of moral perfection was popular throughout fifteenth-century Europe.
It was also maintained by several later authors. Marc
Vulson de la Colombière, the well-known historian of late
medieval chivalry, states that the principal object of his
history is to banish *l'oysiveté et la molesse, où la pluspart des
Gentilshommes se plongent*,[3] and for their edification relates
stories of jousts and tournaments, drawn in great part
from French medieval fiction. His Preface bears a striking
verbal resemblance to Caxton's, and his object in restoring
the 'true image of honour and chivalry' is not much different from Malory's 'noble entente'.[4]

But words are misleading, and the apparent similarity
between Malory's 'entente' and that of the fourteenth-
and fifteenth-century restorers of knighthood should not be
allowed to conceal their differences. What chiefly attracted
these late admirers of chivalry was not its doctrine but its
outward splendour. Chivalry having lost its material basis

---

[1] Caxton's Preface, p. 3; *v. supra*, p. 13.

[2] *History of the Most Noble Order of the Garter*, 2nd ed., 1715, p. 125.

[3] *Le Vray Théâtre d'honneur et de chevalerie*, Paris, 1643.

[4] It has been remarked that Spenser's letter to Sir Walter Raleigh also
contains some obvious analogies with Caxton's Preface, doubtless due to
deliberate imitation. Cf. Marie Walther, *Malorys Einfluss auf Spensers
Faerie Queene*. Diss. Heidelberg. Eisleben, 1898, pp. 5–7.

could not retain its moral ascendency. 'When the heavy-armed knight became a mere trooper, and rode to the war side by side with paid men-at-arms as well accoutred, horsed, and trained as himself, he began to lose his prestige in war and society.'[1] Here as elsewhere the formal aspect proved more permanent than the ideal, and the great devices of medieval knighthood degenerated into mere love of luxury and theatrical pomp. An example is found in the history of the Order of Santiago de Compostella, which, like the great military and religious Orders of Knighthood, originally had a definite aim—the protection of pilgrims who came to worship the relics of the tutelar saint of Spain. Eventually the Order assumed not only the defence of the passage to the shrine of St James, but also a general defence of the Kingdom against the enemies of the Christian faith. With the expulsion of the Moors from Spain, however, the main purpose of the Order disappeared, the vows were broken, and religious aims were replaced by others. The Order gradually developed into an order of merit, and sank to the position of a 'feather in the plume of Spanish dignity'.[2] The cross, finished like the blade of a sword, remained the ensign of the Brotherhood of St. James, but lost its allegorical significance.[3]

Nor was the Order of the Garter established for the 'advancement of Piety, Nobility and Vertue', as Ashmole thinks. Nicolas rightly contends [4] that it had no loftier immediate origin than a joust or tournament. It consisted of the King, the Black Prince, and twenty-four knights divided into two bands of twelve, like the tilters in a 'hastilude'. The real object of this Order was to exhibit the brilliancy of Court festivals. How great an importance was assigned to the forms of ceremony is shown by the proceedings at the great annual feast at which all the Knights of the Order had to be present with their

[1] F. W. Cornish, *Chivalry*.
[2] Cf. Mills, *A History of Chivalry*, vol. i, p. 333.
[3] Cf. Prutz, *Die geistliche Ritterorden*, p. 451.
[4] *History of the British Orders of Knighthood*, vol. i.

attendants and in their best dress. In Ashmole's own words, 'Lest the honour of the Order might receive diminution from too small an appearance at its public solemnities, it was further decreed, that none of the Knights should depart the Kingdom without first acquainting the Sovereign'; and if any Knight 'was so sick as to keep his bed', his habit was laid upon his Stall. At the procession 'the Habits were so ordered that the more grave and civil being placed between those that are rich and gallant, entertained the beholders with a more delightful prospect'.[1] This is perhaps the most typical expression of the chivalric temper of the late Middle Ages. The ideal of a knight combining bravery, generosity, and devotion was no longer a reality, and picturesque parades had taken the place of arms and prayers. In the words of Pierre de Blois, 'the knights had their shields beautifully gilt, but they were kept in a virgin and unused condition'.

A no less theatrical conception of chivalry prevailed at the court of Philip of Flanders. He brilliantly revived the pageant of medieval tournaments, but these had already degenerated into mere games. The competitors in the lists ran no risk, for their armour was too strong for the awkward and obsolete weapons used against it. King René of Anjou, *le bon roi René*, whom Marc Wlson considers one of the champions of knighthood, with the sole object of holding annual festivals and tournaments similar to those of the Burgundian court, founded in 1448 the order of the Crescent. 'Tout cela,' says Michelet, 'commençait à paraître puéril.'[2] And indeed, many a fifteenth-century knight seems to foreshadow Don Quixote. Jacques de Lalain, *le Bon Chevalier*, one of the most accomplished knights of his day, was, according to Michelet, 'le dernier héros de cette gymnastique'. He worshipped an imaginary 'Dame de pleurs' and established his stronghold at a cross-roads near Dijon, but could find no one willing to fight, and complained that 'personne n'a pitié de la Dame de plours et n'i veut toucher'. Olivier de la Marche, the chronicler of the Burgundian court, also men-

[1] Ashmole, *History*, &c. [2] *Histoire de France*, vol. vii, p. 150.

A TOURNAMENT

MS. Bibl. Nat. Fr. 112

A SINGLE COMBAT

MS. Bibl. Nat. Fr. 118

tions 'un escuyer anglois nommé Thomas Qué (qui venoit de Galles)' who was a prominent figure in these comic performances. Thomas Kay, Jacques Lalain, and the 'bastard de Sainct Pol' [1] were Malory's contemporaries, and the quixotic exploits of these upholders of knightly dignity must have been common knowledge at the time when he began his book.

William Caxton witnessed and deplored the degeneration of chivalric customs in the society of his day. He concluded his translation of the *Order of Chivalry* [2] with the following appeal to the 'knights of England':

'O ye knyghtes of Englond, where is the custom and usage of noble chyvalry that was used in those dayes? What do ye now but go to the baynes [3] and playe atte dyse? And some not wel advysed use not honest and good rule, ageyne alle ordre of Knyghthoode. Leve this, leve it, and rede the noble volumes of Saynt Graal, of Lancelot, of Galaad, of Trystram, of Perceforest, [4] of Percyval, of Gawayn and many mo. Ther shalle ye see manhode, curtesye and gentylnesse.'

Caxton's lament over the decay of chivalry clearly expresses Malory's object in compiling the *Morte Darthur*. Unlike the founders of the orders of merit, he was attracted first and foremost by the moral significance of knighthood. It was 'manhode, curtesye and gentylnesse' that he desired to restore to the world, not the pompous

[1] Olivier de la Marche describes this knight in the following terms: 'Au temps desus-dict, messire Jehan, bastard de Sainct Pol, signeur de Hanbourdin (qui fut de son temps un moult chevalereux chevalier), tint un pas pour faire armes pres de Sainct-Omer, le terme de six semaines, luy sixième de compaignons (qui se nommoyent pélerins); et se fonda son pas et emprise sur la belle Pélerine: lequel pas il fit signifier par tous les royaumes et pais voisins, et s'atendoit d'avoir beaucoup de gens-de-bien, et principalement du royaume de France; mais ainsi advint que l'on commença des lors a murmurer, tant de la paix comme des trèves, et par François et par Anglois: tellement que chacun se disposa pour la guerre, et vindrent à celuy pas peu de gens.' (*Mémoires de messire Olivier de la Marche*, t. i, pp. 455–6; edited by M. Petitot in the *Collection complète des Mémoires relatifs à l'histoire de France*, Paris, 1825.)

[2] Reprinted by W. Morris, Hammersmith, 1893.   [3] = baths.

[4] A French prose romance composed towards 1330. It traces an ideal picture of chivalrous society—of its courtesy, bravery, magnificence, and spirit of adventure.

ceremonies of medieval festivals. And he was certainly
well advised in his choice of sources. The medieval romances of chivalry supplied him with the 'ensample' which
he sought, but he went further. Whereas his French
sources often related bare adventures and left them un-
explained, Malory desired that the reader should understand the significance of every episode which involved
problems of chivalric conduct. He makes Sir Ector recall
Lancelot's chivalrous character in a remarkable threnody
which is entirely of his own invention:

'A Launcelot,' he sayd, 'thou were hede of al crysten knyghtes;
and now I dare say,' said syr Ector, 'thou, sir Launcelot, there thou
lyest that thou were never matched of erthely knyghtes hande; and
thou were the curtest knyght that ever bare shelde; and thou were
the truest frende to thy lovar that ever bestrade hors; and thou
were the trewest lover of a synful man that ever loved woman; and thou
were the kyndest man that ever strake with swerde; and thou were
the godelyest persone that ever cam emonge prees of knyghtes;
and thou was the mekest man and the jentyllest that ever ete in
halle emonge ladyes, and thou were the sternest knyght to thy
mortal foo that ever put spere in the breste.' [1]

This is Malory's own code, and the leading *motif* of
his story. It comes out not only in the praise of the 'curtest
knyght that ever bare shelde', but in the reprobation of
the unworthy, such as King Mark, whom Lamorak quali-
fies as 'a grete enemy to alle good knyghtes ... for he hath
chaced oute of that Countrey syr Tristram that is the
worshipfullest knyght that now is lyvynge'.[2] Tristan is,
indeed, the very embodiment of the proud virtues of perfect knighthood, and no one can mistake the noble pathos
of his farewell to the Irish barons:

'yf there be ony man here', he says to them, 'that I have offended
unto, or that ony man be with me greved, lete complayne hym here
afore me or that ever I depart, and I shal amende it unto my power.
And yf there be ony that wil profer me wronge or sey of me wrong
or shame behynde my bak, saye hit now or never, and here is my
body to make it good body ageynst body.' [3]

[1] p. 860.   [2] p. 425.
[3] p. 292. None of the passages quoted here is traceable to Malory's
French source.

Knighthood confers privileges, for, as Guinevere says to
Palomides, 'he that is curtois and kynde and gentil hath
favour in every place'[1]; and Tristan succeeds in the battle-
field because 'all that the noble syre Tristram dothe is
thorou clene knyghthode'.[2] The power of chivalric love is
illustrated in the description of Tristan's fight with Elyas.
At the most dangerous moment he
'remembryd hym of his lady la beale Isoud that loked upon hym,
and how he was lykely never to come in her presence. Thenne he
pulled up his shelde that erst henge ful lowe, and thenne he dressid
up his shelde unto Elyas and gaf hym many sadde [3] strokes twenty
ageynst one.' [4]

But the 'high order of knighthood' [5] also carries with
it paramount duties which often come into conflict with
the surrounding world. In the French Romance the conflict is not always successfully solved, with the result that
Tristan and Lancelot are sometimes inconsistent. In the
course of his adventure at Castle Pluer, Tristan cuts off
the head of Sir Breunor's lady because such is the custom
of the castle. Here Malory follows, perhaps too servilely,
the version of his source, and it surprises one to find that
the 'noble knyghte' Sir Tristram 'strode unto hym [6] and
toke his lady from hym and with an auke [7] stroke he smote
of her hede clene'. But we know that Malory was not
always master of his subject, and an inconsistency with
his leading thought is not surprising.[8]

---

[1] p. 557.   [2] p. 553.   [3] = heavy.
[4] p. 463. On Malory's chivalric temper see W. H. Schofield, *Chivalry in
English Literature* (chapter on Malory), and *Rom. de Trist.*, pp. 137–44.
[5] The phrase is Malory's own (p. 469). As against his source (cf. MS.
B.N. fr. 99) he makes Anglides say to her son: 'Now I requyre the and
charge the upon my blessing and upon the hyghe ordre of knyghthode,
that thow be revengyd upon Kynge Marke for the dethe of thy fader.'
[6] Breunor.
[7] p. 312. *Auke* here means *prompt* (see *Oxf. Engl. Dict.* under *awke*), not
perverse or *sinister*, as Sommer in his Glossary suggests (ii, p. 188), or
backward (Strachey).
[8] Miss Scudder (*op. cit.*, p. 241) wrongly attributes this incident to
Malory's general tendency to 'degrade' Tristan. Justice demands that it
should be attributed to his source. In fact none of Malory's additions and
alterations would justify the theory that 'in Malory, Tristram . . . is pur-

His own theory of chivalrous conduct is clearly illustrated elsewhere. The French Prose *Lancelot* relates that,
after leaving the daughter of Baudemagus, Lancelot rode
for some time without finding shelter, till at last he discovered a pavilion. Finding nobody in it he put out the
lights and went to bed. But soon the owner of the pavilion
returned and lay down beside Lancelot, whom he took for
his mistress. Embracing him and perceiving his mistake, he grew angry, and throwing Lancelot out of the
bed, took flight. Lancelot seized his sword, overtook the
knight, and killed him.[1] This adventure stands in glaring
contrast with Lancelot's otherwise chivalrous character.
Instead of reproducing this incident as he did Tristan's
adventure at Castle Pluer, Malory transforms it into another 'ensample' of Lancelot's courtesy. True, the latter
wounds the knight 'sore nyghe unto the deth', but then
the knight surrenders to Lancelot, explaining that the pavilion belongs to him and that he expected his lady to come
there that same night. Lancelot regrets having wounded
him, 'and soo they wente bothe in to the pavelione, and
anone syre Launcelot staunched his blood'. He is so
'courteous and gentle' that when the lady arrives and, on
seeing her lord Belleus grievously wounded, begins to
lament, Belleus bids her hold her peace, 'for this knyght
is a good man and a knyght adventurous'. When the lady
learns Lancelot's name she says: 'soo me thought ever by
your speche', and makes him promise that when Belleus
comes to Arthur's court he will be made a knight of the
Round Table. Lancelot is pleased to fulfil her wish, and
bids the knight and the lady come 'unto the courte the
next hyhe feest'.[2]

posely and systematically degraded'. There are several instances to the
contrary. In the scene of Tristan's departure from Ireland, Malory makes
Tristan say, 'gyve me la beale Isoud youre doughter not for my self but
for myn unkel Kynge Marke'. And when King Anguish suggests that
Tristan should wed her, Tristan proudly retorts: 'And I dyd, than I were
shamed for ever in this world and fals of my promyse' (p. 309). This is
not in the French (Cf. MS. B.N. fr. 103, f. 56ʳ, col. 1).

[1] Cf. *The Vulgate Versions of Arthurian Romances*, ed. Sommer, vol. v,
pp. 95-7.   [2] p. 189.

This unusually extensive addition to the story is characteristic of Malory's idea of the accomplishments of a
chevalier and gentleman. A knight should not indulge in
useless fighting—his bravery is a means not an end, and
those who abuse their physical superiority forfeit their
claims to perfect knighthood.

The *Merlin* section contains a curious alteration. After
their exile from Arthur's court, Gawain and Ywain enter
a forest and find there twelve damsels dancing around a
tree on which hangs a white shield. 'And ever as the
damoysels cam by it, they spytte upon it and some threwe
myre upon the sheld.' [1] Gawain marvels at the custom,
but Ywain [2] explains to him that the shield belongs to
Morholt, who 'hateth al ladyes and gentylwymmen'. According to the French source, Gawain thinks it incredible
that Morholt should suffer the ladies to insult him, and
wishes Morholt would remove the shield. 'It grieves me
to see them do this', he says, 'for this is a knight's armour.' [3]
Malory clings to this latter remark, and makes Gawain
violently reprove the damsels for dishonouring the shield.
'And paraventur', he says, 'though he hate yow, he hath
somme.[4] . . . And paraventure he loveth in somme other
places ladyes and gentylwymmen.' He further contends
that he 'sawe hym [i.e. Morholt] ones preued at a justes
where many knyghtes were gadered, and at that tyme ther
myghte no man withstande hym'. 'Damoysels', he goes
on, 'me thynketh ye are to blame, for hit is to suppose,
he that henge that sheld ther he wille not be longe ther
fro, and thenne may tho knyghtes matche hym on horsbak.
*And that is more your worship than thus, for I wille abyde no
lenger to see a knyghtes sheld dishonoured.*' [5]

The symbolic meaning of this emblem of knighthood
is emphasized in another passage [6] where Malory's text is
at variance with his source. Tristan refuses to lend his

---

[1] p. 140.   [2] 'The damsels' in Malory.
[3] Huth MS., f. 222^r, col. 1: 'che que je voi que elles font me fait mal,
pour chou que chou est arme a chevalerie'.
[4] Probably a corruption for: 'he hath somme certayne cause'.
[5] p. 141.   [6] p. 374.

shield to Dinadan because it is his lady's gift, and solemnly declares to his companion in arms: 'I will not departe from my sheld for her sake that gaf it to me.'[1]

Loyalty 'fyrst unto God and next unto the joye of them that he promysed his feythe unto',[2] bravery in a 'ryghteous quarel', but kindness to enemies and courtesy to all—these are the foremost virtues of a real chevalier. And if Lancelot is the 'flower of Christian knighthood', it is because he combines the qualities of a warrior with those of a gentleman, because he is at one and the same time 'the sternest knyght to his mortal foo' and 'the kyndest man that ever strake with swerde'.[3]

Such is Malory's simple creed. His book is an earnest endeavour to revive the moral grandeur of what he thought was 'the old custom and usage of this land'. And though the path was fraught with danger, he followed the interminable quests of knights-errant and shared their strange adventure with the sole object of seeking

> the moated castle's cell
> Where long through talisman and spell,
> While tyrants ruled, and damsels wept,
> Thy Genius, Chivalry, hath slept.

It was the humour of the situation that Malory failed to appreciate. It was not easy to preserve the chivalric temper in romance when the institution of knighthood had lost all its significance. Chivalry as a purely literary product was a perilous endeavour. It could easily turn into parody. The more seriously it was treated by romance writers, the more easily it was compromised. But of this danger Malory is unconscious to the last. He does not notice that in his stories there is enough humour to ridicule and discredit the whole fabric of chivalrous morality.

---

[1] In the French source (MS. B.N. fr. 103, f. 171ᵛ, col. 1), Tristan parts with his shield without hesitation: 'Dynadan, fait Tristan, je crois bien que vous diés voir. Or portés mon escu et je porteroy le vostre.'
[2] p. 771.
[3] Similar additions are found on pp. 344₁₈₋₃₈, 534₃₀₋₇, and 541₂₈₋₃₅. Cf. the corresponding passages in my collation (*Rom. de Trist.*, pp. 143, 171, and 203).

When Tristan and Palomides dismount to drink water from a fair well [1] they see a knight sleeping near by. As 'true knights' they cannot leave the matter alone. 'What is best to doo?' asks Tristan. 'Awake hym', says Palomides, and Tristan awakes the knight 'with the but of his spere'. Naturally enough, 'the knyght arose up hastely, and putte his helme upon his hede, and gat a grete spere in his hand, and without ony moo wordes he hurled unto sir Tristram, and smote hym clene from his sadel'. The situation is thus rendered more serious still, and Tristan hears the call of his knightly duty. 'And eyther asked counceylle of other what was best to be done. "By my hede", said sir Tristram, "I wyll folowe this strong knyght."' All through the next chapter he follows the knight in all solemnity and earnestness. In the world of Tristan, Lancelot, and Palomides, such farcical incidents were frequent. The French Prose Romances of the Arthurian Cycle contain many, and so does the *Morte Darthur*.

There is reason to believe that the French Arthurian writers of the Middle Ages were awake to the difficulties of their theme and possessed the sense of humour which Malory so completely lacked.[2] Even Chrestien's attitude towards his fantastic world was somewhat detached: a smile played upon his lips and there were touches of irony in his subtle psychological discussions. The attitude of the writers of the Cycle towards the tales of chivalric magic is often one of scepticism. When Guinevere goes

[1] p. 415.

[2] Though it is generally believed that Malory had a great sense of humour, I have not been able to detect any proof of this in his additions and alterations. Among the instances of 'Malory's vein of humour' mentioned by Sir E. Strachey in his Introduction to the *Morte Darthur* (1923, p. xi), only two may be regarded as Malory's additions: the words 'the kynge was gladde for she made suche a noyse' (pp. 104–5) about a lady who was forcibly carried out of the hall by a strange knight; and the reference to the Bishop of Canterbury who after Mordred's treachery retired to live 'in poverte & in holy prayers, for wel he understode that myschevous warre was at honde' (p. 840). 'For she made suche a noyse' may be a touch of humour, though the real humour of the scene lies in the description of the noise, which Malory copied from his source. As for the Bishop of Canterbury, only modern sophistication can attach a sarcastic meaning to Malory's

to the Fountain of Fairies the author of the Prose *Lancelot*
adds: 'As no one knew who they were they were said to
be fairies.' [1] But few romance writers were so well aware
of the comic aspect of the 'warriors wrought in steely
weeds' as the author of the Second Version of the French
Prose *Tristan*.[2] In that version we find a familiar character, Dinadan, engaged in an artful attack on the theory and
practice of chivalry. He is not a lover, and when he hears
true lovers sighing for their ladies, pokes fun at them.
He expounds his views on love to Palomides and tries to
persuade him to give up his obsolete idea of eternal
longing. 'A love that thus torments and kills its servants,
punishes them for their folly. . . . May God guard and
protect me against such a love!' [3] His own love is
different:

'the love that I have in my heart gives me merriment, joy, and
delight. . . . Never has love deceived me, for never have I made a
request to it without having my fill. And never have I lost my
heart: I always hear it beat and move within my bosom.' [4]

His is a hedonistic conception of love. He seeks pleasure,
not suffering. In the conversation with the nuns of the
Abbey,[5] he suggests that the only thing he might ask of
God is to be defended against ladies and damsels, *car ceulx
ci sont en trop fort prison qui pensent a dame et a damoiselle*.

Dinadan's most serious attacks are directed, however,
against the chivalric conception of duty and valour. He
mocks at the way in which knights greet each other. When
he meets a knight (not named in any of the French MSS.)
who demands that he shall joust, he smiles and says: 'Sir
knight, canst thou not greet a knight-errant without say-

solemn description of his retirement to the monastery. There is unmistakable humour in the adventures of Beaumains (Book VII), but in the
absence of sources it would be hazardous to trace it to Malory's invention.
[1] 'si ne povoit on riens savoir de lor estre, et por ce disoit on que ce
estoient fees' (*The Vulgate Versions*, iv. 305).
[2] On the differences between the First and the Second Versions cf. my
Études sur le Tristan en prose, pp. 27–9.
[3] MS. B.N. fr. 334, f. 318ʳ, col. 1. Cf. *Études*, &c., p. 96.
[4] *Ibid. Études*, p. 97.
[5] MS. B.N. fr. 99, f. 389ʳ, col. 1. *Études*, pp. 97–8.

ing: "joust with me"? By God, this greeting is not too gentle.' [1] The succeeding debate between the two knights affords Dinadan fresh opportunity of commenting upon the inconsistency of the customs of chivalry. He argues that, since a knight is so often challenged by those who are his friends and are supposed to love him, it would be better to be their enemy and to avoid the consequences of an overdose of such love. So he declares himself the enemy of the rival knight, whose answer is 'all the more reason for a fight'. Dinadan is pleased at the success of his stratagem and misleads his opponent still more by pretending to be serious: 'Thou knowest', he says, 'that knights sometimes have good cause for quarrel, sometimes not; and as thou knowest not my reason for being thy enemy, I shall tell thee when thou comest to King Arthur's court in his presence.' The knight, hearing Dinadan speak so wisely, 'noticed not that Dinadan spoke these words in mockery'. In another passage [2] Dinadan tells his friend Agravain, who has been smitten to the ground by a stronger knight: 'My cowardice makes me live, and thy prowess has tumbled thee down from thy horse'; and he defines his position in the world of chivalry: 'I am a knight who seeks the meaning of the world, but nowhere can I find it.' [3]

Dinadan's unconventional criticisms of the chivalrous code are a redeeming feature in the monotonous picture of 'perfect' chivalry as set forth in the French romances. But Malory fails to appreciate this. He has no sympathy with anything that reveals a critical attitude towards his favourite ideal, and tries hard to delete Dinadan's most characteristic comments. To remove all suspicion of Dinadan's opposition to the rules of chivalry, Malory expressly states that Dinadan 'hadde suche a customme

---

[1] MS. B.N. fr. 334, f. 327ʳ, col. 1; *Études*, p. 94.
[2] *Ibid.*, f. 334ʳ, col. 2; *Études*, p. 96.
[3] On the character of Dinadan in the French romance, see *Rom. de Trist.*, pp. 134–7, and *Études*, p. 29. For the sake of completeness I reproduce here with slight changes the account of Malory's treatment of Dinadan which I have given in *Rom. de Trist.*, pp. 144–7.

that he loved every good knyght and every good knyght loved him'. Again, Dinadan's jokes about chivalrous love are given in one sentence: 'And there Sir Tristram told la beale Isoud how Sir Dinadan held against all lovers.'

Owing to such alterations Dinadan's ironical speeches on knighthood have been reduced to mere *bonhomie*, and some of the episodes in which he plays the predominant part have become pointless. In the encounter with the unknown knight Dinadan misses the opportunity of attacking the chivalrous ideals of duty, and so makes the rest of the scene almost unintelligible:

'Soo on the morne' [says Malory] 'sir Dynadan rode unto the court of Kynge Arthur, and by the way as he rode he sawe where stoode an erraunt knyght and made hym redy for to juste. "Not soo," said Dynadan, "for I have no wylle to juste."—"With me shalle ye juste," said the knyght, "or ¹ that ye passe this waye."— "Whether aske ye justes by love or by hate?" The knyght ansuerd: "Wete ye wel, I aske hit for love and not for hate."— "Hit maye wel be soo," said syre Dynadan, "but ye profer me hard love whan ye wylle juste with me with a sharp spere. But, fayre knyghte," sayd syre Dynadan, "sythe ye wylle juste with me, mete wyth me in the Courte of Kynge Arthur, and there shalle I juste with you."'

The knight is quite content that Dinadan should fight with him later, and says he loves him 'hertely'. And 'soo they departed'.²

Malory has made a clean sweep of all Dinadan's mockery of that peculiar 'love' among knights which expressed itself in a desire to battle with its object. It is therefore impossible to understand why Dinadan should refuse the fight. The scene is motiveless throughout, because Malory at the expense of plausibility consistently avoids any criticism which may possibly nullify the naïve but firm morality of his book.

But *naïveté* and the habit of moralizing on how to 'bring yow to good fame and renommée' have survived to this day. Ever since Malory's time poets and critics have regarded the *Morte Darthur* as a means of moral and

¹ =ere.   ² p. 446.

spiritual perfection. In his Introduction to the book Sir Edward Strachey maintains that Malory was able 'to embody the ideals of chivalry in actual and serious personages, and so to influence the national character and manners of his countrymen in the best way'. He finds in the book 'a real effort to distinguish virtue from vice', and an upward progress in that 'the brutish vice has dwindled to half its former size, while virtue is more avowedly triumphant over the evil'.[1] With less faith in the moral elevation and educational value of Malory's romance, we can only accept his modest effort as an expression of his simple and narrow ideal. His was not a crusading chivalry raised to its highest energy by the reunion of the knightly and monastic ideals of service, love, and sacrifice. What he advocated were the comfortable virtues of a righteous gentleman who 'does after the good and leaves the evil', but whose spiritual attainments are limited to social discipline and gentle manners. Malory may have been inspired in his youth by the 'Father of Courtesy', but he had little in common with the great founders of medieval chivalry. We can no longer think that he ever approached the height of their idealism, unless we refuse, in John Denham's phrase,

> To stoop with disenchanted wings to truth.

---

[1] *Ibid.*, p. xxiii.

Chapter Six

CAMELOT AND CORBENIC

I

Die ich rief, die Geister,
Werd ich nun nicht los.

GOETHE, *Der Zauberlehrling.*

WHEN, in his seclusion, Malory began to turn over his faded folios of the French Arthurian Cycle, he must have felt as did Goethe's *Zauberlehrling* when the spirits he had set free refused to obey him. For in the famous French books which at first seemed so attractive there were more evil than good spirits. Not only were Malory's sources overburdened with adventures of the sort he disliked, not only did they introduce Dinadan's displeasing criticisms of knightly customs, but they had as their base a conception of chivalry which was the very opposite of Malory's. From his point of view, the central figures in the story were Lancelot and King Arthur. To him the Arthurian stories were a monument to the glory of earthly chivalry and its virtuous deeds. According to Caxton, the book depicts 'noble chivalry, humanity, friend- liness, hardiness, love, friendship', and for these virtues there could be no better symbols than Lancelot and Arthur. In Malory's eyes the quest of the Holy Grail is only one of their adventures, perhaps the most attractive and the most pious, but hardly a sustaining chord in the whole epic. The point of view of the French authors of the Arthurian Cycle was different. The *Queste* was its central part and gave the key to the whole work.

I have mentioned before that the French Prose Cycle was lacking in sequence or unity, that having diminished the importance of sentiment it yielded a series of uncon- nected and uninspired adventures.[1] But behind its ap- parent shapelessness there was in the Cycle a definite

[1] *V. supra*, pp. 25–6.

meaning and method. Its meaning was not in the nature of Chrestien's *sen*, and its method was not artistic: what the author of the Cycle attempted and partly attained was a moral unity and a religious purpose.

Two theories have been recently advanced with regard to the Prose Cycle. One was formulated by M. Ferdinand Lot as follows: 'Le corpus *Lancelot-Graal*, déduction faite du Merlin et de ses suites, qui sont certainement postiches, est dû à un seul auteur. Il présente sous une diversité apparente une unité de conception et de plan certaine.'[1] The other was first proposed by M. Albert Pauphilet[2] and further developed by M. Étienne Gilson.[3] Their contention is that the *Queste del Saint Graal* is the work of Cistercian monks and contains the doctrine preached particularly by St. Bernard of Clairvaux. Both theories have been slightly overstated by their exponents. The evidence furnished by Lot does not make it imperative to trace the Cycle to a single hand, and permits the supposition that it may have been produced by a few authors working in close contact.[4] On the other hand, Gilson seems to exaggerate the Bernardine inspiration of some passages in the Grail section.[5] Yet it is hard to escape the conviction that in essentials both theories are right. It can no longer be gainsaid that the 'corpus Lancelot-Graal'—i.e. the *Estoire del Graal*, the *Lancelot*, the *Queste del Saint Graal*, and the *Mort Artu*—was the work, if not of one man, at least of one group of authors working simultaneously. It must also be ad-

[1] *Étude sur le Lancelot en prose*, Paris, 1918, pp. 7–8. Lot has, in my opinion, proved the point conclusively. The most convincing chapters in his book are: 'Du principe de l'entrelacement' and 'Du procédé chrono-logique'. His discussion of the 'unity of plan and spirit' (pp. 65–107) is far less conclusive.

[2] *Étude sur la Queste del Saint Graal*, Paris, 1921.

[3] *La mystique de la grâce dans la Queste del Saint Graal* (*Romania*, li. 323–47).

[4] Lot seems to work on the assumption that the unity of spirit and method implies the unity of authorship. There are many examples to the contrary.

[5] e.g. his discussion of the 'cognitive terms' (*voir ouvertement, montrer ouvertement*, &c.) used in the *Queste* (pp. 344–6). Their bearing on the point is insignificant.

mitted that the man who wrote the *Queste* was closely associated with the Cistercian order and had a definite religious purpose. The obvious conclusion to be drawn from these two results is that the whole of the *Lancelot-Grail*, except the *Merlin* section, was the product of a religous mind steeped in the doctrines of Cîteaux.

This might seem at first incredible. It is not surprising that the *Queste* itself had a religious purpose and belonged to a definite religious movement which flourished in France in the twelfth and thirteenth centuries. But it is certainly surprising to find that this religious movement also inspired the 'secular' sections of the Cycle, the stories of Lancelot, Guinevere, and Arthur, and the whole epic of the Round Table with its profane ideals of courtly love. The antagonism between these two parts of the cycle is, indeed, striking. Camelot, where Arthur held his court, and Corbenic,[1] the Grail castle, appear to embody two distinct faiths and to serve two conflicting purposes. The love-romance of Lancelot shows the triumph of earthly chivalry, while the story of the Grail has more in common with the lives of the saints than with any romantic tradition. And yet it is possible to establish a close connexion between the purpose of the *Queste* and that of the *Lancelot*, and so to justify on grounds of internal evidence the theory of their common authorship.

The clue to the problem may perhaps be found in the prophecy of the 'preudons' to Hector: 'when thou comest thither . . . the king shall tell thee that he cares not for men who have risen as high as thou hast, to wit, who dwell in deadly sin and in pride'.[2] The worldly achievements of the knights of the Round Table are described in the secular section of the Cycle with the greatest care and profusion of detail. Yet the object of such descriptions is not to praise earthly chivalry, but to condemn it; to show how he 'who rises high' in the world of Arthur will sink to the

---

[1] *Corbyn* in Malory.
[2] MS. B.N. fr. 120, f. 547ʳ, col. 2: 'quant vous veinrés la . . . le roy vous dira qu'il n'a cure de tels hommes qui si haut soient montés, c'est a dire qui gisent en pechié mortel et en orgueil.'

lowest depths in the world of the Grail: 'For know thou well that in this Queste thy earthly chevalry cannot avail thee, if the Holy Spirit help thee not in all the adventures that may befall thee.' The case of Gawain is particularly interesting. He is one of the most famous knights of the Round Table, second only to Lancelot. Most devoted to his king, he is generous and noble, courageous and strong. He possesses all of man's earthly virtues and is very much loved and honoured by both 'countrymen and strangers': 'Car sans faille il estoit l'ome del monde qui plus ert amez d'estrange gent.' But since God has no part in his career, his brilliant qualities do not help him, and he ends as a vile criminal.[1] It was dangerous, perhaps, to make a sinner so attractive, and it was in any case essential to show that his virtues and successes could lead to no result. By preserving the attractive aspects of Gawain's character the author attempted to demonstrate their futility and the contrast between man's human virtues and Christian duties.

Lancelot's case is no less illustrative. In poetry he was the traditional 'meilleur chevalier du monde', the unquestioned hero of the courtly Arthuriad. Had the romance of Chrestien been accurately reproduced, the perfect knight would have superseded all the other characters and proclaimed the superiority of his courtly philosophy. This would have had disastrous consequences. Lancelot, the sinner, would have held the most important place in the romance and would have prevented the Pure from establishing their rule. The Cistercian who wrote this part of the Cycle therefore took precautions to deprive Lancelot of his moral prestige. In the Prose Romances he still appears as the perfect knight and the perfect lover. He is, in the actual words of the romance, 'le plus beau chevalier, le meilleur, et le plus gracieux et le plus desiré a

---

[1] MS. B.N. fr. 120, f. 547ᵛ, col. 1: 'Gauvain, Gauvain, il a moult long temps que tu fus premier chevaillier, ne oncques puis ne servis ton Creatour se petit non. Tu es mais si vieulz arbres que il n'a mais en toy fueilles ne fruit. Car pense tant au mains que Nostre Sires ait la mouelle et l'escorce, puis que Nostre Sires en a le fruit et l'autre grain.'

veoir de toutes gens, et le mieux aimé qui onques naquist a nos temps.' His love for Guinevere is faithful, moving, and full of charm. It is the model of courtly love in its less sophisticated, human form. But here again the author presents the case *a contrario*: the greater Lancelot's excellence in this world, the more is he condemned in the world of the *Queste*. Lancelot has his first religious experience at the Dolorous Gard. There, from one of the tombs in the mystical burial ground, comes a voice asking him his name, and telling him that he is not the best knight of the world: 'for he who is to become the best knight shall deliver me from the grave; and he shall achieve the greatest feats which thou hast missed through thy love of luxury and of thy body, which is unworthy of attaining the Holy Grail; for thou hast done evil things and thy body is poisoned'. In the *Lancelot* branch this is the first direct announcement of the Quest. It comes when Lancelot is yet far from repenting of his sins; and, moreover, in the very middle of a pure *conte d'aventures*, where one scarcely expects disturbing elements. The *motif* of the Holy Grail is already heard, seemingly in disharmony with the atmosphere of the romance. But it is only an anticipation: the horn is sounded only to urge the Knights of the Round Table to remember their paramount duties.

There follows a series of similar anticipations. They fill all the intermediate part between the *Lancelot* and the *Queste* proper. Lancelot is gradually brought to complete repentance, and the worldly error in him yields its place to religious truth; virtuous love becomes sinful, and all Lancelot's thoughts and deeds henceforth belong to God. His conversations with the priests and hermits mark the various stages of his approach to the ideal of the *Queste*. And yet the sinner must, because of his sin, be precluded from ultimate spiritual perfection. He cannot entirely rid himself of human frailty, of the 'coulpe' of his earlier life. If he is rewarded for repentance, the reward is partial. His virtue is incomplete; he cannot fully understand the power of God. Thus, when he sees two lions barring his way, he draws his sword and forgets that the sign of the

LANCELOT VISITING THE HERMIT

MS. Bibl. Nat. Fr. 116

cross will suffice to drive them off.[1] There are, then, two
sides to Lancelot's character: as a sinner he is punished,
but because he repents he is rewarded. He is permitted
to enter the castle of Corbenic, but only furtively, unlike
the pure knights; he will never cross the threshold of the
sanctuary. The author of the *Queste* will always treat him
as a symbol of earthly chivalry desperately and sincerely
attempting to approach a higher ideal. His successes and
failures are carefully measured, and his punishment is in
direct proportion to his earlier greatness.[2]

Here, as with Gawain, the author applies his method
of antithesis. He does not fear to display the fascinating
world of earthly chivalry, and at great length tells us of the
secular beauty of Arthurian knighthood. He knows how
to subordinate the secular to the divine, and how to de-
velop the teaching of the Grail romance *a contrario*. He is
not afraid to place it on the ground of *coincidentia contra-
dictoriorum*, much as, later on, Nicholas of Cusa conceived
of God as the 'blending of all antitheses'. Lancelot's failure
is as eloquent as Galahad's achievement; the attractions of
courtly love, since they are treated as vicious and futile, are
rendered harmless, and instead of undermining the elaborate scheme of religious romance, they yield an exact measure
of the power of divine truth and serve to support it.[3]

[1] Pauphilet, *op. cit.*, p. 129.
[2] Generally speaking, the knights of the Round Table represent the various
scales of perfection in the enjoyment of grace. According to St. Bernard,
there are three states of mystical experience: dreams, visions, and *pura mens*
(cf. *Sermo XXXI in Cantica canticorum*, in Migne, *Patr. Lat.* 183).
Though revelation through dreams is granted to Lancelot, he can only
attain to a partial understanding of it. He will never experience supreme
ecstasy, a privilege accorded only to the pure: Bohort, Perceval, and
Galahad. Visions attained through the medium of the senses enable these
knights to see the marvels of Corbenic and to reach the second state of
mystical experience. True, Lancelot partly sees such visions, but what
distinguishes him from the three pure knights is that his vision is incomplete, and that he is precluded from the third state which alone yields a
comprehension of the mysteries of God. Cf. E. Gilson, *op. cit.*, pp. 336–40.
[3] 'Le dualisme qui semblait scinder en deux l'œuvre, en apparence con-
tradictoire, et qui en est la base même, aboutit donc à une unité har-
monieuse, à une haute synthèse. A l'intérieur de chaque "branche" de

The philosophic dilemma of the *Lancelot-Grail* was in
this way satisfactorily solved. There remained, however,
an important problem of structure. Lancelot, the pro-
tagonist of the secular section of the Cycle, could not
assume the same part in the *Queste*. A sinner, he could
not achieve the Grail, for to make him do so would mean
impairing the purity of the Christian symbol. The blending of the two *motifs*—the *Lancelot* and the *Grail*—if it
did not result in an impossible plot, would have altered
the fundamental philosophic conception of the work. The
author sees but one solution: to give Lancelot a son who,
though he succeeds in the quest of the Grail, will by his
birth be a punishment for his father's sinful love. All of
the author's efforts tend toward making that solution
both tragic and inevitable. Perceval vanishes, and Lancelot, whose sins cry for punishment, is precluded. It is then
that he begets a son by (Malory's) Elaine[1] whom by reason
of a spell he mistakes for Guinevere. Learning his error,
he goes mad, and wanders in the forest like a hunted

cet arbre si riche en sève, on retrouve aisément et la thèse et l'antithèse'
(M. Lot-Borodine, *Le double esprit et l'unité du* Lancelot *en prose, Mélanges
d'histoire du moyen âge offerts à M. Ferdinand Lot,* Paris, 1925, p. 488).
This is an excellent formula, but Mme Lot-Borodine is often inconsistent
with it, and I cannot concur in her general interpretation of the *Lancelot.*
She thinks that the Prose Cycle shows a spiritual affinity of earthly and
divine chivalry, and that 'la chevalerie "terrienne" mène en ligne droite à
la chevalerie "célestienne" '. She sees in the prose romance a gradual transition from one to the other: 'La filiation mystique de Lancelot et de
Galaad nous paraît certaine, et c'est au sens le plus profond du mot que le
premier engendre le second.' These theories may seem attractive in
themselves, but none of them is borne out either by the facts of the story
or by the principles of the Cistercian doctrine. It is easy to show by quotations from the *Queste* that the author was conscious of an acute conflict
between the two kinds of chivalry, and never derived the one from the
other. Galahad's mysticism can by no means be fathered upon Lancelot.
Yet it is probably true that, as Mme Lot-Borodine suggests, the author
of the *Queste* treated earthly chivalry with considerable sympathy and
broadness of mind, e.g. in the words of the Lady of the Lake: 'Les péchés
du siècle ne peuvent aller sans folie, mais celui-là a raison qui trouve en sa
folie sagesse et honneur.' The Cistercian author was certainly not a narrow
dogmatist: he could see the attractive side of profane things.

[1] She is anonymous in the French romance.

beast. The begetting of Galahad is an irretrievable offence against courtly love. It symbolizes the failure of Lancelot's earthly endeavour—the tragic end of his love for Guinevere. The birth of the pure knight brings about a cataclysm and a deliverance. The same tragic event defiles the purity of earthly love and inaugurates the realm of divine grace. It is a link between earthly error and the truth of religion,[1] and through the final phrase of the threnody of the Round Table runs the liturgical chant of Galahad.

But the real catastrophe comes after the completion of the Quest, when the theme of the Death of Arthur—the *Mort Artu*—creeps into the story.[2] The knights of the Round Table must be punished, and the court of Arthur must perish. There is in the early sections of the *Mort Artu* a sudden revival of the secular aspects of Arthur's glory: the intrigues of Lancelot and Guinevere are renewed, Lancelot again shines in tournaments, and Arthur resumes his victorious campaigns and defeats the Roman Emperor. But all this is only a preparation for the denouement of the drama which destroys the court of Arthur. This, like almost every medieval drama, is of a didactic character: it concerns itself with the rise, decline, and fall of the chivalric ideal as it was originally set forth in the heyday of the Round Table. The unlawful love of Lancelot and Guinevere is reintroduced merely to explain

---

[1] It is often held (cf. M. Lot-Borodine, *op. cit.*, pp. 482–3) that Galahad, being a reincarnation of Lancelot's virtues without the burdens of his sins, provides a material link between his father and the Grail: '. . . son instinct de chevalier, accru d'une puissance surnaturelle, . . . l'intensité du sentiment qui l'inspire, orienté seulement dans un autre sens [*sic*], lui sont directement transmis par Lancelot en personne, lui viennent de lui'. But this is a very superficial view. Lancelot does not survive in Galahad, and their 'virtues' are fundamentally different.

[2] On the connexion between the *Mort Artu* and the other branches of the cycle, see J. D. Bruce's edition of the romance (Halle, 1910), pp. xxxiii, 266–70, and 272–3. Bruce expressly states that the *Mortu Artu* 'has the same author as the *Agravain*—the last division of the *Lancelot* proper'. The latter contains a number of episodes which can only be understood with the help of the *Mort Artu*. Cf. also P. Märtens, *Zur Lanzelotsage*, in Boehmer's *Romanische Studien*, pp. 557 ff.

the decay of Arthur's kingdom. Arthur, betrayed and
slain by his nephew, will pass away to Avalon; Lancelot will forsake the vanities of this world; and Guinevere,
in the silence of a cloistered abbey, will pray for both their
souls.

The good-humoured Chrestien de Troyes, content with
the magic beauty of his Arthurian world, probably never
thought of suggesting any such serious change. But the
ecstatic inspiration of the followers of St. Bernard gave
the Romances new life and meaning: the Arthuriad was
to be exploited for a new, a mystical purpose. It presents,
therefore, a queer mixture of lay and Christian ideals, and
its colour is certainly neither purely religious nor purely
sentimental; but it is intensely medieval in its equal inclusion of both. A double current seems to flow through
the *Lancelot-Grail*—a mixture of two chivalries, one earthly
and the other divine—and the mysticism of the Grail rests
equally upon both.

II

It is doubtful whether Malory could fully appreciate
the religious doctrine of his source; but his point of view
was certainly very different. He did not seek a condemnation of the Arthurian world. On the contrary, he was
anxious to restore and exhibit its moral values and its brilliance. Fascinated by its spectacular side, he overlooked
the essential point of the French Prose Cycle; and where
the French monks attempted a moral tale of sinful knights,
he saw the earthly beauty and the undying charm of
Arthur's kingdom. The greater their mundane achievements the greater their sin; such must have been the view
of the Cistercian author who wrote the stories of Lancelot
and Arthur. Malory only half followed him. He relent-
lessly cut out the theological comments of the *Queste*, and
said nothing that could arouse a suspicion of the sinful
nature of knighthood. Thus, unwittingly, he reasserted
the ideals of earthly chivalry. In his work, the events and
ideas which, in the French romances, had been presented

'HOW LANCELOT AND THE GRAIL KNIGHTS RELATED THEIR
ADVENTURE AND HOW THE CLERKS WROTE IT DOWN'

MS. Bibl. Nat. Fr. 122

a contrario, acquired a direct meaning;[1] and the Round Table, instead of forming an antithesis to the Grail ideals, itself became the symbol of all good. And if in the end it must fail, it will fail not because of a religious condemnation, but because of a human tragedy, which rests upon the conflict of love and loyalty.[2]

Arthur and his knights are not to be made a prey to theological argument, and Malory unhesitatingly deletes most of the theological 'explanations of adventures' which he finds in his source. When Galahad uncovers the magic tomb he hears a voice saying: 'Syr Galahad, the servaunt of Jhesu Cryste, come thow not nyghe me, for thow shalt make me goo ageyne ther where I have ben soo longe.' Galahad then lifts up the stone and a 'foul figure' leaps out from the grave and a voice says: 'Galahad, I see there envyronne aboute the so many angels that my power may not dere the.' Galahad sees a corpse at the bottom of the grave and orders it to be removed, 'for hit is not worthy to lye in this chircheyerd, for he was a fals Crysten man'.[3] To explain this mysterious episode Malory confines himself to a few lines: the body, he says, 'betokeneth the duresse of the world and the grete synne that our Lord fond in the world. For there was suche wretchydnesse that the fader loved not the sone, nor the sone loved not the fader. And that was one of the causes that oure lord took flesshe and blood of a clene mayden, for oure synnes were so grete at that tyme that wel nyghe all was wickednes.' This passage tells us besides that although Malory was 'the servaunt of Jhesu bothe day and nyght', theological interpretation was beyond his range; for the Virgin Birth has nothing at all to do with the problem. In place of the well-ordered sermon of the French *Queste*, he makes an irrelevant reflection on the wickedness and wretchedness of the world. He either failed to understand or de-

---

[1] Paolo and Francesca had made the same mistake: 'En dépit des efforts désespérés de l'auteur, le but moral est, par la faute même du sujet, très imparfaitement atteint. Il échappa à Paolo et à Francesca, qui eurent le tort de ne pas poursuivre leur lecture jusqu'à l'*Agravain* et jusqu'à la *Quête*' (F. Lot, *op. cit.*, p. 289).

[2] Cf. E. K. Chambers, *Sir Thomas Malory*, p. 9.   [3] *Morte Darthur*, p. 628.

liberately omitted the 'senefiance de l'aventure': the parallel between the adventure of the tomb and the passion of Our Lord. According to the *Queste*, the tomb is the symbol of the great punishment inflicted upon the Jews; the body signifies their eyes and ears made blind and deaf by their deadly sin; and the voice signifies the doleful word they spoke to Pilate: 'Li sans de lui soit sor nos et sor nos enfanz!' The coming of Galahad echoes the advent of Jesus Christ: 'For as error and folly disappeared through His advent, and truth became manifest and open to all, so Our Lord has chosen thee above all other knights to send thee into strange lands to achieve grievous adventures' (*por abatre les grevoses aventures*).

Among these 'grievous adventures' there is one group which Malory is particularly anxious to free from suspicion: the adventures of the knights of King Arthur. The French text has it that before Galahad came to the tomb various knights errant had been there, and *as they were vile and unclean sinners*,[1] when they heard the fiend's voice they lost all their courage. But this is not in the *Morte Darthur*. When the *Queste* attacks his heroes, Malory stubbornly resists. The opening sentences of Book XV run as follows: 'Whanne the heremyte had kepte syr Launcelot thre dayes, the heremyte gate hym an hors, an helme, and a suerd. And thenne he departed about the houre of none.' After the word 'suerd' Malory has left out nearly two hundred lines of the original *Queste*.[2] For before Lancelot left him, the hermit spoke to him at great length and reproved him for his deadly sins. 'Thou wilt go on this Queste in vain', he said, 'unless thou pledgest thyself to forsake all deadly sins, and to free thy heart of all earthly thoughts, and of the crimes of this world.'[3] Lancelot stays with the hermit for three days, and before leaving asks the hermit to pray for him. He rides through a forest and there meets a varlet who inflicts an even greater humiliation upon him: 'I did not

---

[1] *pecheurs vielx et ors* in MS. B.N. fr. 120, f. 528ᵛ, col. 2; *vilz* in other MSS. [2] Cf. *infra*, pp. 156 ff.
[3] MS. B.N. fr. 120, f. 540ʳ, col. 2.

seek thee,' the varlet says, 'for thou art the most ill-fated
knight in the world. . . . No wonder thou makest dole,
for thou hast shown thyself . . . the most vile and disloyal
of knights.' ¹ Lancelot, knowing that the varlet speaks
the truth, listens patiently, but his knightly pride makes
him answer: 'Thou canst say what thou wilt, fair friend,
and I shall listen to thee, for a knight must not be wroth
at the words of a varlet.' 'What canst thou do but listen?'
is the retort. 'Will any other good ever come from thee?'
He reproaches Lancelot with his love for Guinevere: a
love which has caused him to lose all the joys of heaven.²
Lancelot, having listened, departs 'weeping and lament-
ing', and prays God to grant him mercy.³ Unwilling to
throw the slightest slur on the reputation of his hero,
Malory dismisses all these scenes. Later in the *Queste*
another hermit says to Lancelot: 'thou hast fallen into sin
since thou hast received the order of chivalry; for ere thou
werest a knight, thou hadst in thee all the virtues'.⁴ Here
again, by omission, Malory defends Lancelot's character
and the 'noble order of chivalry'.

In the *Queste*, other knights are even more severely
treated. If Lancelot is a repentant sinner, Gawain and
Hector de Mares have lost grace for ever. The hermit
says to Hector: 'And thou who shalt always ride upon the
big horse, that is to say who shalt always remain in deadly
sin, in pride, in envy, and in many other vices, thou
shalt go wandering hither and thither.' ⁵ Hector shall
come to the house of the Fisher King where the just and

¹ MS. B.N. fr. 120, f. 540ᵛ, col. 1; *infra*, p. 157.
² ' "Elle vous a si atorné que vous en avés perdue la joye des cieulz et la
compaignie des anges et toute honneur terrienne, et estes venuz a toutes
hontes recevoir." . . . Et le varlet le va ledangant et honnissant et dissant
la greigneur villenie qu'il oncques scet' (*ibid.*).
³ For a complete collation of this passage with Malory's text see Appendix III.
⁴ 'Tu cheïs en pechié, ce est puis que tu receus l'ordre de chevallierie.
Car devant ce que tu fusses chevailliers, avoies tu herbergié en toi toutes
bones vertuz' (MS. B.N. fr. 120, f. 541ᵛ, col. 1).
⁵ MS. B.N. fr. 120, f. 547ʳ, col. 2: 'Et vous qui tous diz chevauchié(e)s
le grant cheval, ce est a dire qui tous diz demouriés en pechié mortel et en
orgueil et en envie et en maint aultre visce, yrés forvoiant ça et la.'

the true knights shall hold their festival, and the King
shall refuse to admit him because of his deadly sins. But
'there is no rehearsal' of these passages in Malory's plain
account.

When a hermit addresses Gawain, he interprets the
latter's vision with a reference to the Round Table, and
uses language that leaves us in no doubt as to the misdeeds
of King Arthur's knights: 'By the three bulls thou shalt
understand the fellowship of the Round Table that by
their luxury and pride had fallen into mortal sin.' [1] Unable to omit this entirely, Malory makes a slight conces-
sion to his original and says: 'By the bulles is to understande the felaushyp of the round table, whiche for their
synne and their wyckednes ben black.' [2] But he consistently refrains from specifying the 'sin' of Arthur's fellowship.

His interpretation of the Grail itself is typical of his
method. King Pelles, who is vaguely described as 'cosyn
nyghe unto Joseph of Armathye', speaks as though he
were estimating the price of a precious jewel when he
tells Lancelot that the Grail is 'the rychest thyng that ony
man hath lyvyng'. Moreover, Malory deprives the Holy
Vessel of its symbolic significance, and is at a loss to explain the conflict between it and the Round Table: 'and
whanne this thynge goth aboute', says King Pelles, 'the
Round Table shall be broken'.[3] No further comment is
added, and we are left to wonder why the Round Table
is to suffer for the seemingly harmless movement of 'the
rychest thyng'.

Since the Grail is neither a mystic symbol nor yet a
sign set up to confound a sinful world, there is no conflict
between the *Lancelot* and the *Grail*. This was Malory's
judgement. The structural problem of the French *Queste*

---

[1] MS. B.N. fr. 120, f. 546ᵛ, col. 2: 'Par les troiz torieaux puet on entendre des chevailliers de la Table Ronde qui par leur orgueil et par leur
luxure estoient cheüz en pechié mortel si durement que leur pechiés ne
pueent mie taper par dedens eulz, ains lez estuet apparoir par dehors, si
qu'il en sont vairié et tachiez et ors si comme lez toreaux estoient.'

[2] p. 669₄₋₅.   [3] p. 573.

—the necessity of condemning Lancelot and yet keeping him in the foreground—presented no difficulty to the English author. He therefore treats Galahad's birth, not as an act of redemption and purification through sin and repentance, but as an ordinary event in family life. Lancelot, he says, was brought to Elaine 'for this entent: the kyng knewe wel that syr Launcelot shold gete a chyld upon his doughter the whiche shold be named sir Galahalt the good knyghte, by whomme alle the forayn countreye shold be broughte oute of daunger and by hym the Holy Graale shold be encheved'.[1] What is meant by this 'danger' is not clear,[2] and the words 'by hym the Holy Graale shold be encheved' throw no light on it. Malory, since he has abolished the main purpose and the sole reasonable justification of the Quest, has to be vague about its object. The Quest thus assumes the guise of a pageant full of strange adventures; and Galahad, from being its mystical leader and inspirer, becomes but a good and valiant knight on whom his grandfather rests great hopes. Malory flatly contradicts his source when he insists on Lancelot's superiority to Galahad.[3] The latter, says Elaine,

---

[1] *Ibid.*

[2] The word may well mean 'power' (as in p. 777, l. 22: 'a good man is never in daunger, but whan he is *in the daunger of a coward*', where it is used in both meanings), but even so the sentence remains obscure.

[3] i.e. in the passages traceable to his own invention. In other passages where Malory simply reproduces his source, the traditional conception of Galahad's mission remains unaltered, as in the following sentence, which is merely a condensed rendering of the French:

Malory, p. 636:	*MS. B.N. fr.* 120, f. 531ʳ, col. 1:
'I may lyken the good Galahad unto the sone of the hyghe fader that lyghte within a mayde and bought alle the soules oute of thralle. Soo dyd syre Galahad delyver all the maydens oute of the woful Castel.'	'li Peres le pere de ceans . . . envoia son fil en terre por delivrer lez bonnes puceles, c'est leur bonnes ames. Et tot aussi comme il envoia son fil qu'il avoit fait devant le commencement du monde, tout einsi envoia il son bon chevalier esleu, son sergant, qu'il despoullast enfer, c'est a dire qu'il despoullast le chastel des bonnes pucelles.'

The words reminding Lancelot of his sins are also drawn from the French

'shal preve the best man of his kyn *excepte one*' [1]—that is
except Lancelot, the 'floure of chivalry'.[2] And so Malory
is unable to explain, and perhaps to understand, the fundamental *motif* of the story: the substitution of Galahad
the pure for Lancelot the sinner.

Malory's *Quest* is indeed a confused and almost pointless story, a beautiful parade of symbols and bright visions.
It is deprived of its spiritual foundation, of its doctrine,
and of its direct object.[3] The Quest is no longer an antithesis to the Round Table, but an ornament of Arthur's
kingdom: the fortunes of Arthur and his fellowship do
not decline with the coming of the Grail Knight, and the
ultimate debate is not between the ideals of Camelot and
the ideals of Corbenic. Faced with two main themes and
forced to subordinate one, Malory made Corbenic a province of Camelot.

Queste, and the translation here is almost literal:

Malory, p. 639:	*Ibid.*, f. 532ʳ, col. 1:

'Ryght so he herd a voys that said: 'si ot une voix qui lui dist:
"Syr Launcelot more harder than   "Lancelot, plus durs que pierres,
is the stone, and more bytter than is plus amers que fus, plus nus et plus
the wood, and more naked and   despris que fueille de figuier, co-
barer than is the leef of the fygge   ment fus tu si hardiz que tu en lieu
tree, therfore goo thow from hens,   ou le Saint Graal repairast osas re-
and wythdraw the from this hooly   pairer?"'
place!"'

---

[1] p. 605.

[2] The idea was not entirely foreign to some French scribes, as may be seen
from the miniature in MS. Bibl. Nat. fr. 116, Part III, f. 5ʳ, where Lancelot is shown presiding over the Round Table which is graced at that moment
by the appearance of the Grail. The miniature used here as a frontispiece
illustrates the traditional conception: Galahad has taken the place of
Lancelot.

[3] For further examples see Appendix III.

Chapter Seven

THE NEW ARTHURIAD

I

LAYAMON was the first Arthurian poet to write in English.[1] He translated Wace's *Brut*, but altered it in a number of passages and added some new incidents. His alterations and additions [2] are of great interest: they reflect his attitude towards the Arthur story, an attitude which is characteristic of all the English Arthurian tradition, including Malory.

If Wace's romantic chronicle was a contribution to the polite literature of the Normans, Layamon has transformed it into a primitive epic with a distinct national flavour. Not only has he added a long series of 'historical' details: wars, rebellions, treasons, hunts, combats, and flights, but he gives his story considerable directness of action and clarity of narrative.[3] It possesses all the weight and solidity of early epic,[4] without the epic 'indifference'. It is, above all, a chronicle of the national past of England. Layamon's Arthur is no international knight errant, but a patriotic and practical Saxon chieftain, almost entirely unaffected by the romantic tradition. Wace had made him into a figure resembling an Anglo-Norman king, and Layamon transformed him into a king in whose veins pulsed much English blood. In the story of the foundation of the Round Table Layamon expands Wace's few

[1] Written between 1189 and 1207, edited by Sir Frederick Madden under the title: *Laȝamon's Brut or Chronicle of Britain, a poetical semi-Saxon paraphrase of the Brut of Wace*, 3 vols., London, 1847. There are two MSS.: Cotton Caligula A ix and Cotton Otho C xiii (*c.* 1250–75). The latter is, according to Madden (vol. i, p. xxxvi), 'an abbreviated recension of Layamon's work'.

[2] A list of all the most remarkable additions of Layamon is given by Madden, *op. cit.*, pp. xiv–xv.

[3] Cf. the description of the murder of Constantin (MS. Cotton Otho C. xiii, ll. 12950–67; Madden's edition, vol. ii, pp. 116–17).

[4] Cf. W. P. Ker, *Epic and Romance*, p. 4.

details into a long and vivid description. 'It was on a
Yule-day, that Arthur was in London,[1] and there were
come to him from all his kingdoms, from Britain, from
Scotland, from Ireland, from Iceland, and from all the
lands that Arthur had in hand, all the highest thanes, with
horses and with swains. There were seven kings' sons,
with seven hundred knights. . . . Then Arthur sat down,
and by him Guinevere; next sat the earls, and then the
barons; next the knights, as they were placed.' Then the
author introduces a story of a savage fight for precedence:
'The high born men [2] bore meat, in order, to the knights,
then to the thanes, then to the swains, then to the porters
forth at the board. The people became angered, and blows
were rife. First they threw the loaves while they lasted,
and the silver bowls filled with wine, and afterwards fists
approached to necks.' One of the knights grasped three
knives and with one of them smote in the neck the knight
that first began the fight, so that his head fell to the
ground. 'There was an exceeding great fight; each man
smote another; there was much blood shed, and bale was
among the folk.' This, Layamon tells us, was the immediate cause of the fashioning of the Round Table, 'where-
at sixteen hundred and more may sit all round, so that
none be left on the outside' (i.e. there will be no end

[1] Madden's edition, vol. ii, pp. 532–3.
[2] *Ibid.*, p. 534:   'þa heȝe iborne
þene mete beoren
æfne forð rihten,
þa to þan cnihten,
þa touward þan þæinen,
þa touward þan sweinen,
þa touward þan bermonnen
forð at þan borden.
þa duȝeðe wærð iwraððed;
duntes þer weoren riue.
Ærest þa laues heo weorpen,
þa while þa heo ilæsten,
and þa bollen seoluerne
mid wine iuuled;
& seodden þa uustes
uusden to sweoren.'

seats).[1] The barbarous character of this episode is typical
of the crude pre-romantic tradition which Layamon followed. But it is perhaps also true that by divesting the
Arthur story of its courtly elegance Layamon gave it
greater simplicity and force.[2]

After Layamon, it was long before an English poet
made any important additions to the plot; but when in
the fourteenth century the English rediscovered the
Arthurian stories, they were actuated by the same feelings
and proceeded on the same lines as their predecessor.
Since the French romances and a few unreliable chronicles
were the only available material, they were not easily used
for patriotic purposes. The first and the last acts of the
long drama of the Round Table—the *Merlin* and the
Mort Artu—afforded an opportunity for developing the
story along national lines, but the elaborate attempts of
the French prose writers to join the Grail *motif* to the
Arthurian plot met with little favour in England. The
majority of fourteenth-century English Arthurian romances dealt with the Arthuriad proper and wove their
stories around the figure of the great king. The romance
of *Arthoure and Merlin* is a rendering of the French *Merlin*, and relates the story of Arthur until he is betrothed to
Guinevere. Composed perhaps in the reign of Edward II,
'it reveals a lingering taste for the more heroic aspects of
the tale, and a survival of that patriotic enthusiasm which
caused the chroniclers to dwell on the legendary glories
of England.'[3]

The alliterative *Morte Arthure* [4] follows the same tendencies. It consists of three parts, the first and third
based upon the Arthurian chronicles, i.e. Geoffrey, Layamon, and possibly Wace. The second part, not directly

[1] ll. 1174–5. Cf. H. Krautwald, *Layamons Brut verglichen mit Waces
Roman de Brut in Bezug auf die Darstellung der Culturverhältnisse Eng-
lands*, Breslau, 1887, pp. 3–32.   [2] Cf. L. A. Paton, *Arthurian Chronicles*,
p. xvi.   [3] V. D. Scudder, *op. cit.*, p. 149.
[4] Edited by J. O. Halliwell (1847), G. G. Perry (1865), E. Brock
(1871, 1898, 1904), Mary M. Banks (1900), and E. Björkmann (Heidelberg and New York, 1915). The only extant MS. of the poem is now in
the library of Lincoln Cathedral, Thornton a, 1, 17.

traceable to any of the known Arthurian sources, recounts Arthur's campaign against the Duke of Lorraine and Gawain's fight with Priamus, the latter admittedly borrowed from the Old French Romance of *Fierabras*.[1] The whole poem, however, is intensely and patriotically English. Its writer possessed a deep sense of reality; his point of view is epic rather than romantic; his interest military and political; his mood heroic. Here is the scene in which Arthur, the good King, seeking the knights of the Round Table, finds Sir Gawain the Good. Gawain grips the grass with his hands, his face to the earth, his banners beaten down, his sword and his broad shield all in blood: never was King Arthur—*oure semliche Kynge*, as the poet says—so sorrowful in heart. 'He kneels down by the body [2] and takes it in his arms, he lifts up the umberer and kisses him, looks at his eyelids that are fast locked, his lips like lead and his pallid face. Then the crowned King cries out full loud—"Dear cousin by blood, I am left in grief, for now my honour is gone and my war ended. Here is the hope of my welfare, my good-fortune in arms; my heart and my boldness were all in him, my counsel, my comfort that delighted my heart! . . ." Then the king loses strength and falls into a swoon, but soon feebly rises and lovingly kisses him, till his great beard drips with blood, as if he had been cutting up beasts he had slain.' [3] 'Let us win back the Kingdom', is the *motif*

[1] Cf. R. H. Griffith, *Malory, Morte Arthure, and Fierabras*, in *Anglia* 32, pp. 389–98.

[2] ll. 3951 ff.:

> Knelis down to þe cors and kaught it in armes,
> Kastys vpe his vmbrere and kyssis hym sone,
> Lokes one his eye-liddis, þat lowkkide ware faire,
> His lippis like to þe lede, and his lire falowede.
> þan the corownde kyng cryes full lowde:
> 'Dere kosyn o kynde, in kare am I leuede,
> For now my wirchipe es wente and my were endide.
> Here es þe hope of my hele, my happynge of armes,
> My herte and my hardynes hale one hym lengede,
> My concell, my comforthe, þat kepide myn herte!'

[3] It is interesting to compare this scene with the corresponding passages in Wace and in the French *Mort Artu*. Wace confines himself to the remark

frequently repeated in the course of the poem; and Arthur's last farewell is full of profound epic sorrow: 'Fair
King with thy crown, I am left in sorrow; for all my lords
in the land have been slain! They who did me honour by
grace of God and upheld my manhood by the might of
their arms, made me great in the world and master in
earth: in a direful time the disaster took place, that I,
through a traitor, have lost all my true lords. Here rests
the rich blood of the Round Table overthrown by a
ribald, the greater the pity!'[1] It is significant that the
chronicles from which the author of the *Morte Arthure* borrowed his account say very little about Arthur's farewell.
Wace dismisses it in two lines: 'there perished the brave
and comely youth Arthur and also the renowned knights
of the Round Table'. Layamon amplifies this account but
is yet very far from the version of the *Morte Arthure*. It is
also noteworthy that the idea of Arthur's eventual return

that 'Arthur made over him great sorrow, for the knight was dearer to him
than any other man' (ll. 13507–8). The *Mort Artu* expands this into an
address to fortune: 'Ha! fortune', says Arthur, 'cose contraire et perverse,
la plus desloiaus cose ki el monde soit! Por coi me fus tu onques si debon-
naire ne si amiable, por vendre le moi si chier au derrain? Tu me fus jadis
mere et m'asesis el plus haut de ta roe. Or mi es devenue marastre; si m'as
mis de si haut si bas, et, por moi faire plus de duel morir, as apielee en
t'aide la mort, si ke tu en deux manieres m'as honni, de mes amis et de
ma tiere. Ha! mors desloiaus et vilaine! tu ne deüsses pas avoir asali tel
home comme Gavains, mes niés, estoit, ki de chevalerie et de bonté avoit
passé tot le monde!' . . . 'Molt est li rois Artus dolans de ceste mort et
molt en a grant pesance, tant k'il ne set k'il doie faire ne dire. Il en fait
duel si merveilleus et se pasme si souvent ke si baron ont grant doutance
k'il ne muire entre lor mains' (MS. B.N. fr. 342, f. 219ᵛ, col. 2). The
Morte Arthure alone gives a realistic description of the scene.
[1] ll. 4275–83:

> 'Kyng comly with crowne, in care am I leuyde;
> All my lordchipe lawe in lande es layde undyre!
> That me has gyfen gwerdons be grace of hym selven,
> Mayntenyde my manhede be myghte of thine handes,
> Made me manly one molde and mayster in erthe;
> In a tenefull tym this torfere was rereryde,
> That for a traytoure has tynte all my trewe lordys.
> Here rystys the riche blude of the rownde table,
> Rebukked with a rebawde, and rewthe es the more!'

to life was first suggested by Wace, but with a sceptical comment: 'Arthur is yet, he says, awaited of the Britons, but men have ever doubted and will always doubt whether he lives or is dead.' Layamon does not follow Wace in his scepticism, and makes Arthur himself say: 'I will fare to Avalon, to the fairest of all maidens, to Argante the queen, and she shall make my wounds all sound. And afterwards I will come again to my kingdom, and dwell with the Britons with mickle joy.'

The author of the *Morte Arthure* still more firmly insists on Arthur's return, and on his own behalf states in the *explicit*: 'Hic jacet Arthurus, rex quondam rexque futurus.' [1] There is in this poem, despite its French descent, a peculiarly English chord. The older alliterative form is revived, the patriotic note is struck with great poignancy, and the 'crowned King Arthur' is duly restored to the heart of the Romance.

II

In at least one respect Malory remains within the English tradition. With Layamon and the author of the alliterative *Morte Arthure* he shares a disposition to treat romance as fact and to attach an historical and national importance to Arthurian legends. One of Caxton's principal reasons for preferring the story of Arthur to that of Geoffrey of Boulogne 'or ony the other eyght' was that 'he was a man borne wythin this royame and Kyng and Emperour of the same'.[2] Malory, himself a victim of Yorkist revenge,[3] did not cease to be a loyalist. In his book he insists on the sanctity of the royal title, and as much as says that there is no greater misfortune for a country than civil strife, and no greater sin than sedition: in a passage already quoted [4] Mark, asking Dinas to

---

[1] It is not unlikely, as some critics have suggested, that in the thin disguise of Arthur the author of the *Morte Arthure* commemorates the deeds and character of Edward III, his barons, and his sons, and reflects the events of the years 1346–64. [2] Preface, p. 2.
[3] *V. supra*, p. 7. [4] *V. supra*, pp. 8–9.

'putte doune alle the peple that he had reysed', promises to go with the Pope 'to warre upon the miscreauntes', for *this is a fayrer werre then thus to areyse the peple ageynst your kynge*.[1] But the real champion of kingship in the *Morte Darthur* is King Arthur. In Malory's eyes he is neither a mere personage in a fairy tale nor a king of a non-existent kingdom: he has the importance and the dignity of a real hero. Malory delights in describing Arthur's chivalric character and insists upon making him every inch a king.[2] He is 'the nobyl Arthur' or 'the nobyl kyng', and in battle he does 'ful nobly as a noble Kynge shold'.[3] He is 'ful of prowesse' and of unequalled bravery. In fighting with Accolon he 'pressed unto Accolon with his sheld, and gaf hym with the pomel in his hand suche a buffet that he went thre strydes abak'.[4] But above all he is 'the crowned king', who during all his troubled reign has never shrunk from the oath made on his coronation day: 'to be a true kyng to stand with true justyce fro thens forth the dayes of this lyf'.[5]

[1] According to the French Prose *Tristan*, Mark told the Seneschal of Léonois that the land which the latter had invaded belonged to the Pope, and that as the result of his invasion 'la saincte terre de Jherusalem sera en aventure'. This misled the Seneschal and he retired with his men. Cf. E. Löseth, *Le Roman de Tristan en prose*, p. 203.

[2] Malory often calls Arthur '*the King*' and thus unwittingly follows the example of earlier English writers.

[3] The French source only praises the prowess of his men. Cf. MS. B.N. fr. 342, f. 228ʳ, col. 2: 'Si peussiés veoir a l'encontrer lances brisier et chevaliers cheoir, mais li home le roi Artu ki estoient boin chevalier et aduré et acoustumé de celui mestier, les rechiurent si bien et si vigoureusement ke il en abatirent ben cinquante en lor venir.'

[4] The French *Merlin* has nothing corresponding with these words. Cf. Huth MS., f. 210ᵛ, col. 2: 'lors commencha il un poi a alentir et a guenchir encontre les caus que chius li gietoit. Mais a toutes voies a la parfin il fust mors sans recouvrier, a chou qu'il se laissast anchois occhire qu'il criast mierchi, se ne fust la damoisele dou lac,' &c.

[5] p. 44. The oath is not in the French (cf. Huth MS., f. 75ʳ, col. 1). Against all existing versions, Malory makes Arthur an Emperor. As early as Book V (p. 182) Arthur is crowned by the Pope in Rome: 'And at the day appoynted, as the Romaunce telleth, he came in to Rome and was crouned Emperour by the Popes hand with all the ryalte that coude be made.'

'The dayes of this lyf' are only one part of his glorious mission. More than a good king, he is a God-sent messenger who has only descended upon earth to reshape the destinies of his chosen country. As a knight, however brave and strong he may be, he is liable to suffer defeat; but as a hero-king guarded by God he triumphs over all adverse circumstances and conquers his 'wycked day of desteyne'. When Fate turns against him and his prowess can no longer resist the attacks of his enemies, another magic force intervenes and takes up his defence. Early in the story he is 'in grete fere to dye', for 'fals treson was wrought for hym to have had hym slayn'. But the good forces conquer the evil, and come to his rescue in the shape of the 'damsel of the Lake', by whose enchantment Excalibur falls 'oute of Accolons hande to the erthe'.[1] Even Mordred's treacherous blow 'wyth his swerde holden in bothe his handes on the syde of the heed', which 'persyd the helmet and the brayne panne',[2] only causes him to 'chaunge his lyf in thys world'[3] and depart to the sublime realm whose message he had been chosen to fulfil. When his earthly power and glory are broken down by treason, Excalibur, the token of their duration, must return to its element and thus put an end to his ill-hap. As soon as Arthur's magic weapon is caught by the mysterious arm, a boat with fair ladies in black hoods comes to the bank of the river and Arthur is taken into it. He 'changes his life' as *rex futurus*; and his departure to Avalon, like the death of Roland in Roncevaux, is a scene not of mourning but of triumph.

The glorification of Arthur is not peculiar to Malory: in the French romances which he adapted and 'reduced' Arthur's figure also looms large. In these romances the transformation of fairy tales into an Arthurian epic had been almost completely achieved, and the ground for Malory's new Arthuriad had been prepared. In the French *Lancelot-Grail* Arthur was no longer a 'mere puppet', as in the poems of Chrestien de Troyes,[4] nor an abstract centre of the Round Table, but a character of

---

[1] p. 131.   [2] p. 847.   [3] p. 851.   [4] Cf. W. Förster, *op. cit.*, p. 14.

primary importance. It is easy to discover the reason for this change. Since the various romances of the 'Breton' group were to be brought together and put into the form of a Cycle, it was necessary to have one central figure. Arthur was the best choice, for although he had frequently been relegated to the background, he was to some degree associated with all parts of the Cycle. It became essential, therefore, to make him into a more conspicuous person, and to seek beyond the purely romantic stories of Chrestien de Troyes for information concerning him. The French writers of the Arthurian Prose Romances went back to the Chronicles of Wace and Geoffrey of Monmouth, and so restored their story to its historical or rather pseudo-historical place. They unknowingly gave it an English atmosphere, and the *Merlin* and the *Mort Artu*, though written by French authors, became romances of English history.

It was fortunate for Malory that the versions of the Arthur story which fell into his hands belonged to this particular group of romances. Had he used Chrestien de Troyes he would have had little opportunity to show his patriotic tendencies, for beyond a few additions and alterations he never departed from his 'bokes'. For the purpose of his Arthuriad, as well as for his chivalrous doctrine,[1] the *Lancelot-Grail* cycle supplied him with an unequalled wealth of material, and his epic ambitions could well be realized through a simple reproduction of the story. But Malory found that his source had one serious fault. The Prose Cycle, although it generally centred upon Arthur, was devoid of epic unity. Each branch referred to some particular period of Arthur's reign, but the six branches when combined contained no consistent plot. Their meaning and structure could only be discovered when they were cleared of subsidiary matter.[2] Then, but only then, was it possible to find, unobscured by adventitious material, the germ of an epic plot capable of being dramatically developed.

Malory's solution of his structural problem could not

[1] Cf. *supra*, p. 60.   [2] Cf. *supra*, pp. 30–2.

have been more simple.[1] He realized that his source
might lead him too far away from his main theme, and
so he simply cut it down to a more reasonable size. He
knew that the Epic of Arthur was there, but that it had
to be freed from its adventurous trappings, and by sheer
'reduction' he caused it to acquire a straightforwardness
and an internal balance which it had never before attained.

There were, in the French romances, two main 'historical' parts which could have supplied a basis for the
Arthuriad: the *Merlin*, or the early history of the Round
Table, and the *Mort Artu*, or the history of its downfall.[2]
The stories between these, such as the *Lancelot* or the
Queste, were perhaps from the point of view of the French
authors the most important, but surely from Malory's
point of view the least attractive. He could only use them
as a background for his main plot, as another illustration
of the 'custom and usage' of Arthur's reign. It is therefore
not surprising that the transition from the *Merlin* to the
Mort Artu section in Malory occupies not more than 320
folios in Caxton's print, while in the French Cycle it extended over 700 manuscript folios.[3] The Prose *Lancelot*,
condensed beyond measure and with all its early section
deleted, is very inadequately represented in the *Morte
Darthur*. The *Queste del Saint Graal* is reduced to a series
of events, and their 'significacyon' is omitted. But since
these stories were irrelevant to Malory's subject the omission was justified. It is only to be regretted that he did
not sacrifice other irrelevant matters. There was no real
necessity to interpolte the *Tristan* and the *Gareth*, which
add little to the background and divert the reader from
the main point of the narrative. As Sir Edmund Chambers
justly remarks, Malory 'would have done better to have
left the *Tristan* alone'.[4] He would have done better still
without the *Gareth*. Half-way through his work he himself seems to realize that he has lost the thread of the
Arthur story proper, and leaves out the third book of
Tristan. Again, at the end of his Nineteenth Book, he

[1] Cf. *supra*, p. 30.   [2] Cf. *supra*, p. 87.   [3] Cf. *supra*, p. 30, note 3.
[4] *Op. cit.*, p. 5.

shows obvious signs of impatience. He wishes 'to shorten thys tale' (the story of Sir Urre's healing), which has indeed little to do with his 'noble hystorye'. He is weary of tournaments and courtly intrigues, and replaces them all by the words: 'thus they lyved in all that courte wyth grete noblesse and joye long tyme. But every nyghte and day Sire Agravayne, Sir Gawayns broder, awayted Quene Guenever and Sir Launcelot du Lake to putte them to a rebuke and shame.' This is an old story, and Malory knows that he is repeating himself. It is time to proceed to more vital matters. 'And soo I leve of this tale and over-hyp [1] grete bokes of Sir Launcelot du Lake.' A little further he adds: 'And by cause I have lost the very mater of la chevaler du charyot, I departe from the tale of Sir Launcelot, and here I goo unto the morte of Kynge Arthur.'

The problem is solved by 'over-skipping' the rambling stories of the French Cycle. From the middle of the *Grail* section attention is no longer diverted by episode or secondary pageant and is focussed on a few figures who, standing in clear light, move with force and speak with energy. The dramatic curve is disengaged from unnecessary ramifications, and its progress is direct. It is revealed in the rise and fall of Arthur's kingdom, a kingdom that realizes the heroic ideals and the noble ambitions of patriotic chivalry. The decay of Arthur's kingdom comes with a tragic reversal of fortune:

> Toutes faillent telles plaisances,
> Et la coulpe si en demeure.

The 'plaisances' bulk large in the *Morte Darthur* and form a strange contrast to the final catastrophe. The Nineteenth Book opens with an idyll: 'How quene Guenever rode on mayeng with certeyn knyghtes of the Rounde Table and clad al in grene.' 'And soo upon the morne they toke their horses with the quene, and rode on mayenge in woodes and medowes as hit pleasyd hem in grete joye and delytes.' [2] And 'as the quene had mayed and

---

[1] =over-skip.   [2] p. 772.

alle her knyghtes, alle were bedasshed with herbys, mosses
and floures in the best maner and fresshest'.[1] But the
unhap is already upon them; for Sir Meliagrance has cap-
tured the queen, and Lancelot at the peril of his life must
rescue her. He succeeds, and the book closes upon a
peaceful scene. The knights perform 'many noble dedes'
and live 'wyth grete noblesse and joye long tyme'.[2] But
a few lines further on we learn that 'here after foloweth
the moost pytous history of the morte of Kynge Arthur',[3]
which is again contrasted with a scene of idyllic beauty
and repose:

'In May whan every lusty herte floryssheth and burgeneth, for
as the season is lusty to beholde and comfortable, soo man and
woman rejoycen and gladen of somer comynge with hys fresshe
floures. For wynter with his rough wyndes and blastes causeth a
lusty man and woman to coure and sytte fast by the fyre. So in
this season as in the monethe of May it byfelle a grete angre and
unhap that stynted not til the floure of chyvalry of alle the world
was destroyed and slayn.' [4]

The Round Table is doomed not because it has forsaken
Christianity, as in the French *Lancelot-Grail*, but because
of a 'prevy hate' of 'two unhappy knyghtes', one of whom
is the child of Arthur's sin. In Malory 'mayenge' scenes
are not intended, as in the *Queste*, to contrast the earthly
and the divine, but to mark the human tragedy of Arthur.
The Grail quest is but a prelude to the tragedy. Malory
uses it to deepen the background of his romance, a background full of peace and beatitude. There is a serene
light breaking from the Holy Vessel, and there is secular
rejoicing in chivalrous festivities. One is the feast of
divine grace, the other is the pageant of beauty and love;
but instead of being contrasted as in the Cistercian
romance, in Malory they coalesce to form a powerful dramatic antithesis to the coming crisis. Malory, instead of
stressing their antagonism, combines both for artistic
effect. He is concerned with neither philosophy nor
theology, and desires neither to teach nor to expound.

[1] p. 773.   [2] p. 795.   [3] p. 796.   [4] p. 797.

His contribution is but a scenic arrangement laid for a play of light and shadow.

But the shadows thicken and the 'doleful day' is at hand. Arthur decides to punish Guinevere for her breach of loyalty. 'For my Quene he (i.e. Lancelot) shalle never fyghte more, for she shall have the lawe.' She is ordered to be brought 'to the fyre there to have her jugement and receyve the dethe'.[1] Gawain's brothers, Gaheris and Gareth, are against their will forced to watch over her. Lancelot, getting word of Guinevere's danger, hurries to the spot and rescues her from the stake. But 'in this rassynge and hurlyng . . . it myshapped hym to slee Gaherys and Syr Gareth the noble knyghte, for they were unarmed and unware'.[2] Gawain, who has for long been true to Lancelot, now solemnly promises Arthur to revenge the death of Gaherys and Gareth: 'Now I shal make yow a promyse that I shalle holde by my knyghthode, that from this day I shalle never fayle Sir Launcelot untyl the one of us have slayne the other.'[3] He besieges Lancelot and Guinevere in Joyous Gard, until one day the Pope sends 'bulles under lede [4] unto Kynge Arthur of Englond chargynge hym upon payne of enterdytynge [5] of al England that he take his quene dame Guenever unto hym ageyne and accorde with Syr Launcelot'.[6] Peace is sealed, but Gawain's sinister promise cannot be altered. Lancelot is exiled from the court and departs amidst 'sobbynge and wepynge for pure dole of his departynge'.[7] And the knights of the court 'spoke all at once' and said: 'he have shame that wylle leve yow, for we alle understande in this realme wyll be now no quyete but ever stryf and debate, now the felauship of the Round Table is broken. For by the noble felauship of the Round Table was Kynge Arthur up borne, and by their nobles [8] the Kynge and alle his realme was in quyete and reste.'[9] The prediction comes true. Arthur and Gawain, at the cost of 'moche slaughter of peple on both partyes', wage a war on Lancelot. Lancelot is unwilling to fight Gawain, but the latter forces him

[1] p. 809.　[2] p. 811.　[3] p. 814.　[4] =lead.　[5] =interdicting.
[6] p. 821.　[7] p. 828.　[8] =nobleness.　[9] p. 829.

to accept a challenge. Gawain is unhorsed and wounded, but Lancelot refuses to kill him: 'to smyte a wounded man that may not stonde . . . God deffende me from suche a shame'.[1] Now while Arthur and Gawain have been waging war against their true friend, the real traitor, Mordred, has entered the field. Hearing of his treason, they hastily return to England, meet with his host at Dover, and 'put Sir Mordred abak, that he fledde and alle his peple'. But Gawain's wound proves fatal, and on his deathbed, repenting, he says to Arthur: 'Myn unkel Kyng Arthur . . . wete you wel, my deth day is come, and alle is thorou myn owne hastynes and wilfulnes, for I am smyten upon th'old wounde the which Sir Launcelot gaf me. . . . And had Sir Launcelot ben with you as he was, this unhappy werne [2] had never begonne, and of alle this am I causer.'[3] He asks for pen and ink, and writing a 'schedule' to Lancelot begs his forgiveness and beseeches him to come to Arthur in all haste and 'rescowe that noble kynge . . . for he is ful streyghtly bestadde [4] with a false traytour'.[5] At noon Gawain dies. That same night his ghost appears to Arthur and warns him that he should not fight the next day, but ask for a month's truce, 'for within a monethe shalle come Syr Launcelot with alle his noble knyghtes and rescowe yow worshipfully'. It turns out otherwise. Lancelot fails to rescue the king, and the battle ends in catastrophe. When Arthur 'loked aboute hym, thenne was he ware of al hys hoost, and of al his good knyghtes were lefte no moo on lyve but two knyghtes, that one was Sir Lucan de Butlere and his broder Syr Bedwere, and they were ful sore wounded. "Jhesu mercy," sayd the kyng, "where are al my noble knyghtes becomen? Alas! that ever I shold see thys dolefull day! For now," sayd Arthur, "I am come to myn ende."'[6] Then begins his fatal struggle with his traitor nephew: ' "Tyde me deth, betyde me lyf," says the King, "now I see hym yonder allone, he shal never escape myn handes, for at a better avaylle [7] shal I never have hym." '[8]

_____

[1] p. 838.   [2] =war.   [3] p. 841.   [4] =beset.   [5] p. 842.
[6] p. 846.   [7] =opportunity.   [8] p. 847.

THE FIGHT BETWEEN LANCELOT AND GAWAIN

MS. Bibl. Nat. Fr. 116

But 'before the father killed his son, the son had wounded his father to death'.[1] 'And therwythall syr Mordred fyl starke deed to the erthe, and the nobyl Arthur fyl in a swoune to the erthe.'[2] Here comes the miracle of Arthur's sword, told less circumstantially and therefore more convincingly than in the French *Mort Artu*, and with a finer sense of dramatic preparation than in the stanzaic *Le Mort Arthur*. Then the crowned king of England departs to Avalon in 'a lytyl barge with many fayr ladyes in hit, and emonge hem al was a quene, and al they had blacke hoodes, and al they wepte'.[3] Among the innumerable medieval versions of the legend there is none so artistically told and so skilfully woven into the framework of Arthur's story. For this sword—with an arm holding it above the water—had appeared once before in the First Book of the *Morte Darthur*: 'in the myddes of the lake Arthur was ware of an arme clothed in whyte samyte that held a fayr swerd in that hand'[4]; and with the help of a fair damsel Arthur obtained the sword—his Excalibur—the emblem of his power. Now that the spell is broken and his 'tyme hyeth fast', he must return it to the magic hand. The lake scene in the First Book thus foreshadows the last act in Arthur's tragedy, and it comes upon us as the inevitable completion of a magic circle. Malory did not create this circle: he merely narrowed it, and by so doing obtained a remarkable succession of scenes. The story, disentangled from its original context, formed the Arthurian epic which, but for Malory, would not have been.

[1] MS. B.N. fr. 342, f. 228ᵛ, col. 2: 'Ensi ocist li peres le fil et le fius le pere navra a mort.'   [2] p. 847.   [3] p. 849.   [4] p. 73.

Chapter Eight

TRANSLATION AND STYLE

'Mystérieux pouvoir du goût, d'une langue saine, d'un beau style! Ce Malory ne fut qu'un traducteur, un adaptateur: sans lui pourtant, dans l'Angleterre d'aujourd'hui, ni la poésie, ni la pensée, ni l'art ne seraient tout-à-fait ce qu'ils sont.'—JOSEPH BÉDIER.

WE may question Malory's merit as a story-teller, disagree with his interpretation of the Romance, and even whittle down his claims to originality; but his *Morte Darthur*, whatever its failings, possesses one important and unchallengeable quality: its style. We know that Caxton was puzzled as to the form in which to give his translations, for, in his time, there was no common standard of English: 'and thus', he said, 'betwene playne and rude and curyous termes I stand abasshed; but in my judgemente, the comyn termes that be dayli used ben lyghter to be understonde than the olde an auncyent englysshe'. Doubtless Malory shared this view and indirectly helped Caxton to solve his problem. In his translation of the 'French books' he also used words which, slightly archaic though they were, sound even now as 'comyn termes that be dayli used', and for this reason his work has preserved the same appeal it had four hundred and fifty years ago, when it was first brought within the reach of 'al noble lordes and ladyes wyth al other estates, of what estate or degree they ben of'.

As far as we can judge, Malory had a good reading knowledge of contemporary and medieval French. He occasionally misread his original[1]; most of his errors, however, are due to carelessness, and on the whole his

---

[1] He takes *li rois regarde contre mont la riviere* (meaning: 'the king looked up the stream', MS. Huth, f. 198r, col. 1) to mean *the kynge loked aboute the world* (p. 125); translates *il beast* by *he was . . . open mouthed* (*v. infra*, p. 152), and *abandonement* by *secretly*. The French (MS. B.N. fr. 99,

translation is correct.[1] What is more, he can hit upon exact idiomatic equivalents and condense long French periods without changing a single shade of meaning. 'He that hath a privy hurt is lothe to have a shame outwardly' reads like an English proverb; but it is a literal translation. The words 'et s'escrie . . . tout come il peut: Seigneurs chevaliers, voulez vous jouster?'[2] are rendered: '. . . dressid him to juste'.[3] Tristan's speech to Breuse sans Pitié, though considerably 'reduced', has more power and meaning than the French:

'Ne place a Dieu . . . ne je ne vouldroie en nulle maniere qu'il fust mors pour cestui afaire, car se il heue folie en pensee, il en a receu le gueredon. Remontés tost et prenés son glaive, tant vueil je bien que vous l'y tolliés.' . . . Et le fait rendre et lui dit: 'Prenés vostre cheval, sire chevalier!'	'Lete be,' sayd syr Tristram, 'slee hym not,\n\nthe knyghte is but a fool, hit were shame to slee hym.\n\nBut take away his spere,\n\nand lete hym take hys hors and goo wher that he wylle.'

Indeed, the passages which Malory translates from the French are not inferior in literary finish to those he himself invents; when his translation is most literal he still remains a master of simple exposition. Andrew Lang was mistaken when he said that Malory's style was 'based on the fresh and simple manner of his French originals'.[4] The manner of his French originals is neither fresh nor

---

f. 401ʳ, col. 2) *le roy Artus cuidoit que la royne Yseult y deust venir abandonement* means that Arthur desired Iseult to come (to the tournament) quite *freely*; Malory says, instead (p. 499): 'la beale Isoud shold behold the justes in a *secrete place* that was honest for her estate'. He apparently confused the adverb *abandonement* with the adjective *abandoné*, meaning 'secret'. Cf. *Rom. de Trist.*, p. 151. For other inaccuracies, see App. III.

[1] In some places he consciously refrains from translating the meaning and introduces English words that are similar in sound to the French. The *ryuer* mentioned in Ch. II of Book XIII (p. 614, l. 27) corresponds to *rive* in the French *Queste*; and *meuer of blood* (p. 700, l. 3) is supposed to render *memoire de sanc*.

[2] MS. 99, f. 421ᵛ, col. 2.   [3] p. 510.

[4] *V.* Sommer's edition of the *Morte Darthur*, p. xx.

simple, but confused and cumbrous. Not only is the syntax loose, but the long-winded periods lack both simplicity and force. Here, then, Malory is distinctly superior to his French books [1] and can securely face the ordeal of minute textual collation. For the sophisticated patterns of his original he substitutes direct and plain designs:

La Queste del Saint Graal.

Et bien doit estre senefiez par le cerf. Car tot ausi com li cers se rajuvenist en lessant son cuir et son poil en partie, tout ausi revint Nostre Sires de mort a vie, quant il lessa le cuir terrien, ce fu la char mortel qu'il avoit prise ou ventre de la beneoite Vierge.

Malory, p. 703.

And wel oughte Oure Lord by sygnefyed to an herte. For the herte whanne he is old, he waxeth yonge ageyne in hys whyte skynne. Ryght soo cometh ageyne Oure Lord from dethe to lyf, for he lost erthely flesshe that was the dedely flesshe wyche he had taken in the wombe of the blessid Vyrgyn Mary.

Not only is the French *tout ausi com . . . tout ausi* simplified by being divided into two parallel sentences; but the image of the hart who 'waxes young again in his white skin' is changed from a rhetorical and abstract figure into a vivid and positive one. But perhaps the easiest way to demonstrate Malory's superiority is to take a stock scene such as the encounter of two knights:

MS. Huth, f. 208r, col. 2–208v, col. 1.

Quant li dui chevalier se virent ensamble parti des autres, li uns d'une part et l'autre, ils laissent courre les chevaus tout maintenant et s'entrefierent en lour encontres des grans aleure des destriers si durement que li escu ne li haubert qu'il tenoient as boins (*poins?*) ne les garandissent qu'il ne se metent es chars nues les fers des glaives . . . (*7 lines*) . . . si durement qu'il chaïrent a la terre tout enviers.

Malory, p. 130.

And thenne they dressyd hem on bothe partyes of the felde and lete their horses renne so fast that eyther smote other in the myddes of the shelde with their speres hede, that bothe hors and man wente to the erthe.

[1] Cf. *Rom. de Trist.*, p. 152.

The intrinsic qualities of Malory's style have often been analysed, and it is well to quote here some of the more successful appreciations. According to Sir Edmund Chambers, Malory's language is 'as finished an instrument in its way as any prose the sixteenth century can show, but with the freshness of the early world still upon it'.[1] Andrew Lang, in his essay on the *Morte Darthur*,[2] notes the remarkable 'fluency' of Malory's English: 'Perhaps it is just because he does follow a French copy, and so is familiar with words derived from the Latin, that Malory possesses his fluency and facility. . . . On the whole it may be said of the narrative manner that it is well fitted to the wandering tale, just old enough and quaint enough to allure and to mark the age, without disturbing or delaying even the youngest reader of the noble and joyous history.' Miss A. D. Greenwood [3] finds in it 'a transparent clarity':

'There is a kind of cadence, at times almost musical, which bears the narrative on with a gradual swell and fall proportioned to the importance of the episodes, while brevity, especially at the close of a long incident, sometimes approaches to epigram. . . . Too straightforward to be archaic, idiomatic with a suavity denied to Caxton, Malory, who reaches one hand to Chaucer and one to Spenser, escaped the stamp of a particular epoch and bequeathed a prose epic to literature.' [4]

There are, then, in Malory two distinct aspects: archaic cadence and crisp idiom, an 'alluring archaism' and an

[1] *Sir Thomas Malory*, pp. 6–7.   [2] In Sommer's edition, loc. cit.
[3] *Cambridge History of English Literature*, ii. 337.
[4] Walter Scott, while warning his readers against 'this work, which misrepresents the adventures', recognized that it was 'curiously written in excellent old English' (*Sir Tristrem: a Metrical Romance of the Thirteenth Century*, Edinburgh, 1819, p. lxxxi). J. A. Symonds thought that it was written 'at a lucky moment in our literary history, when the old Saxon fountain of speech was yet undefiled, and when printing had not introduced stereotyped forms or enforced the laws of a too scrupulous grammar; at the same time the language is truly English—rich in French and Latin words, as well as Saxon, and not so archaic as to be grotesque or repulsive' (*Pall Mall Gazette*, 23 June 1868). Sir Edward Strachey recognizes in Malory's style defects as well as merits: 'Malory's style is often unartificial; he is not always able to master the huge masses of his materials, and fails to fuse and mould them into a perfect whole—but there is an infant beauty

almost colloquial straightforwardness. These correspond to the two common methods of telling an old tale in a modern tongue; that of restoring the old manner and avoiding conflict between form and matter; and that of using modern idiom and deliberately creating a contrast between matter and form. The former method is that of the restorers of chivalry—from *Amadis* to Spenser and Honoré d'Urfé—and of all the conscious archaists who cling to what Spenser described as the 'monuments of ruder antiquity'.[1] The latter is that of the satirists, and is represented by Sir Thopas, Sancho Panza, and, in our days, by Mr. John Erskine's *Galahad*.[2] For men of little genius there is no third alternative: they imitate or ridicule; they lack the skill of reproducing the spirit of an old story without being artificial; and they cannot adapt it to their own times without being consciously or unconsciously coarse.

Malory is one of the few writers who found a 'third way' and steered clear of both coarseness and artificiality. His fundamental merit is not so much his Latin fluency and facility as his art of combining pathos and simplicity, romance and epic straightforwardness. His language has all the strength of an oration, all the ease of a popular tale. It is traditional and fresh at the same time, and this is why it is so well fitted to its theme. Malory's subject was conventional; the world in which his characters lived and acted was artificial. Any less able author treating it artificially and bombastically would have rendered it un-

in Malory's style which is full of promise of the perfect manly form that is to be.' Further, he quotes an instance of this ineffectual beauty of style, where 'the thoughts and images spontaneously utter themselves in words without any attempt at rhetorical balance and arrangement'. In the lament of Ector over Lancelot, 'Malory does not ask himself whether there is a logical connection between courtesy and bearing a shield, or between true friendship and bestriding a horse, as a modern writer would have done, and so brought those sentences into a more finished though more monotonous correspondence with the rest. The flow of feeling is true, direct, and simple, and that is enough' (*Introduction*, p. xx.)

[1] Preface to *The Shepheards Calendar*.
[2] *Enough of His Life to Explain His Reputation*, London, 1926.

readable; or, by using an inappropriate, popular manner, would have parodied the original. Malory avoided both dangers, and without being unjust to the old Romance endowed his story with a wide and undying appeal. Lancelot's words to Guinevere in Ch. III of Book XX are characteristic of his manner: ' "O Jhesu mercy", sayd Sir Launcelot, "this shameful crye and noyse I may not suffre, for better were deth at ones than thus to endure this payne." Thenne he took the quene in his armes, and kyste her, and sayd: "Moost noble crysten Quene, I byseche yow as ye have ben ever my specyal good lady, and I at al tymes your true poure knyghte unto my power, and as I never fayled yow in ryghte nor in wrong sythen the fyrst day kynge Arthur made me knyghte, that ye wylle praye for my soule yf that I here be slayne." ' [1] The pride, daring, and nobility of a perfect knight find their expression in the remarkable lines added to the description of Tristan's farewell to the Irish Barons: [2] they bear a strange resemblance to the terse and rugged language of Brutus.[3] And the sublime virtues of the 'hede of al crysten knyghtes' were never expressed in less strained or more forceful terms than in Ector's famous lament over Lancelot.[4]

This simplicity and elevation of Malory's style is found in every page of the book, and one more quotation must suffice to illustrate it. To the accusation raised against him by Gawain and Arthur, Lancelot replies proudly: 'And where hit please yow to saye that I have holden my lady youre Quene yeres and wynter,[5] unto that I shal ever make a large answer and preve hit upon ony knyghte that bereth the lyf excepte youre person and sire Gawayne, that my lady Quene Guenever is a true lady unto your persone as ony is lyvyng unto her lord, and that wylle I make good with my handes.' [6]

[1] p. 801.   [2] p. 292. Quoted above, p. 60.
[3] Cf. Rom. de Trist., p. 144, footnote.   [4] p. 860; v. supra, loc. cit.
[5] This is an answer to Arthur's words: 'thow hast layne by my Quene and holden her many wynters'. Note the rhetorical amplification: 'yeres and wynter'.
[6] pp. 815–16. The first of the passages quoted here has no parallel in

Akin to these qualities of style is Malory's handling of rhythm and sentence-balance. Long before Bohours, he discovered the advantage of the 'rounded period', i.e. a sentence consisting of four main periods of unequal length [1]; long before Bossuet he gave it the harmony of a musical cadence. He introduced pauses for the voice corresponding to pauses in the progression of thought, and so established an exact balance between logical periods and rhythmical units.

Lancelot's 'long answer' to King Arthur is a case in point:

And at suche tymes, my lord Arthur, sayd sir Launcelot, ye loved me, and thanked me whan I saved your quene from the fyre;
and thenne ye promysed me for ever to be my good lord;
and now me thynketh ye rewarde me ful ylle for my good servyse.

The structure is here characterized by a symmetrical disposition of periods: two long periods, of sixteen syllables each, enclose two shorter ones (twelve and fourteen), and serve to 'round off' the sentence. It is also interesting to note the succession of verbs: *loved*, *thanked*, *promysed*, *rewarde*, indicating, by the simplest means, the growth of Lancelot's indignation.

Iseult's farewell to Tristan (p. 371) presents another example of numerous prose:

> And ever whan I maye I shalle sende unto you,
> and whan ye lyst ye may come to me,
> and at alle tymes erly and late
> I wille be at your commaundment
> to lyve as poure a lyf as ever dyd quene or lady.

the French source except the words: 'Si ot a l'uis grant cri et grant noise de gens ki voelent l'uis brisier, mais il ne pueent . . . "Voire", fait-il, "or ne vous caille. Si voirement m'ait Dex, il a sa mort porcachié, car ce sera il tos premiers ki en morra, se je puis . . ." ' (M.S. B.N. fr. 342, f. 183ᵛ, col. 1). Tristan's farewell, Ector's threnody, and the last passage quoted are Malory's own.

[1] Cf. P. Bohours, *Doutes sur la langue françoise proposez a Messieurs de l'Académie Françoise par un gentilhomme de province*, Paris, 1674, p. 220: 'Une des règles générales de la Rhétorique en toute langue est que les plus longues périodes ne passent point quatre membres: de-sorte qu'une période

Here the balance is produced by the lengthening of the
last period, which widens the movement and enhances the
effect of the final pause.[1]

Malory knows, besides, the secret of slow and swift
movements, which he alternates according to the meaning.
The slow movement is used in solemn discourse, and the
swift in narrative and description. The two passages just
quoted illustrate Malory's *andante* and *largo*; elsewhere,
in the more dramatic scenes, the periods are short and the
general impression is that of an *allegro* or *allegro moderato*:

> Thenne it befel upon a daye,
> in hervest tyme,
> Syr Launcelot loked over the walles
> and spak on hyghe
> unto Kynge Arthur and Sir Gawayne.[2]

Unnoticed by the inattentive ear, these varying harmonies
lend Malory's prose the grace of a musical rhythm and
atone for the length and monotony of his stories.

There are no doubt in the *Morte Darthur* a number
of passages in which sentence-balance and rhythm will
be sought in vain. Sometimes, from the very nature
of his task, Malory could not help choosing his sentences
at haphazard, or translating the innumerable *ore*, *et*, and
ainsi of his source by no less tedious *and*, *then*, or *so*. But
we must confess the like of the greatest early prose-
writers—even of Bossuet, whose sense of measure and
structure failed him in the middle of some of his most remarkable sermons. Unlike Bossuet, Malory is seriously

de six membres est quelque chose, à mon gré, d'aussi monstrueux que
seroit un homme qui auroit quatre mains et quatre pieds.' I can find
nothing resembling this device either in Chaucer or in Sir Thomas More.

[1] This is an important device in prose rhythm, and it warrants a comparison between Malory and other great writers of prose. In the orations
of Bossuet there is a similar alternation of periods of unequal length concluded by a long rhythmical group. 'Dans les assemblages de deux ou
trois groupes', says M. Lanson (*L'Art de la Prose*, p. 102), 'celui qui est
placé le dernier est le plus long. L'impression est celle qu'on ressent,
lorsque, en poésie, un vers de dix ou de douze pieds vient après un ou
deux vers de sept ou de huit. Ainsi, l'éloquence s'élargit et s'étale.'

[2] p. 815.

handicapped by the colossal proportions of his work, by the endless variety of scenery and character it presents. This often destroys the harmony of the movement and breaks the unity of tone. But now and again, especially in the crucial and tragic moments of his story,[1] his voice rises, and, with a sense of greatness and majesty unequalled in Romance, sustains the pathos of his 'noble and joyous book'.

[1] In some such passages Malory has recourse to alliteration and assonance, e.g. in the scene of Arthur's death: 'Syr,' says Bedivere, 'I sawe no thynge but the *w*aters *w*appe and *w*awes *w*anne.' When Guinevere is 'led forth withoute Carleil' and 'despoylled in to her smok', there is '*w*epynge & *w*aylynge and *w*ryngynge of handes of many lordes and ladyes' (p. 810); Lancelot departs from the court, amidst 'so*bb*ynge and we*p*ynge for *p*ure dole of his de*p*artynge' (p. 828). Malory seems to have realized the musical effect of the *ynge* ending of the present participle (cf. C. S. Baldwin, *The Inflections and the Syntax of the 'Morte d'Arthur' of Sir Thomas Malory*, Boston, 1894, p. 79): 'foining, tracing and traversing like two wild boars', 'racing and hurling', &c., are his most common *clichés*. Cf. also his use of the modifying participial phrase: 'there he fond a careful wydowe *wryngynge* her handes and *makyng* grete sorrowe, *syttynge* by a grave' (p. 167).

Conclusion

There came a bark that, blowing forward, bore
King Arthur, like a modern gentleman.
TENNYSON, *The Morte d'Arthur.*

THE discussion of Malory's work as set forth in the
foregoing chapters resolves itself into two main problems: that of Malory's literary character and that of his
contribution to Arthurian romance.

On the first it would be perilous to generalize. Malory's
ideas, methods, and general outlook cannot be expressed
in a few words, and the preceding survey would gain
little from a summary. One thing, however, appears certain, and follows naturally from all that has been said
before: Malory is a modern, both in his sympathies and
in his idiosyncrasies. He shares the moderns' dislike of
shapeless stories of adventure, their interpretation of
chivalry, and their misunderstanding of the medieval
romantic spirit. For the medieval courtly idealism he
attempts to substitute the philosophy of a practical and
righteous fifteenth-century gentleman; and where the
French romantic writers seek to set forth an ideal remote
from reality he sees but a moral doctrine to be followed
by all those who desire honour and 'renommée' in this
world.[1]

His contribution is easier to summarize, but it leaves
an impression as surprising as that left by his personality.
He added little—much less than critics have hitherto believed. By condensing his sources, he occasionally achieved

[1] This doctrine is suited to the moral and practical temper of Malory's
age, just as much as Tennyson's didactic purpose is suited to the moral and
sentimental temper of the Victorian era. The only real difference is that
Tennyson is able to carry out his design, while Malory is 'a moral child
without the craft to rule' and only succeeds in indicating his intentions.
It would have surprised and grieved him to have learnt that his book was
regarded by Ascham and Tennyson as a glorification of 'open manslaughter'
and 'guilty love'.

greater ease and directness of narrative, especially in detail. But on the whole he failed to weld the rambling episodes of the French cycle into a harmonious whole, and retained a mass of stories unconnected with each other and often irrelevant to the main theme. He also failed—and this was unavoidable—to restore to those stories their original psychological basis. His 'glosings over' usually disfigure the meaning of episodes, and his additions reveal no vaguest glimpse of the long-forgotten world of medieval romance. It is not Malory who can lead us back to the enchanted realm of Arthur and Lancelot; to understand its message we must return to the ruins of its battered stronghold, not to the 'virtuous deeds' recounted in the *Morte Darthur*.

In one respect, however, Malory has improved on older versions: he has disentangled the Arthurian plot proper from its ramifications, and so created his 'most piteous history of the morte of King Arthur'. He was inspired throughout his task by a definite national and political purpose, and it is doubtful whether the book would have been written had it not been for the events of 1454–85. Faced with the horrors of internecine strife and the uncertainty of the future, Malory naturally enough fell back on remembrances of the past and tried to find in them a picture of glory and prosperity, as well as the causes which had led to the decay of the great kingdom of Arthur. By adapting the Arthurian romances to the needs of his day, he made them into a record of the national past of England, and endowed them with the greatness and importance of a national epic. In this sense, and in this sense alone, it is true to say that he holds out one hand to the Middle Ages and one to us. The epic of Arthur, whose roots go deep into medieval soil, is a living drama which, owing to Malory's contribution, has preserved all its powerful appeal for the modern mind.

But neither the dramatic quality of this story, nor its national and patriotic inspiration, would have sufficed to save Malory's book from the ravages of time. If the *Morte Darthur* has survived in modern poetry and has

succeeded in transmitting to many generations of English
readers the records of Arthurian chivalry, it is because the
form in which it is written possesses a strange magnetism.
A comparison with the fortunes of Arthurian romance in
France may once more throw light on the nature of
Malory's work. Soon after the close of the Middle Ages
the French Arthurian tradition came to an end. In the
fourteenth and fifteenth centuries the French Arthurian
manuscripts are far fewer and far more luxurious than
they were in the thirteenth, and their popularity is more
and more limited to aristocratic circles. The last printed
edition of *Lancelot* appeared in 1533,[1] and until quite
recently no French author made any notable attempt to
renew the epic of the Round Table.[2] The French romanticists, unlike their English contemporaries, knew little
about the Arthurian legacy. In one of Alfred de Vigny's
letters there is a curious remark about the 'tower of
Tristan'. He affirms that it was so called, not after 'the
rascal of Louis XI', but after the Tristan of medieval
romance: 'Qui songe à ce roman du moyen âge? Personne; et il est délicieux.'[3] Knowledge of the Arthurian
stories was then limited to a narrow circle of scholars,[4]
and had ceased to be the patrimony of poets and prose-
writers. The reason for this was given by Joachim du

---

[1] The edition of 1591 (Rigaud) is a condensed version.

[2] Paulin Paris published in 1868–77 a résumé of the romances, but his
work had little success. 'Paru au moment où la littérature naturaliste
triomphait chez nous, son livre passa presque inaperçu' (F. Lot, *Étude sur
le Lancelot en prose*, p. 3). In recent years, M. Jacques Boulenger has published a modern version of the Arthurian Romances (*Les Romans de la Table
ronde nouvellement rédigés*) in four volumes, which in spite of its outstanding
literary quality enjoys no great popularity. The only notable exception is
M. Bédier's reconstruction of the Tristan romance (*Le Roman de Tristan
et Iseut*), undoubtedly one of the finest prose works of our century.

[3] *Revue des Deux Mondes*, January 1897, p. 80.

[4] The eighteenth century contributed nothing to Arthurian romance,
except the brief accounts of the *Lancelot*, the *Mort Artu*, the *Queste*, and
the *Estoire del Graal* which were published in the *Bibliothèque universelle
des romans* in 1775. In 1788 Tressan wrote his *Histoire de Tristan de
Léonois*, a free rendering of the Prose Romance of Tristan. None of the
great French romanticists used Arthurian themes.

Bellay as far back as 1549. Du Bellay had no particular admiration for magic fountains and enchanted forests, 'assez suffisans pour degouter tout lecteur sçavant d'en lire davantaige',[1] but at the same time he recognized the obvious merits of the old stories contained in the romances of chivalry. Their chief defect, according to him, was that they were badly written. Had some good author undertaken to rewrite them in the correct style, he would have produced, thought Du Bellay, a new *Iliad* or another *Aeneid*.[2] The same view was expressed a few years later by Jacques Peletier, who found the romances of adventure 'happily invented', but regarded them merely as a stock of stories which had to be divorced from their obsolete form. Peletier wanted them to be revived by a 'poète héroïque', and Du Bellay could only accept them as material for a work in the proper epic style.[3] But since no one undertook the rewriting of the old romances, and their unrefined language lost its appeal for the French, they were finally condemned by the 'learned readers', and their 'adventures, travels, enchantments and combats' failed to save them.[4] 'On vit renaître Hector, Andro-

[1] *La Deffence et Illustration de la Langue françoyse*, édition critique par Henri Chamard, Paris, 1904, p. 310.

[2] 'Comme luy (=Ariosto) donq', qui a bien voulu emprunter de nostre langue les noms et l'hystoire de son poëme, choysi moy quelque un de ces beaux vieulx romans françoys, comme un *Lancelot*, un *Tristan*, ou autres: et en fay renaitre au monde un admirable *Iliade* et laborieuse *Eneïde*. Je veux bien en passant dire un mot à ceulx qui ne s'employent qu'à orner et amplifier notz romans, et en font des livres, certainement en beau et fluide langaige, mais beaucoup plus propre à bien entretenir damoizelles qu'à doctement ecrire: je voudroy bien (dy-je) les avertir d'employer cete grande eloquence à recueillir ces fragmentz de vieilles chroniques francoyses, et comme a fait Tite Live des annales et autres anciennes chroniques romaines, en batir le cors entier d'une belle histoire' (*Ibid.*, pp. 235-8).

[3] *L'Art Poëtique, departi an deus livres*, Lyon, 1555; II. viii. 78-9: 'Je trouve noz rommans bien invantiz. E dirè bien ici an passant, qu'an quelques uns d'iceus bien choesiz, le poëte heroïque pourra trouver a fere son profit: comme sont les avantures des chevaliers, les amours, les voyages, les anchantemans, les combaz, e samblables choses.'

[4] It would be an exaggeration to say that they enjoyed no popularity in the sixteenth century. Rabelais was certainly familiar with them, and Étienne Jodelle records in his *Epistre au Lecteur*, which prefaces *L'Histoire*

maque, Ilion, mais non pas les chevaliers d'Arthur, et la forêt de Broceliande.' [1]

The contrast between the decay of the Arthuriad in France and its success in England naturally suggests itself. The last black-letter edition of Malory appeared in 1634, a century later than the last edition of the French *Lancelot*. In the subsequent period the Arthur story continued its existence in chap-books [2] and was probably read by many, but Malory's *Morte Darthur* was not known. Like the old romances in France, Malory in England suffered from the anti-Gothic tendencies of the age of reason. But long before the close of the eighteenth century there are signs of his return,[3] and with the romantic revival he definitely reconquers the sympathies of English readers. Nineteenth-century poets not only hold his work in reverence

Palladienne of Claude Colet, that the latter was very fond of the old romances. Jodelle also states that they were much appreciated by 'des gentilz-hommes et des damoyselles de nostre siecle, qui fuyent l'histoire pour sa severité et rejettent toute autre discipline pour leur ignorance'. In the seventeenth century the old romances of chivalry were severely criticized by Labbé and ignored by Boileau, but favourably treated by Chapelain (cf. *Continuation des Mémoires de littérature et d'histoire*, ed. Desmolets, vol. vi, Part i, p. 334). P.-D. Huet (*Lettre sur l'Origine des Romans*, 1670) like Du Bellay condemns the medieval romances on literary grounds: 'tous ces ouvrages, ausquels l'ignorance avoit donné la naissance, portoient des marques de leur origine, & n'estoient qu'un amas de fictions grossierement entassées les unes sur les autres, & bien éloignées de ce souverain degré d'art & d'élégance, ou les François ont depuis porté les Romans' (7th edition, pp. 174–5).

[1] Joseph Bédier, Preface to the *Romans de la Table Ronde* by Jacques Boulenger, p. iii. He further adds: 'De nos jours, hors du cercle étroit des érudits, quel lettré l'a jamais lu ? Les noms mêmes des héros qu'il met en scène ne sont plus que des grelots vides. Nous ne connaissons plus que par un vers de Dante Galehaut, seigneur des Iles Lointaines, — et Perceval, en français d'aujourd'hui, se prononce Parsifal.'

[2] Dryden's dramatic opera and Blackmore's *Prince Arthur* and *King Arthur* are examples of the neglect of the traditional themes of the Arthur story. The underground literature of chap-books and popular tales no doubt contained more valuable material which was most probably borrowed from Geoffrey's *Historia*.

[3] Thomas Warton's *Observations on the Faerie Queene*, published in 1754, show a keen interest in Malory, and *The Grave of King Arthur* is not altogether free from his influence.

as the most authentic record of Arthurian chivalry, but regard it as one of the fountain-heads of romantic fiction. Ascham may have fulminated against Malory's crudities,[1] and Tennyson may have disapproved of the 'grey King'

> Of Geoffrey's book, or him of Malleor's, one
> Touched by the adulterous finger of a time
> That hover'd between war and wantonness.

But the mere fact that such warnings were thought necessary in Ascham's time and in Tennyson's shows that 'Malleor's book' was never a negligible quantity. Four and a half centuries after its publication, it continues to inspire poets and prose-writers to renew their quest of the 'grey King'. And, if it is still living and strong, it is largely because it possesses what is denied to the 'French books': the mysterious power of style—the only immortal merit in the world of books.

[1] 'In our forefathers' tyme, when Papistrie, as a standyng poole, covered and overflowed all England, fewe books were read in our tongue, savyng certaine bookes of chevalrie, as they said, for pastime and pleasure; which, as some say, were made in the monasteries, by idle monks or wanton chanons. As one, for example, *La Morte d'Arthure*; the whole pleasure of which book standeth in two speciall poynts, in open manslaughter and bold bawdrye; in which booke they be counted the noblest knightes that do kill most men without any quarrell, and commit fowlest adoulteries by sutlest shiftes: as Sir Launcelot, with the wife of King Arthur, his master; Sir Tristram, with the wife of King Marke, his uncle; Sir Lamerocke, with the wife of King Lote, that was his own aunt. This is good stuffe for wise men to laugh at; or honest men to take pleasure at: yet I know when God's Bible was banished the Court, and La Morte d'Arthur received into the Prince's chamber.'—Ascham's *Scholemaster*.

APPENDIX ONE

MATERIALS FOR MALORY'S BIOGRAPHY

1. *Malory's Identity*

IN Chapter I of this study I assume that the author of the *Morte Darthur* was Sir Thomas Malory of Newbold Revel. The evidence on which this theory is based is as follows:—

The *Morte Darthur* contains the following indications concerning its author: (1) his name was Thomas Maleore; (2) he was a knight; (3) he was alive between 4 March 1469 and 3 March 1470, and was then old enough to write a book; (4) a large part if not the whole of the book was written in prison.

The first three indications are given by Malory himself in the concluding lines of his work.[1] The fourth is suggested by the two passages in which he speaks of 'good deliverance': the reflections on the hardships of seclusion in the Ninth Book, and the prayer for deliverance at the end of the work.[2] The 'deliverance' for which he prayed was undoubtedly deliverance from prison, as a comparison of the two passages readily suggests. The *Oxford Eng. Dict.* quotes 'good deliverance' as a legal term for release from prison, but gives a fairly late example (1660). In France, on the other hand, 'mettre à pleine délivrance' was a common technical term in the fourteenth and fifteenth centuries.[3] The only other meaning of the word might be 'deliverance from sickness', but this is put out of question by the first passage: 'For alle the whyle a prysoner may have his helthe of body, he maye endure under the mercy of God, and in hope of good delyveraunce. But whanne sekenes toucheth a prysoners body . . .', &c. Hence both passages would seem to refer to Malory's imprisonment.

The four conditions necessary for the identification of our author are fulfilled in the life of Sir Thomas Malory of Newbold Revel:

(1) His name was Thomas, but his surname was spelt in many different fashions. The records quoted below give the following readings: *Malore* (Dugdale, Bridges), *Mallore* (Bridges, *Calendar*

---

[1] Cf. *supra*, p. 1.   [2] Cf. *supra*, pp. 7–8.

[3] Cf. *Choix de pièces inédites relatives au règne de Charles VI* ed. by L. Douët-D'Arcq, vol. i, p. 118: 'que les personnes des dessudiz de la Rivière et le Mercier soient mis à plaine délivrance'. This 'délivrance' dates from 1394. A later document quoted by Douët-D'Arcq in *La Chronique d'Enguerran de Monstrelet en deux livres avec pièces justificatives 1400–1444*, vol. i, p. 409, says as follows: 'son corps et ses biens non confisqués, se aucuns en sont pour ce prins, saisiz, levez ou arrestez, lui mectent ou facent mectre sans délay à plaine délivrance'.

of Pat. Rolls), *Mallere* (*Sepulchral Inscriptions*), *Malorie* (*Liber
Albus III*), *Malarie* (*Liber Albus II*), *Malorey* (Wilkinson), *Malory*
(Burton, Nichols, Dugdale, *Calendar of Pat. Rolls*, Caxton),
Malorye (Caxton). There is therefore nothing strange in the fact
that the author spelled his name *Maleore*.

(2) He was a knight (cf. the records below).

(3) He died in 1471. Before 1422 (in Henry V's time) he
served in the train of Richard of Warwick, so that he must have
been at least 14 in 1422, and not under 62 in 1470.

(4) He was arrested in 1451 and 1452 for a local dispute, and
excluded from two successive general pardons in 1468. Consequently he must have been in prison up to 1469, and perhaps several
years before that date.

This identification was first suggested by T. W. Williams in his
letter to *The Athenæum* (11 July 1896, No. 3585, pp. 64–5), and
by G. L. Kittredge in his article *Who Was Sir Thomas Malory?*
It is open to criticism in assuming that in 1469–70 there could
exist only one knight of the name of Thomas Malory, who had
spent several years in prison. This assumption is highly probable,
but it cannot be proved, and until further clues are found to connect
Sir Thomas Malory of Warwickshire with the book written by a Sir
Thomas Maleore in 1469–70, our author's identity must be a little
less than certain.

2. *Malory's Ancestors*

There existed in the fifteenth century several families of the
name of Malory (also spelt *Malorie, Malore, Malorey*, &c.). The
three main families of that name were the Yorkshire Malorys,[1] the
Cambridgeshire Malorys, or the Northants family,[2] and the Warwickshire Malorys. The latter were divided into two branches: the
Kirkby family and the Draughton family, probably closely related to
one another. The Malory who is supposed to be identical with the
author of the *Morte Darthur* belonged to the Draughton family.

Our information about the Draughton Malorys is based on the
following authorities:

A. *The Description of Leicester Shire containing Matters of An-
tiquitye, Historye, Armorye, and Genealogy*, written by William

---

[1] Cf. *The Itinerary of John Leland in or about the years* 1535–1543, ed. by L. T.
Smith, Lond. 1908, vol. v, p. 144.

[2] One of their descendants was personally known to Leland, cf. *op. cit.*, vol. ii,
p. 30.

Burton, Esqu. London, 1622. Burton's pedigree of the Draughton Malorys is as follows (pp. 279–80):

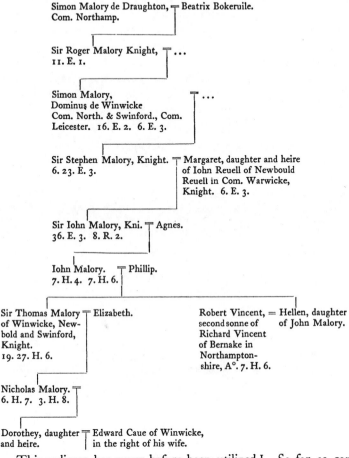

Simon Malory de Draughton, ⊤ Beatrix Bokeruile.
Com. Northamp.

Sir Roger Malory Knight, ⊤ ...
11. E. 1.

Simon Malory,   ⊤ ...
Dominus de Winwicke
Com. North. & Swinford., Com.
Leicester. 16. E. 2. 6. E. 3.

Sir Stephen Malory, Knight. ⊤ Margaret, daughter and heire
6. 23. E. 3.   of Iohn Reuell of Newbould
                                Reuell in Com. Warwicke,
                                Knight. 6. E. 3.

Sir Iohn Malory, Kni. ⊤ Agnes.
36. E. 3. 8. R. 2.

Iohn Malory.   ⊤ Phillip.
7. H. 4. 7. H. 6.

Sir Thomas Malory ⊤ Elizabeth.   Robert Vincent, = Hellen, daughter
of Winwicke, New-   second sonne of   of John Malory.
bold and Swinford,   Richard Vincent
Knight.   of Bernake in
19. 27. H. 6.   Northampton-
                                        shire, A°. 7. H. 6.

Nicholas Malory. ⊤
6. H. 7. 3. H. 8.

Dorothey, daughter ⊤ Edward Caue of Winwicke,
and heire.   in the right of his wife.

This pedigree has never before been utilized.[1] So far as can be ascertained, the only mistake in it is that it makes Nicholas Malory the son of Sir Thomas instead of his grandson. The omission of Nicholas's father, Robert, may be due to the fact that he died in Sir Thomas's lifetime (see records 2 D and 3 B below).

B. I have found a similar pedigree in MS. Rawl. B. 77 of the

---

[1] Sommer briefly refers to Burton's book in a footnote (vol. ii, p. 1) and Kittredge merely reproduces Sommer's reference (*op. cit.*, p. 85).

Bodleian Library (fo. 134), written in the seventeenth century by
Thomas Wilkinson, vicar of Lawrence Waltham, Berks. We have
it on Hearne's authority that this Thomas Wilkinson was well
versed in English 'history and antiquities, and particularly heraldry',
and that he was ' well acquainted (and held a correspondence by
letters) with Mr. Ashmole'.[1] His MS. belonged to Peter le Neve
(No. 588) and was eventually bought by Richard Rawlinson.

Wilkinson's pedigree of the Draughton Malorys agrees with that of
Burton in every important particular, except that it gives the spelling
Malorey instead of *Malory*. The fact that Wilkinson, like Burton,
leaves out Robert Malory suggests that they had a common source.

C. A less accurate but more comprehensive pedigree is furnished by Nichols's *History and Antiquities of the County of Leicester*,
(London 1807, vol. iv, p. 364). It begins with Richard Malory,
who lived in the time of King Stephen and King Henry II:

Richard Malory.
|
Anketil Malory, 1174.
|
Henry Malory, 1199.
|
Simon Malory, lord of Drayton, 1277.
|
Roger Malory of Drayton, 1293.
|
Simon Malory of Drayton, 1313 and 1317.
|
Sir Roger Malory, knt. 1283.
|
Simon Malory, lord of Winwick, co. Northampton
and Swinford, 1323 and 1333.
|
Sir Stephen Malory, knt., 1333 and 1350.
|
Sir John Malory, knt.   = Agnes.
1363 and 1385.
|
John Malory,   = Philippa.
high sheriff 1406; living 1429.
|
Sir Thomas Malory,   = Elizabeth ...
of Winwick, Newbold, and   died Sept. 30,
Swinford, knt. 1441 and   1479.
1442.
|
Robert Malory.   = ...
|
Nicholas Malory, born 1466,
high sheriff 1502.

Cf. Hearne's note in a priced copy of Le Neve's sale catalogue in the Bodleian,

This pedigree is by no means reliable : the second Simon and Sir Roger are probably identical with the first Simon and Roger respectively. It has also been suggested [1] that the first Simon is at least a generation too late to be Henry's son.

D. Another pedigree is found in *The History and Antiquities of Northamptonshire compiled from the Manuscript Collection of the late learned antiquary John Bridges, Esq.*, by the Rev. Peter Whalley, Oxford, 1791 (vol. i, p. 604). Bridges does not know any of Malory's male ancestors beyond Sir Stephen, and puts down Beatrix de Bokerville as his mother, while in reality she was his great-grandmother. He also puts Peter Malory, Justice of the Common Pleas, at least a generation too early. The pedigree from Beatrix de Bokerville down to Margery, great-granddaughter of Sir Thomas, is as follows:

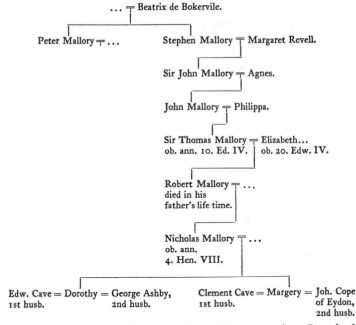

In another place (vol. ii, pp. 28–9) Bridges mentions Beatrix de Blokerville, or Bokervile, widow of *Simon Malore* in 1286, and

Mus. Bibl. III. 8vo. 42, and *Catalogi codicum manuscriptorum Bibliothecae Bodleianae*, p. v, fasc. i, Oxon. 1862.

[1] Cf. G. L. Kittredge, *op. cit.*, p. 91.

her heir *Simon Malore*, lord of Draughton (1316). From the latter *Stephen Mallore* received 'the fourth part of a knight's fee' and was still possessed of it in the twenty-second year of Edward III (1349). Bridges further adds (p. 603) that in the ninth year of Edward III (1336) Stephen Mallore was lord of Winwick. 'Upon levying the aid for the knighthood of the king's son, in the twentieth of *Edw. III*, he accounted for a tenth part of one knight's fee here held of the prior of *Coventre*; . . . By *Margaret* his wife, one of the daughters and coheirs of *John Revell* of *Newbold Revell*, *Sir Stephen Mallory* had issue *John Mallory* Kt his successor, who in the fifty-first year of this reign settled this Manor on *Nicholas Ryvell*, Sir *John Wichemale*, and other trustees.'

E. The career of Sir Thomas Malory's father, John Malory, is fully described by Dugdale in his *Antiquities of Warwickshire*, London, 1656 (p. 56). Dugdale states that John Malory, son of John Malory, lord of Winwick and Northampton, had the manor of Fenny Newbold as well as other lands, and that in 1390 and 1391 he was 'constituted one of the commissioners for conservation of the Peace of this County'. In 1392 'being then a kt. he was made sheriff of these counties'. In 1413 he was M.P. for his County, and in 1417 Sheriff for his county. In 1420 he was 'by speciall Commission, with others, assigned to treat with the people about a loan of money to the King'. In 1428 he was Escheator for Warwick and Leicester, 'and the next year held the Sheriffalty'. From 1419 to 1434 he was Commissioner for the Peace. The earliest date at which he is mentioned is 1383.

This account was first discovered by Professor Kittredge and summarized in his article mentioned above.[1]

F. In a document dated 6. E. 3 (1333) is mentioned *John Malore*, Sir Thomas's grandfather (*Miscellanea Genealogica et Heraldica*, ed. by J. Howard, 1st series, vol. i, p. 54). It is important to note the spelling of his name.

3. *Malory's Life*

A. Bridges (*op. cit.*, p. 603) mentions Sir Thomas Malory as the grandson of John Mallory, Knight, from whom he received in

---

[1] *Ibid.*, p. 88. Kittredge drew his information from the second edition, revised by William Thomas, London, 1730. I have used here the first edition, published in London in 1656.

course of succession the Manor of Winwick. He was 'member of parliament for the county of Warwick in the parliament held at *Westminster* in the twenty third of *Hen. VI* after whose decease being held in dower by *Elizabeth* his widow (Esc. anno 20 Edw. IV, n. 46), in the twentieth year of *Edw. IV* (1481) it fell to their grandson *Nicholas Malory,* son of *Robert Malory* who died before his father, a minor of fourteen years old. This *Nicholas* had issue two daughters, *Dorothy* the wife of *Edward Cave,* and secondly of *George Asby;* and *Margery* first married to *Clement Cave* and afterwards to *John Cope.'*

B. A more complete account of Malory's life is given by Dugdale (*loc. cit.*). John Malory, he notes, 'left issue *Thomas;* who, in K.H. 5 time, was of the retinue to *Ric. Beauchamp* E. 𝔚𝔞𝔯𝔯. at the siege of 𝕮𝖆𝖑𝖊𝖞𝖘, and served there with one lance and two Archers; receiving for his lance and 1. Archer *XX. li per an.* and their dyet; and for the other Archer. X. marks and no dyet. This *Thomas,* being a Kt in 23. H. 6 served for this Shire in the Parliam. then held at 𝔚𝔢𝔰𝔱𝔪. and dying 14. *Martii* 10. E. 4 lyeth buried under a marble in the Chappell of St. *Francis* at the 𝕲𝖗𝖆𝖞 𝕱𝖗𝖎𝖊𝖗𝖘, near 𝕹𝖊𝖜𝖊𝖌𝖆𝖙𝖊 in the Suburbs of 𝕷𝖔𝖓𝖉𝖔𝖓. To whom succeeded Nicholas his Grand-Child, *viz.* son of *Robert,* who dyed in his Fathers life time'. On this record Professor Kittredge [1] based his identification of the author of the *Morte Darthur.*

The only obscure point in Dugdale's account is the reference to the siege of Calais. There was no siege of Calais in Henry V's time.

C. Burton (*op. cit.,* p. 279) states that Robert Vincent, Malory's brother-in-law, first mortgaged his estate in Swinford 'and after sold out-right all his Lands in *Swinford* to *Thomas Malory,* his wives brother, reserving onely an annuitie which was enjoyed by his posterity two discents untill *William* the grandchilde of *Robert* aforesaid, released the same, a° 10. H. 8 to *Nicholas Cave* of *Winwicke* and *Swinford,* in right of *Dorothy* his wife, daughter and heire of *Nicholas Mallory'* (the grandson of Sir Thomas). The dates which Burton assigns to Sir Thomas in the pedigree (1441 and 1449) may refer to these contracts.

D. Malory figures in two commissions of Henry VI (*Calendar*

---

[1] *Op. cit.,* pp. 87–94.

of Patent Rolls, Hen. VI, v. 476; vi. 61). The first, dated 13 July 1451, appoints Humphrey Duke of Buckingham and Richard [1] Earl of Warwick to arrest Thomas Malory, knight, and his servant John Appelby, 'and cause them to find mainpernors who will mainprise for them under a sufficient penalty that they will do no hurt to the prior and convent of the Carthusian house of Axiholme or any of the king's people, and that they will appear in person before the king and council on the quinzaine of Michaelmas next to answer certain charges'. The second commission, of 26 March 1452, directs the Duke of Buckingham, Sir Edward Grey of Groby, and the Sheriff of Warwick and Leicester 'to arrest and bring before the king and council Thomas Malorre, Knight, to answer certain charges'.

Sir Edmund Chambers, who was the first to draw attention to these two documents,[2] suggests that they refer to a local dispute about the priory of Monks Kirby. On the suppression of the alien priories under Richard II, this priory (once a cell of the monastery of St. Nicholas of Angiers) 'was transferred to the Carthusian house of Epworth in the isle of Axholme, Lincolnshire. Henry IV restored it to Angiers, and Henry V in 1415–16 to Epworth again. The last transfer was confirmed by Edward IV in 1468–9'. 'In view of the late date of Edward IV's confirmation of Epworth it is of course possible that some renewal of this dispute and not sedition led to Malory's imprisonment in 1468.'

E. The documents relating to the Inquisition at Nuneaton and the subsequent trial of Sir Thomas Malory have been recently published by Mr. E. Hicks (*Sir Thomas Malory, His Turbulent Career*, pp. 93–102).

F. Nichols (*op. cit.*, vol. iii, p. 302) mentions a transfer of land made by Sir Thomas Malory who 'being seised in fee' of the manor of Swinford 'conveyed the same in fee to *Henry Sharp, John Menely, Eustace Burneby* and *John Malory*, son of *Simon Malory* (?), to hold to them and their heirs for ever'. Nichols gives no date. He says that the transfer was effected a considerable time before 1480, which is obvious enough since Malory was dead in 1471.

In a footnote to 'Sir Thomas Malory' in the pedigree Nichols writes: 'Inter Radulfum Cromwell, militem, & alios querentes,

---

[1] Richard Neville, the 'king-maker'.   [2] *Sir Thomas Malory*, p. 16.

Will. Malory, militem, & Marger. uxorem defendentem messuag'
& terras in Careby East, & Castel Bytham & Edenham; medie-
tatem manerii de Careby, &c. Fines Leic. 21. Hen. VI.' The
connexion of this entry with Sir Thomas is doubtful since it only
refers to a William Malory.

In vol. iv, p. 368, Nichols quotes a conveyance of the lands of
the family of Feilding where 'Thomas Malory, miles' is mentioned
among the witnesses. The date of the conveyance is 12 September 1464.

G. Two MSS. of Wells Cathedral witness that in 1468 Malory
was in prison. *MS. Liber Albus III* (ff. 227–8) contains a general
pardon granted by Edward IV on 24 August 1468, where it is
stated that the pardon 'shall not extend to Thomas Malorie, miles'.[1]
This reference was discovered by T. W. Williams and published
in *The Athenaeum* on 11 July 1896 (No. 3585, pp. 64–5).

MS. *Liber Albus II* (ff. 199–200) contains another general pardon from which Malory is also excluded: . . . 'not to include any
customer, nor Humfrey Nevyll knight, Thomas Malarie knight',
&c. It is dated 1 December 1468.[2] This reference was discovered
by Sir Edmund Chambers, *loc. cit.*

H. Cotton MS. Vitellius F. xii contains the following record:
'In Capella Sancti Francisci . . . sub 2ᵃ parte fenestre 4ᵉ sub lapide
jacet dominus Thomas Mallere, valens miles: qui obiit 14 die men-
sis Marcij, Aᵒ dⁿⁱ 1470, de parochia de Monkenkyrkby in comitatu Warwici.' Quoted by Sir Edmund Chambers, *loc. cit.*

I. The inscription on Malory's tomb is as follows: 'dñs Thomas
Mallere, valens miles, ob. 14 Mar. 1470, de pochia de Monkenkyrkby in coñ Warwici'.[3]

K. Nichols gives some details about Malory's widow, Elizabeth
(*op. cit.*, vol. iii, p. 302). 'By an inquisition taken at Lutterworth
on the Tuesday after the feast of Sᵗ Anne (26 July), 1480, before
William Bristowe, the king's escheator, and returned into the

[1] Cf. *Historical MSS. Commission, Report on the MSS. of Wells Cathedral*, London,
1885, pp. 183–4.
[2] Cf. *H.M.C., Calendar of the Manuscripts of the Dean and Chapter of Wells*,
London, 1907; vol. i, p. 407.
[3] Cf. *Sepulchral Inscriptions in the Church of the Grey Friars, London*, in *Col-
lectanea Topographica et Genealogica*, vol. iii, p. 287.

Court of Chancery, it was found that *Elizabeth*, relict of sir
Thomas Malory knight, died Sept. 30, 1479, seised, in demesne,
as of free tenure, for the term of her life, of the manor of Swynford,
with the appurtenances, and of one messuage and two virgates of
land, with the appurtenances, in Stormefeld; which, after the death
of the said *Elizabeth*, reverted to *Nicholas* Malory, cousin and heir
of the said *Thomas* (being the son and heir of *Robert* Malory, son
of sir *Thomas*), and his heirs; and that the said manor was worth
four marks a year, *in omnibus exitibus suis, ultra reprisas*; and the
messuage and lands in Stormefeld, in like manner, worth 20*s.* 8*d.*
a year; but of whom, or by what services, the said manor and lands,
or any part of them, were held, was wholly unknown: That the
said Elizabeth died on the 30ᵗʰ of September 1479; that the aforesaid Nicholas, her cousin and heir, was then 13 years old and more;
and that, at the time of her death, she held no other lands in
Leicestershire, either of the king or any other person.'

L. Caxton says in his preface to the *Morte Darthur* (p. 3) that
he 'sette it in enprynte' from a 'copye' which 'Syr Thomas Malorye
dyd take oute of certayn bookes of frensshe'. In the colophon
(p. 861) he alters the spelling of Malory's name: the book, he says,
was 'reduced in to englysshe by syr Thomas Malory Knyght as
afore is sayd'.

M. The will of Sir Thomas Malory has not been preserved.
On 11 September 1897 A. T. Martin announced in *The Athenaeum* (No. 3646, pp. 353–4) that he had discovered the will of a
Thomas Malory of Papworth whom he identified with the author
of the *Morte Darthur*. This will makes ample provision for the
education of a family of three daughters and seven sons, and the
testator styles himself 'Thomas Malory de Pappeworth in Comitatu
Huntingdon'. It is dated 16 September 1469. But this Thomas
Malory cannot be identical with the one of Newbold Revell: firstly,
because he was not a knight; secondly, because he had seven sons
instead of one; and thirdly, because he belonged to the Cambridgeshire family of Malorys, Papworth being a hundred partly in Cambridgeshire, partly in Hunts.[1]

[1] Notwithstanding these inconsistencies, A. T. Martin's theory has been
accepted by some critics, notably by A. W. Pollard (see his Introduction to *Le
Morte Darthur*, Library of English Classics, London, 1900, p. vi).

4. *The* Morte Darthur *and Wales*

In his Introduction to the edition of the *Morte Darthur* published by J. M. Dent (London, 1893, vol. i, pp. xi–xii), Professor Rhŷs expressed the belief that Malory was a Welshman. He called attention to the fact that in John Bale's *Illustrium Majoris Britanniae Scriptorum* the author of the *Morte Darthur* is described as 'Britannus natione', and his birthplace as 'Mailoria in finibus Cambriae, Devae flumini vicina' (ff. 208ᵛ–209ʳ). 'Britannus' means Welsh, and Professor Rhŷs naturally concluded that Malory was a Welshman. Although 'Mailoria upon Dee' could not be identified with any locality in Wales, Professor Rhŷs suggested that *Maleor(e)* being dissyllabic may be referred to the name of two districts on the confines of England and Wales: a 'Welsh Maleor' in the county of Denbigh, and an 'English Maelor' in that of Flint. This name could easily become a surname, as in the case of Gruffud Maelawr, lord of the two Maelors in the twelfth century. Professor Rhŷs is therefore inclined to consider our author as a fellow-countryman and namesake of the Welsh poet Edward ab Rhys Maelor (or 'Edward Price of Maelor'). The trisyllabic form *Malory* he regards as an Englished form of the Latinized *Mailorius*.

This theory has been attacked and almost completely invalidated by Professor G. L. Kittredge in his article on Malory's identity quoted above. Professor Kittredge points out, in the first place, that the name *Maleore* is not dissyllabic: the final *e* is not silent, but corresponds to the French *é* (Latin *a*) which regularly develops in English into *y*. Besides, the form Malore had been common in England long before Malory wrote his book, and a Richard *Malore* is mentioned as early as the twelfth century. The name is therefore not necessarily Welsh; it could well exist simultaneously in England and in Wales.

Further, Professor Kittredge questions the accuracy of Bale's testimony, which, as he rightly remarks, is entirely based on Leland's *Syllabus et Interpretatio Antiquarum Dictionum* (London, 1542). It is to this work that Bale refers ('inquit in antiquarium dictionum syllabo Ioannes Lelandus'). He seems to have no first-hand information, and Leland is hardly a reliable authority. In the *Assertio inclytissimi Arturii regis Britanniae* (London, 1544) Leland clearly shows his dislike of the 'fabulae' and his exclusive interest in historical authors (f. 19ᵛ: 'ut fabulas contemno, ita historiae veritatem

amplector, et suavior'). He is aware that Malory's version is a *rifacimento* of the French Romances (*loc. cit.*: . . . 'e Gallicae. Unde et collectio Anglica, autore Thoma Mailerio, prodiit'), but shows no knowledge of the author. His ignorance is, in my opinion, further attested by the fact that in his *Itinerary* he only mentions the Cambridgeshire and the Yorkshire Malorys, and however little we may know of Malory's real identity, it is at least certain that he belonged to neither of these families.

Professor Rhŷs's theory is therefore untenable. But to do justice to the Welsh elements in the *Morte Darthur*, it is important to note here some facts which, inconclusive though they are, may suggest a distant connexion between our author and Wales.

Comparison of the *Morte Darthur* with its French sources has shown me that of all the countries of the legendary England which he describes Malory is most partial to Wales. He often introduces Welsh knights against his source which he otherwise follows very closely. Among the knights who came to the tournament of Lonazep[1] he mentions *the kynge of the best part of Walys with many other countreyes*, and on the second day of the tournament[2] *the kynge of Northgalys*. In both cases he alters his source. The king of Wales also appears, against the French version, on the third day of the tournament of Surluse.[3] In the chapter entitled *How Sir Tristram had a fall with Sir Palomides and how Launcelot overthrew two knights* (Book IX, ch. 28) Malory substitutes for the anonymous 'autre chevalier de Norgales'[4] *two knyghtes of Northgales* and gives each of them a name: *that one hyghte Hewe de la montayne and the other syr Madok de la montayne.*[5]

In another passage[6] Malory substitutes the King of Wales for the King of Ireland: 'and so syr Launcelot smote doune the kynge of Scottes *and the Kynge of walys*' (tournament of Lonazep), and maintains the alteration to the end of the chapter: *the kynges of Walys and of Scotland* help Palomides to resume his armour and his horse. The conscious nature of the substitution of Wales for Ireland is the more evident because the chapter is otherwise an exact reproduction of the corresponding passage in the French original.

The thirty-eighth chapter of Book VIII relates 'how Syr Tris-

---

[1] p. 529.   [2] p. 545.   [3] p. 485.
[4] MS. Bibl. Nat. fr. 334, f. 226ᵛ, col. 2.   [5] p. 383.
[6] p. 555.

tram and his wife arrived *in Walys*, and how he met there with Syr Lamorak'. Tristan, Kehidius, and Iseult of the White Hands sail in a 'little barget', and a wind drives them *in to the coste of Walys upon the Isle of Servage*. All this is to be found in the French source, *except that it does not mention Wales*. Malory's is the only version which places the Isle of Servage on the Welsh coast. Never before or after, in any medieval romance, has Tristan journeyed to Wales.

In his Books VIII—XII, whence all these quotations are drawn, Malory used nothing but the French Prose Romance of Tristan and had no knowledge of any other version. His alterations in this section of the *Morte Darthur* are few and personal; they reflect his own outlook and his own interpretation of the stories. If, therefore, he insists on introducing Wales and Welsh knights contrary to his French source it is for some yet undiscovered reason.

APPENDIX TWO

THE SOURCES OF THE *MORTE DARTHUR*

1. *Introductory*

THE study of Malory's sources is of comparatively recent date. Early critics vaguely described them as French 'romances of chivalry' and seldom committed themselves to more definite statements. Up to 1890 only four important suggestions were made: in 1817 Southey pointed out that Malory had 'drawn liberally' from the prose *Tristan* contained in Vérard's edition of 1495;[1] in 1878 Moritz Trautmann urged that Malory's Book V was derived from the alliterative *Morte Arthure*;[2] in 1886 Gaston Paris, in his edition of the Huth *Merlin*, traced some parts of Malory's first four books to that manuscript,[3] and in the same year he compared Malory's version of the *Conte de la Charrete* with the French.[4]

On the 4th January 1890 there was published in *The Academy* a letter in which Dr. H. Oskar Sommer announced his intention of making public, in the third volume of his edition of the *Morte Darthur*, the conclusions he had reached as to Malory's sources. 'The result of my researches', he wrote, 'surpasses all my anticipations . . . I can clearly show what were the versions of the sources Malory used, and how he altered and added to them to suit his purpose.' The results of these studies have since been published in a voluminous book.[5] Most critics accepted them as the only firm basis for a critical examination of Malory's text, and E. Kölbing went even so far as to say that no further study was required.[6] In reality, however, the promise made in the letter to *The Academy* was only partially fulfilled, and to all those who ventured to under-

---

[1] *The Byrth, lyf and actes of Kyng Arthur; of his noble Knyghtes of the rounde table, theyr marveyllous conquestes and adventures, thacheuyng of the Sanc Greal; and in the end le morte d'Arthur*, ed. by Rob. Southey (London, 1817), Preface.

[2] *Anglia*, i. 145–6.

[3] *Merlin*, roman en prose du XIIIe siècle publié par Gaston Paris et Jacob Ulrich (S.A.T.F.), Paris, 1886, pp. lxx–lxxii.

[4] *Romania*, xii, pp. 498–508.

[5] *Op. cit.*, vol. iii.

[6] *Englische Studien*, xvi. 403: 'Um eine Recension dieses Buches zu schreiben, müsste man die ganze Untersuchung noch einmal machen, eine Arbeit, die sich für jeden, der nicht das Glück hat Jahre lang in englischen Bibliotheken arbeiten zu können, von selbst verbietet. Und ich meine, das ist auch im vorliegenden Fall für eine Formirung unseres Urtheils kaum erförderlich.'

take a further study of the problem it was obvious that Sommer 'exaggerated his originality in regard to most of what was sound in his theories'.[1] Thus, in 'establishing' the source of Malory's Books I—IV (the *Merlin*) he merely adopted the views of Gaston Paris, who as early as 1886 had traced it to the Huth *Merlin*. For Book V Sommer utilized the theory of Trautmann, and for the *Lancelot* proper (Books VI and XIX) confined himself to a long quotation from an article by Gaston Paris. These are, as far as we know, the only 'sound' parts of his theory. The rest is more original, but proportionally less convincing. An examination of Malory's *Tristan* has satisfied me that Sommer's theory on this point is of no critical value.[2] His discussion of the *Prophécies de Merlin* is based on an incomplete knowledge of the French tradition,[3] and his assumption of a lost *Suite de Lancelot* would not have been advanced if he had been more familiar with the Arthurian MSS. in the Bibliothèque Nationale.[4] For Malory's *Quest of the Holy Grail* Sommer used Furnivall's edition of the French *Queste*, because it was 'within the reach of every scholar'.[5] It did not occur to him that the thirty-nine extant manuscripts of the *Queste* might show the imperfection of Furnivall's text. Lastly, for Malory's Books XVIII, XX, and XXI he suggested a theory which has been a subject of controversy ever since, for he left it uncertain whether Malory used the French Prose *Lancelot* or the English poem contained in MS. Harl. 2252.

The real and, perhaps, the only merit of Sommer's studies on the sources of Malory lies not in 'clearly showing what were the versions of the sources Malory used', but in the minute comparisons between the *Morte Darthur* and those sources which had been indicated before. Thus, Sommer's collation of Malory's text with the Huth *Merlin* and with the alliterative *Morte Arthure* is still useful, because there can be no doubt that these works represent Malory's source.

Since the publication of Dr. Sommer's *Studies* the question of Malory's sources has only partially been reconsidered,[6] and a num-

---

[1] *V. The Nation*, 26 May 1910, vol. xc, No. 2343, p. 538.
[2] Cf. *Rom. de Trist.*, pp. 27–86.
[3] Cf. *ibid.*, pp. 59–71.
[4] Cf. *ibid.*, pp. 73 ff.   [5] *Op. cit.*, p. 206.
[6] Valuable suggestions have been made by E. Löseth (*Le roman en prose de Tristan*, pp. xxii–xxiii), Ed. Wechssler (*Ueber die verschiedenen Redaktionen des*

ber of doubtful points have remained unsettled. In the following pages an attempt will be made to detect the nearest extant version of his 'Frensshe booke'. For some parts of this study I claim no originality: whenever I have found the existing theories well established, I have confined myself to restating them with more precision in details. Elsewhere, and particularly in discussing Books VIII—XVII, I have endeavoured to determine Malory's source on the ground of my own investigations and have given larger extracts from my collations. The actual manuscript used by Malory has not been preserved. Some of the extant texts, however, are so closely related to it that they may be conveniently used as a substitute for a considerable part of Malory's source. In this way Books I–V and VIII–XVII (i.e. 600 pages in Caxton's print) can be traced to their originals. And although for the rest (226 pages in Caxton) the result is less satisfactory, the portions traceable to extant MSS. suffice to provide a sound basis for a critical study.[1]

2. The MERLIN (Books I—IV)

The first four books of the *Morte Darthur* relate the birth and coronation of Arthur, his first wars and tournaments, and the various adventures of his knights. In all these episodes Merlin the soothsayer plays a prominent part; and, indeed, down to p. 64, l. 32, Malory's text roughly corresponds to a section of the French prose romance of Merlin. Malory omits the early part of this romance and begins his story with the love intrigue of Uther Pendragon and Igraine, the wife of the Duke of Cornwall, which he relates in a very summary fashion.[2] To give his story a suitable beginning, Malory says in the opening lines of his book (p. 35) that Uther waged a war against the Duke of Cornwall and that 'by the meanes

Robert de Boron zugeschriebenen Graal-Lancelot Cyklus, pp. 22–37), J. D. Bruce (*Anglia*, xxiii, pp. 67 ff.), and E. Vettermann (*Die Balen-Dichtungen und ihre Quellen*, pp. 62–70). See *Bibliography*.

[1] I hope to publish at some later date the bulky collations on which my own commentary is based. Meanwhile the reader may consult the works enumerated on p. 154 *infra*. A collation of Malory's Book XV with the corresponding folios of MS. B.N. fr. 120 will be found in Appendix III.

[2] Cf. G. Paris et J. Ulrich, *op. cit.*, p. lxxi: 'il semble même qu'il manque matériellement quelque chose au début de son livre, car on nous présente tout à coup Merlin mettant en œuvre son pouvoir surnaturel, sans que nous sachions qui il était et d'où il tenait ce pouvoir.'

of grete lordes they were accorded bothe'.[1] Otherwise he follows his source fairly accurately and varies only in details. The narrative is much condensed: Malory's pp. 35–64 correspond to more than 27 folios in his source. The only important addition is found on p. 44 (ll. 3–20), where Malory describes at great length how Arthur heard the complaints of his barons, and distributed lands and offices.[2]

From p. 64_{34} down to the end of Book IV (p. 159_{36}) Malory tells a series of adventures unknown to all the cyclic MSS. of the *Merlin*. He begins by saying that 'after the departyng of kyng Ban and of Kyng Bors, Kynge Arthur rode unto Carlyon, and thyder cam to hym kyng Lots wyf of Orkeney'. This is unintelligible, because King Arthur was at that time already in Caerlion and could not have ridden there. The key to the mystery is found in a French MS. of the British Museum, Huth No. 4, which contains the following sentence (f. 75^v col. 1): 'Ore dist que un rois [3] aprés le couronnement le roi Artu vint a une grant court que li rois semonst a Carduel [4] en Gales la feme le roi Loth d'Orkanie.' It is obvious that 'le roi Artu' is genitive, and that the sentence means: '. . . after *Arthur's* coronation the wife of King Loth of Orkeney came to a court which the king [i.e. Arthur] held at Carduel'.[4] Malory interpreted 'le roi Artu' as nominative, made it the subject of the clause, and so caused Arthur to travel from Caerlion to Caerlion.[5] A further comparison of the Huth MS. with Malory's text shows that from this sentence onwards Malory used a version very similar to that contained in ff. 75^r col. 1–229^v col. 2

---

[1] This is not unlike the addition made by Malory at the beginning of Book VIII. Cf. *Rom. de Trist.*, pp. 156–7.

[2] There may be an echo of contemporary events in Malory's statement that the North 'fro Trent forwardes' 'was that tyme the most party the kynges enemyes. But within few yeres after Arthur wan alle the North Scotland and alle that were vnder their obeissaunce' (ll. 14–17).

[3] The editors of the Huth MS. transcribe this *mois*.

[4] Here as elsewhere, Malory renders Carduel by Caerlion.

[5] Cf. my article in *Arthuriana*, vol. I. Malory says further that the Queen of Orkeney came 'in maner of message'. This again may be explained as a misreading of the French text. MS. Huth has: 'serour le roi i fu mais quoi quelle fust sasuer nen sauoit elle riens'. The correct reading of this line is: 'serour le roi i fu. Mais quoi qu'elle fust sa suer, n'en savoit elle riens.' Malory reads instead: 'serour le roi i fu maisgier, qu'elle fust asuer n'en savoir telle riens', and translates: 'in maner of message, but she was sente thyder to aspye the Courte of Kynge Arthur.'

of the Huth MS. The agreement goes as far as p. 140, l. 1 of Caxton's edition and ends with the following passage:

Malory, p. 140.	Huth MS., f. 229ᵛ, col. 1.
And so the kyng made it to be putt upon her, and forth withal she felle doune dede and never more spake word after and brente to coles.	si le met a son col et l'affuble. Et si tost comme ele l'ot mis entor li, elle chiet . . .[1] et s'estent, et maintenant li part l'ame del cors.

Malory condenses the story more than in the previous section: 76 pages of Caxton's print correspond to 154 folios in the French MS. This version is the only extant source of Malory's pp. 64–140.[2] But it also helps to explain the origin of the first, 'cyclic' section of Malory's *Merlin*. Ff. 19–76 of the Huth MS. contain part of the French cyclic version of *Merlin*, which is put in as an introduction to the main body of the narrative. There is, therefore, reason to believe that thirteenth-century scribes used to connect the two, and to preface episodes such as those contained in the Huth MS. ff. 76–229 by a recapitulation of the ordinary version of *Merlin*. Ff. 76–229 of the Huth MS. may consequently be regarded as a continuation of the cyclic *Merlin* ('La Suite de Merlin'). Malory must

---

[1] The editors of the Huth MS. suggest: 'chiet pasmee'.

[2] The connexion between Malory's *Merlin* and the Huth MS. was first suggested by Gaston Paris in his Introduction to the edition of *Merlin* quoted above. Speaking of Malory's compilation he said (p. lxxi): 'Au ch. xvii, il commence à suivre notre texte, et, sauf quelques modifications et additions que nous ne relevons pas, et surtout sauf de fortes abréviations, il ne le quitte pas jusqu'à la fin du livre I. Il le prend au début, et termine son livre I à la p. 211 de notre édition, avec l'épisode des enfants exposés. — Le livre II, dont le début est assez singulier et semble un commencement de toute l'œuvre, est consacré à l'histoire de Balaain (appelé Balin le Sauvage); il comprend dix-neuf chapitres, et se termine à la p. 60 de notre t. ii. — Le livre III, comprenant quinze chapitres, raconte le mariage d'Arthur, le renouvellement de la Table Ronde et la triple aventure de Gauvain, Tor et Pellinor; il correspond à ce qui, dans notre t. ii, va de la p. 60 à la p. 139 environ; mais la fin est très abrégée d'une part et de l'autre contient quelques traits qui manquent dans notre manuscrit. — Le livre IV, divisé en 28 chapitres, comprend toute la fin du ms. Huth, et en plus, comme nous l'avons remarqué ci-dessus . . . le dénouement de la triple aventure d'Ivain, Gauvain et le Morhout.' Since the publication of Gaston Paris's study of the *Merlin* in 1886, the only substantial addition to his theory has been made by E. Vettermann (*Die Balen-Dichtungen und ihre Quellen*, pp. 62–7) who gives a number of interesting parallels, but does not consider the passages quoted above. Sommer in his studies on Malory's sources (vol. iii of his edition of the *Morte Darthur*) merely reproduces the theory of Gaston Paris in a less lucid form. Whenever he attempts to put forward a theory of his own, he invariably obscures the issue. Thus, in order to explain the relationship of

have used some MS. containing part of the cyclic *Merlin* as well as a 'Suite de Merlin'.

This version was similar, no doubt, to the Huth MS., but not identical with it. It differed from the Huth MS. in two respects: (*a*) it contained a larger section of the *Merlin* than is found in the Huth MS. After Arthur's coronation it related the rebellion against the newly-elected king and the war waged against him by the eleven kings. These episodes form the subject of Malory's pp. 44_{21}–64_{32}. They are found in all the existing MSS.[1] of the cyclic *Merlin*, and occupy an average of twelve folios. (*b*) The MS. used by Malory contained a more complete 'Suite' than the Huth MS. After the story of the magic mantle, whose conclusion has been quoted above, it related the adventure of Ywain, Gawain, and Marhaus, which Malory reproduces in pp. 140_1–159_{36}, 'as it reherceth in the book of Frensshe'.

This 'book of Frensshe' is not extant, but one of the MSS. in the Bibliothèque Nationale seems to have preserved another trace of it. Ff. 17^r col. 2–22^r col. 1 of MS. B.N. fr. 112 contain the

the various *Merlin* MSS. (p. 32), he suggests that 'various MSS. descended from the original MS. . . . were copied either from the original or from one another', and that 'during this process the scribes, who either wished to add matter of their own to their copies or misunderstood their original, introduced variations'. This astounding discovery enables Sommer to draw up a diagram the only meaning of which is that all the derivatives of the *Merlin* romance derived from the *Merlin* romance. He renders it thus:

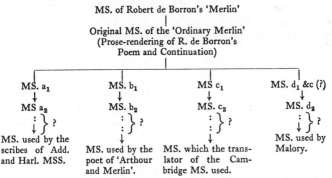

MS. of Robert de Borron's 'Merlin'
|
Original MS. of the 'Ordinary Merlin'
(Prose-rendering of R. de Borron's
Poem and Continuation)
|

MS. a_1	MS. b_1	MS c_1	MS. d_1 &c (?)
↓	↓	↓	↓
MS a_2	MS. b_2	MS. c_2	MS. d_2
: } ?	: } ?	: } ?	↓ } ?
↓	↓	↓	
MS. used by the scribes of Add. and Harl. MSS.	MS. used by the poet of 'Arthour and Merlin'.	MS. which the translator of the Cambridge MS. used.	MS. used by Malory.

To appreciate this table it is well to remember that all except the mysterious MSS. a_1, a_2, b_1, b_2, &c. and the queries was known before Sommer, so that his contribution consists in numbering non-existent MSS.

[1] These are: MSS. Bibl. Nat. fr. 98, 113, 117, 344, 747; Br. Mus. Add. 10292 Harl. 6340; Bodl. Douce 178; Phillipps (Cheltenham) 1046.

same episodes as the last section of MS. Huth No. 4 (ff. 220^r
col. 1–230^r col. 2), and these episodes are followed by an account
of the adventures of Ywain, Gawain, and Marhaus similar to that
found in Malory's Book IV. The agreement ends, however, as
early as f. 28^r col. 1, corresponding to Malory's p. 151:

MS. B.N. fr. 112, f. 28^r, col. 1.	Malory, 151$_{33-34}$.
'Alés dont,' fet elle. Et il sault erranment en son destrier et s'en vait grant erre	'Ye have deceyved me and bytrayd me falsly, that al ladyes and damoysels may beware by yow and me.' And therwith Syr Gawayn made hym redy and wente into the forest.

The last nine pages of Book IV remain untraceable. According to
Ed. Wechssler, Malory has here preserved a more authentic version
of the story than any other extant romance:[1] he must have used
an 'unshortened redaction' of which MSS. Huth and B.N. fr. 112
are only fragments.

The relation of Malory's first four books to their French sources
may be briefly tabulated as follows:

Malory, pp. 35$_1$²–44$_{20}$ correspond to Huth MS., ff. 59^v col. 1–75^r col. 1.
    „   „ 44$_{21}$–64$_{32}$ „   Harl. MS. 6340, ff. 60^r col. 2–83^v
                                  col. 2.
    „   „ 64$_{33}$–140$_1$ „   Huth MS., ff. 75^r col. 1–229^v col. 2.
    „   „ 140$_1$–151$_{34}$ „   MS. B.N. fr. 112, ff. 22^r col. 1–
                                    28^r col. 2.[3]
    „   „ 151$_{35}$–159$_{36}$ are not traceable to any extant version.

3. The Roman Expedition (Book V)

In his Introduction to the Huth *Merlin*, Gaston Paris remarked:
'Avec le livre V, Malory reprend le *Merlin* ordinaire.'[4] This
statement is accurate up to a point. The conclusion of the '*Merlin
ordinaire*', or the common cyclic version of the *Merlin*, contains episodes which roughly correspond to the contents of

---

[1] *Op. cit.*, p. 23: 'Sein Auszug weder auf C (=Huth MS.) noch auf B (=The
Spanish *Demanda*), sondern auf die ungekürzte Redaktion A zurückgeht.'
[2] The *Morte Darthur* begins on p. 35 of Caxton's print.
[3] Published by Sommer in *Die Abenteuer Gawains, Ywains und Le Morholts
mit den drei Jungfrauen* (*Beihefte zur Zeitschrift für romanische Philologie*,
xlvii), Halle, 1913. Sommer gives a brief comparison of Malory's pp. 140–51
with MS. B.N. fr. 112 (p. xxvii, footnote) and an account of Malory's pp.
151–9 (p. xli, footnote).   [4] p. lxxi.

Malory's Book V. It recounts Arthur's expedition against the 'Roman Emperor' Luce (*Lucius* in Malory), and the agreement is fairly close, especially in the early section of the story. Cador's remark on the Roman challenge has a curious parallel in the French:

MS. Add. 10292, f. 204ʳ col. 3.	Malory, 161₁₀₋₁₄.
dist *qu'il avoient grant piece del tans usé en parece et en els deduire*; 'Mais, merci Dieu, ore nos ont esveillé li Rommain.'	Syre, this message lykes me wel, for we have many dayes rested us and have ben ydle.

Yet, further on, Malory diverges from the French *Merlin*, and in such a way as to make it impossible to ascribe the differences to his invention.

A more satisfactory parallel is found in an English fifteenth-century MS. of the Lincoln Cathedral Library. This MS. (Thornton A1, 17) contains a number of verse romances (*Octavian, Isumbras, Erl of Toulous, Sir Degrevant, Sir Eglamour, The Aunturs of Arthur, Sir Perceval of Gales,* &c.),[1] and among them, from f. 53ʳ to f. 98ʳ, an alliterative *Morte Arthure* written about the middle of the fourteenth century.

The alliterative *Morte Arthure*[2] contains a story very similar to that found in Malory, and stands in much closer relation to his Book V than does the French *Merlin*. The earliest instance is the Roman challenge:

Morte Arthure, ll. 112–15.[3]	*Malory*, 160₁₃₋₂₀.
Thy fadyr mad fewtee, we fynde in oure rollez, In the regestre of Rome, who so ryghte lukez: Withowttyn more trouflynge the tre- bute we aske, That Julius Cesar wan wyth his jentill knyghttes.	Commaundyng the . . . to sende hym the truage . . . whiche thy fader and other to fore thy pre- cessours have paid as is of record, and thou as rebelle, not know- ynge hym as thy soverayne, with- holdest and retenest, contrary to the statutes and decrees maade by the noble and worthy Julius Ce- zar, conquerour of this Royame.

This parallel, however, is not close enough to warrant the theory

---

[1] For a full table of contents of this MS. see Sir Frederick Madden's edition of *Sy: ?awayne* (Bannatayne Club, 1839).

[2] Cf. *supra*, pp. 87–90.

[3] I quote from Erik Björkmann's edition (Heidelberg and New York, 1915).

of a direct influence.[1] The real agreement of the two English versions begins with the declaration of war on the Romans. Trautmann and Sommer have carefully collated the two texts, and it will suffice to quote here some of the most convincing examples:

Morte Arthure, ll. 760–84.	*Malory*, V, 4.
He dremyd of a dragon, dredfull to beholde, Come dryfande over þe depe to drenshen hys pople, Ewen walkande owte of the weste landez . . . His sc[h]oulders ware shalyde all in shire sylver . . . Hys wombe and hys wenges of wondyrfull hewes, In mervaylous maylys he mountede full hye . . . He romede, he rarede, that roggede all þe erthe	dremed . . . that a dredeful dragon dyd drowne moche of his peple, and he cam fleyng oute of the west . . . his schoulders shone as gold . . . his bely lyke mailles of merveyllous hewe . . . he rored so hydously that it were merveill to here

Morte Arthure, ll. 801–72.	*Malory*, 165_{21}–166_{25}.
Betwyx þe taile and þe toppe ten fote large . . . And the tatterede taile with tonges so huge . . . I had lever thane all Fraunce, this fyftene wynter, I had bene before thatę freke, a furlange of waye	X foote large fro the hede to the taylle . . . his taylle which is al to tattered. . . . I had leuer than the best Royame that I have that I hadde ben a forlonge way

Morte Arthure, l. 979.	*Malory*, 167_{18}.
and slitt hir to þe navyll.	and has slytte her unto the navyl.

The agreement appears closest in Ch. V (*Morte Arthure*, ll. 840–1262). It goes on as far as Ch. XII—the last chapter in Malory's

---

[1] In the *Morte Arthure* Cador's speech reads as follows (ll. 251 ff.):

> Þe letters of sir Lucius lyghttys myn herte.
> We hafe as losels liffyde many longe dayes,
> Wythe delyttes in this lande, with lordchipez many,
> And forelytenede the loos, þat we are layttede:
> I was abaishite, be oure Lorde, of oure beste bernes,
> For gret dule of deffawte of dedez of armes.
> Now wakkenysę þe were, wyrchipe be Cryste.

This seems less close to Malory than the French text quoted above.

fifth book, ending with l. 3186 in the *Morte Arthure* (p. 182, l. 7 in Malory):

Morte Arthure, ll. 3174–86.	*Malory*, $182_{1.7}$.
But one a Seterdaye at none a sevenyghte thareaftyre	But soone after on a saterday came unto kynge Arthur alle the
The konyngeste cardynall, that to the courte lengede,	senatours that were left on lyue, and the noblest Cardynals that
Knelis to þe conquerour and karpes thire wordes,	thenne dwellyd in Rome, and prayd hym of pees and pro-
Prayes hym for þe pes and profyrs full large,	fered hym ful large, and by-sought hym as governour to gyve
To hafe peté of þe pope þat put was atundere;	lycence for vi wekes for to as-semble alle the Romayns and
Besoghte hym of surrawns for sake of oure Lorde	thenne to crowne hym Em-perour with creme as it bylong-
Bot a sevenyghte daye, to þay ware all semblede,	eth to so hyghe astate.
And they schulde sekerlye hym see the Sonondaye þeraftyre	
In the ceté of Rome as soverayne and lo[ue]rde,	
And crown hym kyndly with kryso-mede hondes	
With his ceptre [and his swerde] as soveraynge and lo[uer]de.	

After this passage the *Morte Arthure* relates Arthur's dream, his return to England, his fight with Mordred, and his death. Of these episodes Malory's fifth book gives no account. The last twenty-one lines of Ch. XII were probably added by Malory. Here he relates Arthur's coronation in Rome (not recorded in the *Morte Arthure*) and his peaceful return to England, where 'he was nobly receyved of alle his comyns in every cyte and burgh, and grete yeftes presented to hym at his comyng to welcome hym with. *Thus endeth the fyfthe booke of the conqueste that Kynge Arthur hadde ageynste Lucius the Emperoure of Rome.*' [1]

It seems hardly necessary to enumerate all the points in which Malory follows the English alliterative poem against the French *Merlin*. Not only do the English texts agree in the minutest details of narrative and description, but they often use the same words, and Malory even preserves some traces of alliteration [2] as well as certain

[1] The colophon was most probably added by Caxton.
[2] Cf. Trautmann, *op. cit.*, p. 146.

archaic expressions. We may conclude, therefore, that Malory used either the *Morte Arthure* itself or some other English poem closely related to it.[1] Until such a work is found, we may regard ll. 760–3186 of Björkmann's edition of the *Morte Arthure* as the best extant representative of the source of Book V.

4. *The Book of Beaumains (Book VII)* [2]

The seventh book of the *Morte Darthur* records the adventures of Gawain's brother, Gareth, otherwise called Beaumains. This story has no close parallel in the extant medieval romances. Renaud de Beaujeu's *Guinglain* and its prose version by Claude Patin bear only a distant resemblance to Malory's story.[3] In all probability, Malory used a French non-cyclic prose romance on some similar theme and introduced a few episodes of his own. It is likely that the name *Beaumains* was added by Malory as a tribute to Richard Beauchamp. The fights with the Black, Green, and Red Knights may have been suggested by the famous adventure of Richard Beauchamp at Calais (cf. *supra*, p. 3) and W. H. Schofield[4] contends that the Duke de la Rowse who plays a prominent part in the book was introduced by Malory as a tribute to John Rous, author of the *Life of Richard Earl of Warwick*, who must have been closely associated with Warwick and, presumably, with Malory.

Apart from these few points which may be due to Malory's own invention, the story of Gareth must have existed in some French romance now lost, which was not very intimately related to the Arthurian cycle. This view, as Sommer rightly remarks,[5] is corroborated by the fact that in none of the known Arthurian stories 'is any, even the slightest, reference made to Gareth's exploits on his way to the castle of Lady Lyonesse, or to this lady, her sister Linet, her brother Gryngamor, or the five brothers whom Gareth overcame and sent to Arthur's court'.

5. *The Tristan (Books VIII—XII)*

These books contain a condensed redaction of the French prose romance of Tristan. The version used by Malory is found in three

---

[1] It seems significant that in this section Malory describes his source as 'the Romaunce', not as the '*French* book'. Cf. p. 182₁₂ and *passim*.
[2] On the sources of Book VI, *v. infra*, p. 148–9.
[3] Cf. W. P. Ker, *Epic and Romance*, p. 343, and *Romania*, xv. 22–4.
[4] *Chivalry in English Literature*, p. 284.   [5] *Op. cit.*, p. 9.

separate MSS. of the Bibliothèque Nationale.[1] From p. 273_1 to p. 379_{28} he agrees in most points with MS. B.N. fr. 103; from p. 379_{28} to p. 455_{22} he follows MS. B.N. fr. 334; and from p. 455_{23} to p. 611_{34} he takes up the version of MS. B.N. fr. 99. The main points of agreement are:

A. Pp. 273_1–379_{28}.

Malory and MS. B.M. fr. 103.	*Other MSS.*
The episode of Tramtrist.	Lacking in all other MSS.
The order of events in the episode of Brunor: *abcmn* in Malory.	*ambcn* in all other MSS.[2]
abmcn in MS. 103.	
The description of the death of Lamorak.	Lacking in all other MSS.
Lancelot's departure for Joyous Gard.[3]	Lacking in all other MSS.

B. Pp. 379_{28}–455_{22}

Malory and MS. B.N. fr. 334.	*Other MSS.*
Palomides' reluctance to fight the unknown knight.	Lacking in all other MSS.
The division between the 'first' and 'second' books of *Tristan*.[4]	Lacking in all other MSS.
The readings:	
Berluse in Malory.	
Berlez in 334.	*Bellet* in all other MSS.
Beale Valet in Malory.	*Belnalhot* (103), *Benalist* (94),
Belvaliot in 334.	*Benaloth* (99).

C. Pp. 455_{23}–611_{34}.

Malory and MS. B.N. fr. 99.	*Other MSS.*
The episodes of Alixander li Orphelin and of the tournament of Sorelois (Surluse).	Lacking in all other MSS. except Br. Mus. Add. 25434 and B.N. fr. 350.
In this section Malory gives the readings: *Cameliard, Seymound*.	These MSS. read: *Tarmelyde, Asmonz*.
MS. 99 has: *Carmelide, Esmont*.	
Tristan is delivered from prison by Iseult.	In 103—*by the people of Loonois*.
The King of Ireland is defeated by Lancelot.	In all other MSS.—by *Arthur*.

[1] In my *Rom. de Trist.* (pp. 31–87) I have given a complete account of my study of these MSS. It must suffice to mention here its most important results.
[2] Cf. *ibid.*, pp. 41–5.
[3] For an additional point of resemblance see *ibid.*, p. 50 note 2.
[4] Cf. *ibid.*, pp. 51–4.

| The episodes of *Lancelot*. | Lacking in all other MSS. except B.N. fr. 97, 101, 379, 758, and Br. Mus. Add. 5474.[1] |
| The division between the 'second' and 'third' books of *Tristan*. | Lacking in all other MSS. |

This table shows that within the limits of each of the three sections, A, B, and C, Malory agrees with one MS. only and differs from all others: he is with 103 in Section A; with 334 in Section B; and with 99 in Section C. This implies that in each case he follows an already existing version and does not himself combine heterogeneous material. The only passages in which he might have changed his sources are pp. 379 and 455; but they show a continuity of narrative which makes it most unlikely that in writing them he passed from one MS. to another. In all probability, therefore, he had no more than one source for his Books VIII—XII.[2] Their relation to the extant French MSS. may be expressed thus:[3]

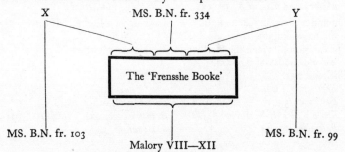

For the study of Malory's treatment of the *Tristan* the following table of concordances may be used:

Malory, pp. 273_1 –379_{28} = MS. B.N. fr. 103, ff. 27^r col. 1–184^r col. 2.
Malory, pp. 379_{28}–455_{22} = MS. B.N. fr. 334, ff. 220^r col. 2–336^r col. 1.
Malory, pp. 455_{23}–611_{34} = MS. B.N. fr. 99, ff. 360^r col. 1–560^v col. 2.4

---

[1] Cf. *ibid.*, pp. 73–5. Although these MSS. also contain the *Lancelot* episodes, they do not represent Malory's source.   [2] Cf. *ibid.*, pp. 81–6.
[3] In a recent review of my *Rom. de Trist.* (*Zeitschrift für französische Sprache und Literatur*, liii. 131–69), Professor E. Brugger questions this theory, especially in regard to MS. B.N. fr. 334. My main argument in favour of the connexion between Malory and that MS. was that they both introduced the division between the first two books of *Tristan* in the middle of the conversation between Arthur and Tristan, and that no other MS. contained a division in this passage. Professor Brugger strongly suspects me of having overlooked some of the evidence on this point. 'MS. 99 soll also beim Gespräch zwischen Arthur und

Note 4, see opposite page.

6. The Quest of the Holy Grail (Books XIII—XVII)

These books contain the 'Quest of the Holy Grail'. In *Rom. de Trist.*, p. 78, I pointed out that Malory's *Tristan* source ended where MS. B.N. fr. 99 f. 560ᵛ col. 2 announced the beginning of the *Queste*. 'The third book of which Malory "makes no rehearsal" is found in MSS. B.N. fr. 99 and Chantilly 317. It was no doubt part of Malory's source and contained the whole of the *Queste*. It remains to be discovered whether the "noble tale of the Holy Grail" of Books XIII to XVII was derived from that compilation or from the *Queste* proper.' The question can now be answered: Malory's version of the *Queste* derives not from any *Tristan* compilation, but from the *Queste* proper.

This *Queste* exists for us to-day in at least thirty-nine MSS., and it is important to decide which, if any, of these MSS. Malory used. Sommer avoided the problem, and instead of submitting all the existing versions of the *Queste* to a close examination used F. J. Furnivall's edition, which is at best unsatisfactory.[5] No attempt has since been made to utilize the extant French MSS. for the study of Malory's version, and I shall here endeavour to consider the whole question afresh.

The *Queste* has been preserved in the following MSS.: *Paris,*

Tristan kein Explicit haben?' he asks. A mere glance at MS. 99 would have made the question unnecessary, and the same applies to MS. Chantilly 316 which, in spite of Professor Brugger's suspicions, has nothing resembling the division in MS. 334. But he himself admits that he has not seen any of these MSS. and his mistake is excusable. His other contentions, however, are not more cogent. He brings to my notice, among other things, that 'Palomides' reluctance to fight' is not peculiar to MS. 334. I never pretended that it was, but it is certainly not in MS. 103, and therefore indicates the end of its influence. Which of the two readings is original we have no means of knowing, and it is clearly impossible to base the study of Malory's direct sources on the distinction between the 'ursprüngliches' and the 'unursprüngliches', as Professor Brugger wishes me to have done. Further, he questions the importance of the reading *Belvaliot* because he has found the same reading in MS. Royal 20 D 11, and exclaims: 'Das ist also dieselbe Form wie in 334 (was Vinaver auch hätte finden können)!' But here again he makes a mistake in method: when I had found the agreement between the *incipits* of the Second Book, I was faced with the necessity of drawing a line of division between MS. 103 and MS. 334 on the one hand and between 334 and 99 on the other. For this purpose I used 'Palomides' reluctance to fight' as the earliest instance of the substitution of 334 for 103, and the form *Belvaliot > Beale Valet* as the latest example of the influence of 334 unsupported by 99. MS. Royal 20 D 11 has no bearing on my point.

⁴ On the rate of abbreviation *v. supra*, p. 30.

⁵ Cf. A. Pauphilet, *Étude sur la Queste del Saint Graal,* p. xxiii.

B.N. fr. 98, 110, 111, 112, 116, 120, 122, 123, 339, 342, 343, 344, 751, 768, 771, 1423–4, 12573, 12580, 12581, 25520, nouv. acq. fr. 1119; Arsenal 3347, 3480, 3482, 5218; *Lyons*, Palais des Arts 77; *Brussels*, Bibl. Royale 9627–8; *Cheltenham*, Phillipps Collection 130, 1046, 3630; *London*, Br. Mus. Royal 14 E III, Royal 19 C XIII, Royal 20 C VI, Add. 10294, Add. 17443; *Oxford*, Rawlinson D. 899 (wrongly cited by A. Pauphilet, *op. cit.*, p. x, as 89), Rawlinson D. 874, Digby 223; and *Manchester*, John Rylands Library, Fr. No. 1 (Crawford MS. 1–2), ff. 182–211ᵛ.

Three of these MSS. differ widely from the rest: MS. B.N. fr. 123 presents an abridged and almost independent version of the story; MSS. B.N. fr. 112 and 343 combine the Grail story with some fragments of the romance of Tristan. This redaction used to be traced to Robert de Borron. After Robert de Borron's authorship had been disproved, it was ascribed to a pseudo-Robert and still believed to be earlier than the ordinary *Queste*. In reality, however, the origin of these two MSS. is much simpler: they were written long after the *Queste* in order to connect the Grail adventures with stories derived from the Prose *Tristan*. They bear distinct traces of late workmanship. MS. B.N. fr. 112 interpolates, among other *Tristan* episodes,[1] a description of the tournament at Louvezerp, borrowed from the Second Version of the Prose *Tristan* (ff. 285ᵛ col. 2–301ʳ col. 2) which is much later than the ordinary *Queste*.[2] MS. B.N. fr. 343 is based on the same version of the *Tristan* and is also much later than the *Queste* proper.

The remaining MSS. fall into two main groups: GROUP A, including MSS. B.N. fr. 110 (*P*), 116 (*N*), 1423–1424 (*Y*), Br. Mus. Royal 14 E III (*S*) and Royal 19 C XIII; B.N. fr. 751 (*V*), Arsenal 3482 (*Ad*); Lyons 77 (*K*), B.N. fr. 344 (*R*), nouv. acq. fr. 1119 (*Z*), fr. 12573 (*T*), 771; 98 (*M*), 111 (*Q*), 122 (*L*), 12580 (*U*), 25520 (*U'*), Arsenal 3347 (*Aa*), 5218 (*Ab*), Br. Mus. Add. 17443; Royal 20 C VI; and GROUP B, including MSS. B.N. fr. 120 (*O*), 339 (*A*), 342 (*D*), 343 (*B*), 12581 (*C*), Arsenal

---

[1] The *Tristan* fragments in this MS. are: II, ff. 8ʳ col. 1–17ʳ col. 1; 18ʳ col. 1–19ᵛ col. 2; 71ᵛ col. 1–78ʳ col. 1; 175ʳ col. 1–206ᵛ col. 2; 236ʳ col. 2; III, ff. 11ᵛ col. 2–15ᵛ col. 1; 52ᵛ col. 2–54ʳ col. 2; 54ᵛ col. 1–56ʳ col. 2; 99ʳ col. 2–128ʳ col. 1; 214ᵛ col. 1–220ᵛ col. 2; *285ᵛ col. 2–301ʳ col. 2*; IV, ff. 6ʳ col. 1–2; 28ʳ col. 2–84ᵛ col. 2; 138ᵛ col. 2–146ᵛ col. 2. The MS. is signed by Micheau Gatelet, 'prestre demeurant en la ville de Tournay' (4 July 1470).

[2] Cf. my *Études sur le Tristan en prose*, pp. 27–9. On the date of the *Queste*, see F. Lot, *Étude sur le Lancelot en prose*, pp. 126–36.

3480 (*Ac*).[1] The three Oxford MSS.[2] may be classified as follows: Rawlinson D 899 (*E*) and Digby 223 (*G*) agree with KRZ (group A); Rawlinson D. 874 (*F*) belongs to group B and often agrees with AD.

Each of these two groups gives an imperfect version of the original. The original *Queste*, now lost, must have been copied by two independent scribes, and it does not seem possible to decide which of the two copies was nearer the archetype.

Below are given fifteen parallel quotations from Malory and the MSS. of the French *Queste*. The MSS. used for this collation are: in the A group—K, R, Z, and S; in the B group—A, Ac, and O. MSS. V (A group) and D (B group) have been used in a few cases only. This list is far from including all the variants; a number of minor points have been left out as inconclusive—in particular, all the variants from the beginning of the story down to p. 656 in Sommer's edition. For the remaining section of the text, only the most important passages have been utilized.[3]

The first column serves to number the variants. The second refers to pages and lines in Sommer's edition. The third gives quotations from Malory; the fourth contains the French readings that are nearest to Malory; and the fifth—all other variants. The readings of MSS. not included in this table are either identical with those cited or entirely unconnected with Malory's version.[4]

1.	656₂₂₋₂₄	and whether he be saved or dampned'. Thenne he said with an horryble voys: 'He is not lost but saved'.—'How, &c.	*OAcAS:* et s'il est perilz ou sauvez'. Lors parle l'ennemi a voix orrible et espoventable et dist [al preudome]: '[Il] n'est mie perils mes sauvés.'—'Et comment, &c.	*KRZ:* et s'il est periz ou sauvez'. 'Comment, &c.
2.	658₃₅	upon their knees	*OAc:* a genoulz; *SA:* a genoillons	*KRZ:* a oroisons
3.	660₁₂₋₁₄	went into Walys and toke there the dough-	*OAcASZV:* s'en ala en Gaulle et prist la fille	*KR:* s'en ala en Gaule et vint

[1] This classification has been suggested by A. Pauphilet in his edition of the *Queste* (p. vii): 'Chacun de ces groupes représente ce qu'on peut appeler une version de la *Queste*. Et ces versions diffèrent entre elles non seulement par leurs fautes, mais par de nombreuses petites variantes de pure forme, dues au caprice individuel des copistes.'
[2] Not classified by Pauphilet.
[3] A number of important divergences which serve to classify the French MSS. occur in passages omitted by Malory.
[4] The French texts are quoted in each case from the MS. mentioned first.

	ter of Manuel, whereby he had the lond of Gaulle, and he came to dwelle in this countrey	Morneus dont il ot le roiaume de Gaulle. De celui issi le roy Lancelot ton aieul qui se departi en Gaulle et vint maindre en cest païs	maindre en cest païs
4. 662₅	were overcome for the defaute of hym	*OAc:* furent maintenant vaincus qu'il lor failli; *ASV:* furent vaincu puis qu'il lor failli d'aide	*KRZ:* furent failli qu'il lor failli
5. 662₂₄	a chappel where was a recluse	*OAcS¹A:* une chappele ou il avoit une rencluse	*KRZ:* une recluse
6. 665₂	twenty knyghtes	*R:* XX chevaliers	*O:* X chevaulx; *AcKZS:* dis chevaliers; *A:* XXX chevaliers
7. 665₂₉₋₃₀	and of the bulles that were so whyte that one came ageyne and no mo	*OAcAS:* des trois sanz tache revenoit li uns et li autres doi remanoient	*KRZ:* des trois sanz tache remenoit li uns et li autre revenoient
8. 665₃₃	one here and another there	*OAcAS:* li uns ça et li autres la	*KR:* li un et li autre; *Z:* li un de l'autre
9. 677₁₇₋₂₀	it went thurgh his shelde and haberion on the lyfte sholder, and thorowe grete strengthe he bete hym doune to the erthe, and at the pullynge oute of Bors spere there he swouned	*AcOA:* li met le glaive par mi l'espaule, mes il ne l'a mie si fort navré qu'il ne puist garir bien legierement, et il l'empeint bien come cil qui estoit de grant force, si l'abat du cheval a terre, et au retraire du glaive qu'il fist cil se pasme de l'engoisse	*KRZS:* li met le glaive et cil se pasme de l'angoisse
10. 679₂₋₄	the whyte foule betokeneth a gentylwoman fayre and ryche whiche loved the peramours	*QAcAV:* le blanc oiseil qui venoit a toy en lieu ¹ de cigne, signifie une damoisele belle et riche ² et de vaillant gent ³ qui t'amera par amours	*KRZN:* li oisiax qui venoit a toi en guise de cisne t'amera par amours
11. 688₁₅₋₁₆	thenne sayd Syre Percyval: 'We lak no thynge but Galahad the good knyghte	*OAcAVD:* et Perelsvaus⁴ dist que or ne li fault il maiz riens fors Galaad que sa promesse ne lui soit rendue. Lors devise a Boort comment il li	*KRZS:* [*all this passage missing until the words:*] Mes a tant lesse ore li contes a parler d'els et re-

¹ So in *OAc. AV:* guise.   ² belle et riche *not in A.*
³ de vaillant gent *not in AcAV.*   ⁴ Perceval *in AVD.*

		avoit esté promis. Mais a tant se taist [1] ores li contes a parler d'eulz deux [2] et retourne a Galaad, [3] car longuement s'en est ores teuz	torne au bon chevalier
12. 694₃	sylver	*KRZS:* argent	*AcAVD:* azur
13. 702₁₁₋₁₄	and thenne they broughte the Erle Hernox oute of pryson into the myddes of the halle that knewe Galahad anone, and yet he sawe hym never afore but by revelacyon of our Lord	*AcOAD:* Lors font oster le conte Hernol de la prison, et quant il l'ont aporté amont el palois et il l'orent mis en la grant sale, si troverent qu'il estoit el point de la mort. Et nonpourquant si tost come il vit Galaad, si le congnut, non mie por ce qu'il l'eust onques mais veu, mais par la vertu de Nostre Seignor li avint	*not in KRZV*
14. 722₉₋₁₀	the Kynge was a Tyraunt and was come of the lyne of paynyms	*OAcSZVD:* et cil fu si desloiaulx et si crueulx comme cil qui tout estoit estrais de la maleoite ligniee de paiens	*A:* et cil fu desloiaux et cruex
15. 7246	a yere and two monethes	*OAcZS:* un an et deux mois	*VA:* un an et trois jorz

This list of variants shows, in the first place, that as long as Malory did not deliberately shorten or alter his story he had none of the lacunae so common in the French MSS.: variants 1, 3, 5, 9, 10, 11, 13, and 14 give ample proof of this. In the second place, the English version appears to be free from certain typical mistakes and contradictions: variant 7 shows that while KRZ gives a reading inconsistent with the context,[4] Malory avoids it by adopting the version of OAcAS. In the next example (variant 8) KR make the bulls depart *li un et li autre*, and Z: *li un de l'autre*. Now the meaning is that the bulls dispersed in all directions, and this happens to be the version of OAcAS (*li uns ça et li autres la*) which Malory here follows (*one here and another there*). When OAc omit to describe Galahad as 'le bon chevalier' Malory rejoins the version of KRZS and calls him 'Galahad the good knyghte' (see variant 11).

[1] lesse *in AVD*.   [2] deux *not in AVD*.   [3] au bon chevalier *in AVD*.
[4] Cf. A. Pauphilet's edition, p. 285.

The following parallel, not included in our list, is also significant:

Malory, 645₂₃₋₂₄: that I may see hym openly that he may encheve the Sancgreal.	*OAcAS:* cil qui doit les merveilles dou Saint Graal veoir appertement.	*KRZ:* cil qui doit les merveilles dou Saint Graal mener a chief.

Malory's version here combines the readings of the two conflicting groups of MSS. The original whence Malory took his story must have had: *cil qui doit les merveilles dou Saint Graal mener a chief et veoir appertement.* With his characteristic freedom he translated *cil qui doit,* etc., by *that I may,* but there is hardly any doubt that his source had both *veoir appertement* and *mener a chief.* All these examples serve to establish one important characteristic of Malory's original: it was superior to the extant French MSS. and probably closer to the original text of the *Queste* than either B or A MSS.

It is noteworthy, too, that wherever these two groups give each an acceptable but different reading, Malory agrees now with one now with the other. He has more in common with the B group, and particularly with OAc: in thirteen places out of fifteen he agrees with OAc, and in three of these he goes against *all* the MSS. of the A group (var. 9, 11, and 13). But in two other passages (var. 6 and 12) he differs from all B MSS. The version he represents is, as it were, 'intermediate'[1] between A and B, though in most points it stands closer to B than to A.

[1] I am using this term in much the same sense as Dom P. Quentin in his *Essais de Critique Textuelle* (Paris, 1926). In a simplified form, Dom Quentin's method may well be applied to Malory's *Quest.* Indeed, we have established that Malory agrees with A against B in two points; he agrees with B against A in three points; and B never agrees with A against Malory, except of course in passages which Malory himself omitted or altered. Representing Malory's source as M* we may describe the relationship of A, B, and M* by the following formulae:

$$M^* B > A = 3 \text{ times}$$
$$M^* A > B = 2 \text{ ,,}$$
$$A B > M^* = 0 \text{ ,,}$$

This would imply one of the following:

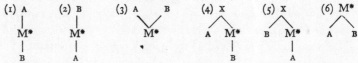

It is easy to show that the superiority of M* to A and B makes it necessary to eliminate the first three alternatives. The conclusion suggested by any of the

Bearing in mind these three main peculiarities of Malory's version, i.e. (*a*) its superiority over A and B; (*b*) its 'intermediate' character; and (*c*) its points of resemblance with B, we may suggest the following diagram:

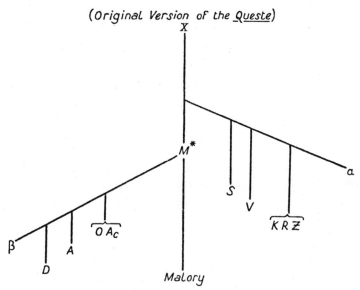

Malory's version thus acquires considerable importance for the study of the French *Queste*, while on the other hand the investigation of the French MSS. becomes less fruitful here than in the *Tristan*. For, if Malory's source was superior to all the extant MSS., none of these can be regarded as his authority, and the search for a suitable representative of M* becomes a choice of evils. My collation has satisfied me, however, that the nearest extant versions are found in O and Ac, and the table of variants shows that these MSS. are tolerably faithful to the version Malory used.[1] Until further notice, and for all practical purposes, we may establish the following concordance:

Malory, pp. 611_{34}–725_2 = MS. Bibl. Nat. fr. 120, ff. 522^r–565^v.

other three would be practically the same as that at which we have arrived above ; our diagram is in the main identical with stemma 4.

[1] MSS. O and Ac are derived from an excellent source, probably very close to M*, but they both contain many scribal errors, mostly quite insignificant. O is slightly better than Ac, and for this reason I have used O in preference to Ac for all quotations as well as for the extract published in Appendix III.

7. The LANCELOT (*Books VI and XIX*)

No satisfactory theory has yet been advanced of the origin of Malory's *Lancelot* proper, i.e. Books VI and XIX. The first seven chapters of Book VI follow fairly closely a portion of the French Prose *Lancelot* as given in a number of MSS.[1] and in the printed edition of 1513.[2] The next four chapters (Ch. VII–beginning of XI) are traceable to a later portion of the Prose *Lancelot*,[3] but the concluding section of the book (end of Ch. XI–Ch. XVIII) has no close parallel in any extant French MS. Sommer has given a detailed comparison of all these sections with the Prose *Lancelot*,[4] but in the absence of a reliable source the comparison is of little importance.[5]

The case of the XIXth book is also puzzling. The book falls into two distinct parts: on p. 780 (l. 22) Malory says: 'and soo leve we of this tale le Chevaler du Charyot and torne we to this tale'. This, according to Gaston Paris,[6] would show that Malory drew from two distinct sources, one of which contained the adventures also found in the Prose *Lancelot* and in the second part of Chrestien's *Charrete*. In spite of the differences between Chrestien and Malory, Gaston Paris was prepared to consider their works as closely related. But he was unable to solve the mystery of the first six chapters. It is, indeed, impossible in the present state of our knowledge to determine their origin, but it seems in any case unnecessary to assume the existence of two different sources. Gaston Paris bases his assumption on Malory's words: 'and soo leve we of this tale'. But this can by no means be taken as an indication that Malory himself used two different manuscripts. In all probability,

---

[1] These are: Bibl. Nat. fr. 98, 110, 111, 112, 114, 118–19, 339, 344, 751, 768 B, 771; Br. Mus. Harley 6341-2, Add. 10293-4, Royal 20 D IV, Royal 20 C VI, Royal 19 B VII, Royal 20 B VIII, Royal 19 C XIII; Phillipps 1046, 3630; Lyons, Palais des Arts 77.

[2] ff. 98–103.   [3] *Lancelot*, ed. 1513, ff. 146–50.

[4] *Op. cit.*, vol. iii, pp. 178–200.   [5] Cf. also Wechssler, *op. cit.*, p. 35.

[6] *Romania*, xii, pp. 498–508. Sommer gives an English translation of this article in vol. iii, pp. 233–41, but refrains from adding any suggestions of his own, and leaves the problem unsolved. I have been compelled to do the same: no extant text can help us to establish the source of Chs. I–VI of Book XIX, and there is no reason to believe that Malory used a different source for the ensuing chapters. We may, of course, attempt to find among the extant MSS. one which would be nearer Malory's Chs. VI–IX than some others, but the result would not repay investigation: the MS. thus found would be still very different from that which Malory used.

his announcement of 'another tale' is but a translation of some similar sentence which he found in his source, and which read roughly as follows: 'Ore laisse li contes a parler du chevalier de la charrete et retourne a parler d'une aultre matiere.' Such announcements were very frequent in the French MSS., and Malory almost invariably reproduced them in his work.

The contents of Chs. X—XII of Book XIX are again untraceable to the French. Much in this section may be due to Malory's own invention: references to the French book, which mostly serve to conceal additions, occur three times in the course of eight pages, and the whole matter is told in a loose and inconsistent manner. Heterogeneous episodes (such as the story of Tristan's death on p. 792$_{21-33}$, and the revenge of Bellangere in ll. 28–9 of the same page) are interpolated, and a number of fantastic personages are introduced, as in the list of the knights who came to handle Sir Urre's wounds, which is most probably Malory's own.[1] The whole thing appears rather as a collection of reminiscences from French romances which the author has read before, than a translation of any definite French text.[2] In concluding Book XIX, Malory himself admits that he has lost his way and that the only course open to him is to give up the Lancelot episodes altogether: 'And by cause I have lost the very mater of la chevaler du charyot, I departe from the tale of sir Lancelot, and here I goo unto the morte of Kynge Arthur' (p. 796$_{13-15}$). 'The very mater' means of course the 'true story' of Lancelot, or what we call to-day the '*Lancelot* proper'. Malory abandoned it as early as p. 788 (Chs. IX—X). He was loath to return to it, for he hastened to relate the *Death of Arthur*.[3] What that *Lancelot* story was, and whether it existed in a separate MS. or was interpolated between the two sections of the *Mort Artu* (corresponding to Malory's Books XVIII and XX), we have no means of knowing. I am inclined to believe that Malory did not interpolate the contents of Book XIX into the Death of Arthur story, but found it already incorporated in the *Mort Artu* MS. which he used for his eighteenth, twentieth, and twenty-first books.

---

[1] Cf. Sommer, *op. cit.*, vol. iii, pp. 248–9.
[2] Wechssler (*op. cit.*, p. 36) thinks that this episode belongs to a lost version of *Lancelot*, and 'ist wohl das jüngste und schwächste Stück der durch Crestien hervorgerufenen Lancelot-litteratur'.
[3] Cf. *supra*, p. 32.

8. The Death of Arthur (Books XVIII, XX, and XXI)

With regard to the origin of Malory's story of the Death of Arthur, Sommer formulated the following view: 'A close examination of the last portion of Malory's compilation shows that he cannot have derived his account from the Prose-Lancelot, to which, however, it is equally certain that his source was intimately related. Malory's source is thus either derived from the Prose-Lancelot, or both come from a common original. In the English metrical romance "Le Morte Arthur", as preserved in the unique Harl. MS. 2252, we possess a version which stands in the same relation to Malory's source as that does to the Prose Lancelot; and of this Malory was aware, for, in his last two books, he often makes use of the very words of the English poem.'[1] This statement is by no means clear, and its very incoherence led to a vivid controversy between J. D. Bruce and Sommer. J. D. Bruce questioned Sommer's theory that the English poem was Malory's immediate source,[2] while Sommer maintained that he had never said anything to that effect.[3] On the whole Bruce gave a more satisfactory solution of the problem, and there is little doubt that the MS. Malory used for his Death of Arthur was French. Nevertheless, the case for Malory's direct dependence on the English *Le Morte Arthur*[4] seems prima facie fairly strong, in view of verbal parallels such as these:

Le Morte Arthur (ed. Bruce).	Malory.
(1) l. 1852: Now, know thou wele, syr Agra-wayne, Thow presons me no more to-Nyght.	p. 802$_{24\text{-}5}$: For wete yow wel, sir Agravayne, ye shall not prysone me this nyghte
(2) l. 1876: Owre knyght*is* have bedrechyd to-nyght, That som nakyd oute of bed spronge.	p. 803$_{31\text{-}2}$: we all . . . were soo dretched that somme of us lepte oute of oure beddes naked
(3) l. 2204: He sayde, 'Allas!' wyth syghynge sore, 'That evyr yit thys werre be-gan.' The parties arne wyth drawen A-waye.	p. 819$_{33\text{-}5}$: . . . and sayd: 'Allas, that ever this werre began.' And thenne eyther partyes of the batails withdrewe them to repose them

[1] *Op. cit.*, vol. iii, p. 220.
[2] *Anglia*, xxiii (1900), pp. 67 ff.; for a summary of his views, see his Introduction to the E.E.T.S. edition of *Le Morte Arthur* (London, 1903), pp. xiii–xx.
[3] *Anglia*, xxix, pp. 529–38.   [4] Ed. Bruce (ll. 1672–3969).

These parallels provide an excellent test, the others being much less close. They have led Sommer to conclude that while writing his account Malory had a copy of the stanzaic *Le Morte Arthur* before him. But the evidence is doubtful. The three passages quoted above are striking, and contain some curious analogies. The question, however, is not whether Malory agrees with the English text, but whether the agreement must be explained by the direct influence of the English text. Let us suppose that there existed a French original whence both the author of *Le Morte Arthur* and Malory drew their stories, and that that original had: 'Or sachiés, sire Agravain, vous ne me mettrés mie en prison ceste nuit' or something to the same effect. Is it not possible that both English authors working independently would translate the sentence exactly as they have done? Nor is it absolutely necessary to explain the other two parallels by direct filiation: they may well be due to a common source which both authors faithfully translated. In short, none of the verbal parallels between Malory and *Le Morte Arthur* make it imperative to assume a direct influence of the latter on the former.[1]

There is, besides, direct evidence that Malory's source for Book XVIII was French. In the first chapter of the book he says that Lancelot and Guinevere 'had suche prevy draughtes to gyder that many in the Courte spak of hit, and in especial sir Agravayne, syr Gawayns broder, *for he was ever open mouthed*' (p. 725$_{22}$). So, according to Malory, Agravain spoke of Lancelot's guilty love for Guinevere because it was his habit to gossip. This seems at first quite coherent, but the reason given in the French *Mort Artu* is distinctly preferable; there the sentence reads: '*por cou k'il(=* Agravain) *beast le roi a vengier de sa honte*'.[2] Why, then, did Malory introduce the 'open mouthed' Agravain? Two explanations are

---

[1] Cf. J. D. Bruce's Introduction to *Le Morte Arthur* (E.E.T.S., Extra Series, No. 88): 'The similarities and occasional coincidences of phraseology which one observes in comparing Malory and the Middle English metrical romance are only such as must occur where two writers are following closely the same original' (p. xv). Perhaps the most striking coincidence is the use of the verb *to dretch* (ME. *drecchen*, to vex, torment, or to trouble in sleep), which is not very frequent in Malory's time. But it occurs again on p. 859 of the *Morte Darthur* unsupported by any English source.

[2] MS. Bibl. Nat. fr. 342, f. 151^r col. 2. So in all MSS. and in J. D. Bruce's edition, p. 3. The sentence literally means: 'because he intended to revenge the King's dishonour'. On this passage see *Arthuriana*, loc. cit.

possible: either he used an imperfect MS. in which the words *le roi vengier de sa honte* were missing, and so naturally took the verb *beer* in the sense of 'to be wide open'; or, if his MS. was as complete as MS. 342, he failed to understand the verb *beer* in the sense of 'to aim', 'to aspire',[1] and took it to mean 'to be wide open'. But in either case the word *beer* must have been in his immediate source, and this source was, therefore, French.

Now Books XX and XXI not only continue the narrative of Book XVIII, but Book XX begins at the very same point where Book XVIII ends. The latter is concluded by reflections on the month of May, followed by Malory's theory of stable and unstable love.[2] Book XX opens with the same *motif* and almost with the same words: '*In May whan every lusty herte florssheth and burgeneth,* for as the season is lusty to beholde and comfortable, soo man and woman rejoycen and gladen of somer comynge with hys fresshe floures.' This is but a reiteration of the concluding section of Book XVIII, where the May season is described in well-nigh identical terms: 'the moneth of may was come *whan every lusty herte begynneth to blosomme and to brynge forth fruyte*', &c. Probably the reflections on the flourishing of love in spring are Malory's own, but his source must have contained here some reference to or description of maying which followed the account of the tournament related in Book XVIII. Later on, after the long digression corresponding to Malory's Book XIX, the author of the 'French book' returned to the place where he had left the story, i.e. to the maying scene, and Malory, faithful to his original, proceeded to relate how 'in this season as in the monethe of May it byfelle a grete angre and unhap that stynted not til the floure of chyvalry of alle the world was destroyed and slayne'.

But if the source of all three books was one, and if the original of Book XVIII was French, we must conclude that the whole of the Death of Arthur story was derived by Malory from a French MS. This MS. has not been preserved. It differed widely from the extant French MSS., and the main divergence occurred no doubt in the order of episodes in the early section of the story: whereas in the extant MSS. (and in *Le Morte Arthur*) the queen's dinner and

---

[1] As in Colin Muset's *Descort*:

> Cil est mout fols qui si haut bee
> Ou il n'en ose aprochier.

[2] Cf. *supra*, p. 47.

Lancelot's fighting for her are related after the story of Lancelot's encounter with the fair maiden of Astolat, in Malory's Book XVIII the dinner and its immediate results precede the episode of Astolat; only in the ninth chapter are we told how Lancelot 'cam to an old Barons place that hyght sir Bernard of Astolat' (p. 739$_{26}$). Sommer gives the following table of concordances, which shows with considerable accuracy Malory's relation to the French *Mort Artu*: [1]

Malory, Book XVIII:	*Mort Artu* (printed edition, 1513):
Chs. I—VIII	ff. 143^v–144^r;
	ff. 160^v–166^r.
Chs. IX—XX	ff. 144^r–160^r.

9. Conclusion

Malory's 'Frensshe Booke' was in all probability a single French MS. divided into three or four volumes. It contained several romances of the Arthurian prose cycle placed in the following order:

(1) *Merlin* with a continuation.
(2) Fragments of *Lancelot*.
(3) *Gareth* (lost).
(4) *Tristan* (complete copy of the Second Version).
(5) *Queste del Saint Graal* (complete copy of one of the earliest versions akin to B).
(6) *Mort Artu* (different from the extant French versions and containing a fragment of *Lancelot*).

The habit of combining all these romances in single MSS. belongs to a fairly late age. Most of the extant MSS. in which such contaminations are found belong to the fifteenth century.[2] It therefore seems probable that Malory's French source was of a late date, not more than a century older than the *Morte Darthur*.

---

[1] *Op. cit.*, p. 221. Sommer suggests the following explanation (p. 229): 'Had the writer of Malory's source—who intercalated the contents of book XIX from a much earlier portion of the Prose *Lancelot*—preserved the sequence of incidents in the Prose *Lancelot*, the two episodes [i.e. that of Guinevere and Mador de la Porte, and that of Guinevere's rescue by Lancelot] would have immediately followed one another, and the one would have thus weakened the effect of the other.' Ed. Wechssler (*op. cit.*, p. 36) thinks that 'Malory auch hier das selbständige Originalwerk übertragen hat'. This statement is correct if by Malory Wechssler means the author of his immediate source. For a different theory cf. *Romania*, xxiv, p. 475 (Gaston Paris).
[2] This also applies to the interpolation of the *Prophécies de Merlin*, cf. *Rom. de Trist.*, p. 86.

Between sections (1) and (2) Malory substituted for his 'Frensshe Booke' an English MS. (the 'Romaunce' as he calls it) which furnished the subject of Book V of the *Morte Darthur* and is now represented by the alliterative *Morte Arthure*.

The study of Malory's methods and of his contribution to the story can only be made by means of a comparison with the extant MSS. which represent his source. For this purpose the following publications may be used:

(1) Sommer's edition, vol. iii, pp. 16–148 (collation of Malory's Books I—IV with Robert de Borron's *Merlin*, the Ordinary *Merlin*, and the Huth MS.).

(2) Sommer's edition, vol. iii, pp. 149–75 (collation of Malory's Book V with the English *Morte Arthure* as preserved in the MS. of Robert Thornton in the Lincoln Cathedral Library).

(3) Sommer's edition, vol. iii, pp. 178–89 (collation of Malory's Book VI, Chapters I—X, with the Prose *Lancelot* as represented in the printed edition of 1513, ff. 98–103 and 146–50).

(4) *Rom. de Trist.*, pp. 155–218 (collation of Malory's Books VIII—XII with MSS. B.N. fr. 103, 334, and 99).

(5) Pp. 156–88 *infra* (Appendix III), containing a collation of Malory's Book XV with MS. B.N. fr. 120.

(6) J. D. Bruce's article in *Anglia*, xxiii, 88–100, and Sommer, vol. iii, pp. 250–72 (collation of Malory's Books XX and XXI with the Prose *Lancelot* as represented in the printed edition of 1513, vol. iii, ff. 166–202; and with the stanzaic *Le Morte Arthur* as preserved in MS. Harl. 2252).

Books VII, XVIII, and XIX cannot be included in this list, and the finding of their immediate sources remains the chief desideratum in the study of Malory.

APPENDIX THREE

MALORY'S VERSION OF THE 'QUEST OF THE HOLY GRAIL'

MALORY'S Book XV contains an account of Lancelot's adventures in quest of the Holy Grail. There is no better way of showing Malory's treatment of the Grail story than by comparing this book with the corresponding portion of the French Romance. In the following pages will be found a complete collation of Book XV with ff. 540^r col. 2–545^r col. 2 of MS. Bibl. Nat. fr. 120 (MS. *O*). Passages common to both texts have been italicized. The non-italicized passages in the French are those which Malory left out. The non-italicized passages in Malory's text are his additions and alterations.

It will be seen that his alterations are due either to carelessness or to over-condensation. The additions, however few, reflect some of his characteristic ideas about Chivalry (*v. supra*, pp. 55–69) and the Grail. The italicized passages show his method of translation, and the extent of his indebtedness to the French source. Perhaps the most important parts of this collation are the non-italicized sections of the French text. They form an elaborate theological treatise and provide a detailed commentary on the Grail story. The way in which Malory dismisses them with brief résumés illustrates his attitude towards the doctrine of the French source (*v. supra*, pp. 78–84) and justifies the conclusion that he was little concerned with the mystical interpretation of the Quest.[1]

[1] In my transcription I have preserved the spelling of the originals, but resolved the abbreviations and introduced modern punctuation. I have also introduced (in both texts) the modern use of *u*, *v*, *i*, and *j*. In the French text, the acute accent has been used only to distinguish the accented final *é* and *és* from the unaccented. Unaccented final *ez* has been transcribed *es*. Square brackets indicate missing words and letters.

THE QUEST OF THE HOLY GRAIL
And here foloweth of Syre Launcelot whiche is the fyftenth

*Or dist li contes que trois jours fist li preudoms demourer Lancelot
avec li.* Et entre tant qu'il le tint en sa compaignie, le sermonna
tous diz et l'amonnesta de bien faire et li dist: 'Bien certes, Lancelot,
pour noient alez vous en ceste Queste, se vous ne vous baés a tenir
de touz pechez mortelx et a retraire vostre cuer de toutes pensees
terriennes et des delis du monde. Car bien sachiez que [en] ceste
Queste ne vous peut riens vostre chevallierie valoir, se li Sains
Esperis ne vous fait la voie en toutes les aventures que vous trou-
verriés. Car vous savés bien que ceste est emprise pour savoir et
pour veoir aucune chose du Saint Graal, que Nostre Sires a promis
a veoir au Saint Chevaillier qui de bonté et de chevaillierie a passé
touz ceulz qui devant li ont esté et qui ores sont, ne ja mais aprés
lui ne sera nulx qui li soit parans. Ce chevaillier veistes vous le
jour de la Penthecouste seoir ou Siege Perilleux de la Table Ronde,
ouquel Siege nulx ne s'estoit assis qui ne moureust. Et ceste merveille veistes vous aucune foiz avenir. Ce chevaillier est li grans

lyons qui mousterra a son temps toute chevaillierie. Et quant il
avra tant fait qu'il ne sera mais terriens mais celestiaux, il laissera
le terrien abit et enterra en la celestial chevaillierie. Ainsi dist
Merlins de ce chevaillier que vous avés maintes foiz veu, comme cil
qui moult savoit des [choses] qui moult grant temps amprés sa vie
estoient a avenir. Et nepourquant, ja soit ce verités que ce chevallier ait plus prouesse en lui et chevaillierie que nulx autres ait,
sachés que, s'il se mouvoit jusques a pechié mortel, — dont Nostre
Seignour le gart, — il ne feroit en ceste Queste nient plus que uns
autres chevaillier. Car ce service ou vous estes entrez, n'appartient
de riens aux terriennes choses, mais aux celestiaux; dont vous povez
bien veoir que qui veult entrer ne venir a perfection, il le convient
avant nettoier et espurgier de toutes ordures terriennes, si que ly
ennemis ne parte en lui d'aucune riens. Et en telle maniere, quant
il avra du tout renoié l'annemy et il sera du tout nettoiez et espur-
giés de touz les orribles pechiés, adonc pourra il seurement entrer
en ceste Queste qui est sainte chose. Et se il est tieulz qu'il soit de
foible creance et de povre, que il cuide plus faire par la prouesce

book. [Capitulum primum.] *Whanne the heremyte had kepte Syr Launcelot thre dayes, the heremyte gate hym an hors, an helme, and a*

que par la grace Nostre Seigneur, sachiez qu'il nen s'en repentira ja sans honte, ne au derrain ne fera il chose pour quoy il s'i mist.' Ainsi parloit li preudoms a Lancelot souventes foiz, *et le tint en telle maniere trois jours avecques lui.* Si se tint Lancelot a boneuré de ce que Dieux l'avoit mené celle part a tel preudomme qui si bien l'avoit conseillé et enseignié, si qu'il en cuidoit mieulz valoir toute sa vie. Et quant le quart jour fu venus, *si manda li preudoms* a son frere qu'il lui envoiast *armes et cheval* a ung chevaillier qui avoit avecques lui demouré. Et il en fist la requeste moult debonnairement. Et au quint jour, quant Lancelot ot oÿ messe et il se fu armés et monté ou cheval, si se departi du preudomme moult tendrement plourant, et moult le requist pour Dieu qu'il priast pour lui que Nostre Sires ne l'oubliast, par quoy il revenist a sa premiere maleurté. Et il li promist que si feroit il, *et tantost s'en parti Lancelot de laiens.* Et quant il s'en fu partis, si chevaucha jusques a eure de prime, et lors encontra ung vallet qui li demande: 'Sire chevaillier, dont estes vous?' — 'Je sui, fait Lancelot, de la court le roy Artus.' — 'Et comment avez vous a nom? Dites le moy.' Et il li dist qu'il a a nom Lancelot du Lac. 'Lancelot, fait il, ou nom de Dieu, vous n'aloie je mie querant, car vous estes le plus maleureux chevaillier du monde.' — 'Biaux amis, fait Lancelot, comment le savez vous?' — 'Je le say bien, fait il. Donc n'estes vous mie cil qui vit venir le Saint Graal devant lui et faire appertes miracles, ne onques pour la venue du Saint Graal ne vous remuastes de vostre siege nient plus que se ce fust ung meschant.' — 'Certes, fait Lancelot, je ne le vi voirement, ne onques ne m'en remuay; si m'en poise plus que bel ne m'en est.' — 'Ce n'est mie merveille, fait li varlet, si vous en poise, car certes vous monstrastes bien que vous n'estiés mie preudoms ne bon chevaillier, mais desloiaux et mescreans. Et puis que vous honnour ne li voulsistes porter ne faire de vous meismes, ne vous merveilliés mie se honte vous avient en ceste Queste ou vous estes entrez avecques lez autres preudommes. Certes, mauvais chevaillier, moult povez avoir grant dueil, qui souliés estre tenus au plus preudomme du monde. Or estes venus a ce que vous estes tenus au plus mauvais et au plus desloial et au plus failli.' Et quant Lancelot ot ceste parolle, si ne scet que [f. 540ᵛ, col. 2]

*suerd, and thenne he departed about the houre of none. And thenne
he sawe a lytel hows, and whanne he came nere he sawe a chappel,
and there besyde he sawe an old man that was clothed al in whyte* ful
rychely. *And thenne Sire Launcelot saide:* 'God save yow!'—'God
kepe yow, sayd the good man, and make yow a good knyghte.'

---

respondre, car il se sent a forfait de ce dont le varlet l'acuse. Et
toute voies li dist: 'Biaux amis, tu me diras ore ce que tu vouldras
et je t'escouteray, car ung chevaillier ne se doit couroucier de chose
que varlet die, se trop grant villenie ne li dist.' — 'A l'escouter,
fait le varlet, estes vous ore tenus, car de vous n'isterra ja maiz ung
aultre preux, qui soulié(e)s estre la flour et la merveille de toute
chevaillierie du monde. Chetifs! bien estes enfantosmés par cele [1]
qui ne vous aime se petit non. Elle vous a si atorné que vous en
avés perdue la joye des cieulz et la compaignie des anges et toute
honneur terrienne, et estes venuz a toutes hontes recevoir.' Et il
n'ose respondre, comme cil qui tant a de couroux qu'il vouldroit
bien estre mors. Et le varlet le va ledangant et honnissant et dissant
la greigneur villenie qu'il oncques scet, et il escoute toutes voies si
entrepris qu'il n'ose neis regarder. Et quant le varlet est touz
lassés de lui dire ce qu'il veult et il voit bien qu'il ne lui respondra
nient, si s'en va tout son chemin. Et Lancelot ne le regarda oncques,
ains s'en va par la forest plourant et doulousant soy et priant Nostre
Seigneur qu'il le remaint a tel voie qui li soit prouffitable a l'ame.
Car il a tant de mal fait en cest siecle et tant meserré vers son
Creatour que, se la pitié Nostre Seigneur et la misericorde n'est
trop grant, il ne pourroit ja maiz avoir pardon. Si est a ce menés
que la vie devant ne li pleut onques tant qu'elle li desplaist assés
plus orendroit. *Et* quant il a chevauchié jusques *a heure de midi,
si voit devant lui une petite maison* hors du chemin. Et il tourne
celle part pour ce qu'il scet bien que ce est hermitage. *Et quant il
est jusques la venuz, si voit une* petite *chappelle* et d'encoste, une
petite maison. *Et devant,* a l'entree, *seoit uns homs vieulz vestu
d'une robe blanche* de homme de religion, et faisoit un dueil trop
merveilleux et disoit: 'Biaux sire Dieux, pour quoy avés vous ce
souffert? Ja vous avoit si longuement servi et s'estoit traveilliez en
vostre service.' Et quant Lancelot voit le preudomme si tendrement plourer, si li en prant grant pitié. *Et il* le salue et *li dist:*

Thenne Syr Launcelot alyghte and entred into the chappel, *and there he sawe an old man dede, in a whyte shert* of passyng fyne clothe. *'Sir,* said the good man, *this man* that is dede *oughte not to be in suche clothynge as ye see hym in, for in that he brake the othe of hys ordre, for he hath ben more than* an C wynter *a man of relygyon.'* *And thenne the good man* and Sire Launcelot *wente in to the chappel, and the good man tooke a stole about hys neck, and a book; and thenne he conjured* on that book. *And with that* they *sawe in an hydous figure* and horryble, *that there was no man soo hard herted nor soo hard but he shold have ben aferd. Thenne saide the fende: 'Thow hast travaylled me gretely. Now telle me, what thow wilt with me?'—'I wille, saide the good man, that thow telle me how my felawe became*

'Biaux sire, *Dieux vous gart!'* — 'Dieux le face! sire chevaillier, *fait* [1] *li preudoms,* car s'il me garde de prés, je ne cuide mie que l'ennemy me puist legierement sousprendre. Et Dieu vous oste du pechié ou vous estes!' Et quant Lancelot entent ce que li preudoms li dist, *si descent* et dist qu'il ne s'en partira huy mais, ains se conseilliera au preudomme qui bien le congnoist, ce li est avis aux parolles qu'il a dittes. Lors atache son cheval a ung arbre et va avant, *et regarde que devant l'entree* du moustier *se gisoit* par semblant *ung vieulz homs mort, vestu de chemise blanche* et deliee, et devant lui a terre avoit une haire aspre et poignant. Et quant Lancelot voit ce, si se merveille de la mort au preudomme. Et il s'assiet et demande comment il est mort, et il li dist: *'Sire chevaillier,* je ne sçay; mais je voy bien qu'*il n'est mie mort* selon Dieu ne *selon l'ordre. Car en celle robe ou vous le veés, ne peut tieulx homs mourir comme il estoit qu'il n'ait religion enfrainte;* et pour ce say je bien que l'ennemy li fait tel assaut par quoy il est mort. Si est trop grant dommage, *car il a demouré ou service Nostre Seigneur plus de* trente ans.' — 'Par Dieu, fait Lancelot, le dommage est grant voirement, pour ce qu'il a son service perdu et de(s) ce qu'il en tel aage a esté souspris de l'ennemy.' *Lors entre li preudoms en sa chappelle et prent ung livre et met une estole entour son col,* et puis vient hors *et commence a conjurer* l'ennemi. *Et* quant il a grant piece lut, il regarde et *voit l'ennemy en si hideuse fourme qu'il n'a si hardi homme* en tout le monde *qui* grand hide *n'en eust* et *paour. 'Tu me travailles trop, fait l'ennemi,* or me di que tu me veulz.' —

[1] MS. *sire.*

dede, and whether he be saved or dampned.' Thenne he said with an horryble voys: 'He is not lost but saved.'—'How may that be? sayd the good man. It semed to me that *he lyved not wel, for he brake his ordre for to were a sherte where he oughte to were none, and who that trespaceth ageynst our ordre dothe not wel.'*—'Not soo, sayd the fende, this man *that lyeth here dede was come of a grete lygnage. And* there was *a lord that hyghte the Erle de Vale,* that *helde* grete *werre ageynste this mans nevewe, the whiche hyghte Aguarus.* And soo *this Aguarus sawe the Erle was byggar than he. Thenne he wente for to take counceylle of his unkel, the which lyeth here* dede *as ye maye* [P. 657] see. *And thenne he* asked leve, and *wente oute of his hermytage for to mayntene his nevewe ageynst the* myghty *Erle; and* so hit happed that *this man* that lyeth here dede *dyd so moche* by his wysedome and hardynes *that the Erle was take* and thre of his lordes by force of this dede man. [𝕮𝖆𝖕𝖎𝖙𝖚𝖑𝖚𝖒 𝕵𝕵] *Thenne was there pees betwyxe the Erle and this Aguarus, and grete seurte that the Erle shold never werre ageynst hym.* Thenne *this* dede *man* that here lyeth *came to*

'*Je veul, fait il, que tu me dies comment cilz miens compains est mort, et* [s]*'il est perilz ou sauvez.' Lors parle* l'ennemi *a voix orrible* et espoventable *et dist: 'N'est mie perils, mais sauvés.'* — '*Et comment puet ce estre? fait li preudhoms. Il me semble* que tu me mentes, car ce ne me commande mie nostre ordre, ains le vee tout plainement *que nulx de nostre ordre ne veste chemise* de lin; *et qui* la vest, il *trespasse l'ordre.* Et qui en trespassant ordre muert, *ce n'est mie bien,* ce m'est avis.' — '*A! fait l'ennemi,* je te diray comment il est alés de lui. Tu scés bien qu'*il fu* gentils homs et *de grant lignage,* et qu'il a encores nepveux et nieces et parens moult en cest païs. *Or* avint avant hier que *li quens du Val commença guerre encontre ung de ses nepveus que on appelle Agaran.* Et quant la guerre fu commenciee, *Agaran,* qui *de la guerre vint au dessoubz,* si ne sçot que faire. *Si s'en vint conseillier a son oncle que tu voiz ci, et* li pria si doulcement que *cil yssi de son hermitage* et s'en ala avec le sien nepveu *pour maintenir la guerre encontre le conte.* Et il revint a ce qu'il seult jadis faire, c'est d'armes porter. Et quant il fut assemblez avec ses parens, *si le fist si bien* de toute chevaillierie *que li quens fu pris* a la tierce journee qu'il assemblerent; *et lors firent paix entre le conte et Agaran, et donna li quens bonne seurté que ja maiz ne le guerroit.* Et quant la guerre fut apaisiee, *si s'en revint cilz homs en son her-*

*this heremytage ageyne; and thenne the Erle made two of his nevewes
for to be avenged upon this man.* Soo they came on a day *and fonde
this dede man at the sacryng of his masse, and they abode hym tyl he
had sayd masse, and thenne they set upon hym and drewe oute swerdes
to have slayne hym. But there wold no suerd byte on hym more than
upon a gad of stele, for the Hyghe Lord whiche he served, He hym
preserved. Thenne made they a* grete *fyre, and dyd of all his clothes
and the hayre of his back. And thenne this* dede *man* heremyte *sayd
unto them: 'Wene ye to brenne me?* It shalle not lye in your power,

---

mitage et recommença son service qu'il avoit maintenu maint jour.
Et quant *li quens* sceut qu'il avoit esté desconfiz par lui, si *pria a
deux de ses nepveuz qu'il l'en vengassent,* et il dirent que si feroient
il voulentiers. *Si s'en vindrent* ceste part. Et quant il furent hier
matin descenduz a l'entree de ceste chappelle, *si virent que li preudoms estoit ou secret de la messe.* Si ne l'oserent mie asaillir en tel
point, *ains dirent qu'il soufferroient tant qu'il* seroit hors de laiens.
Et firent maintenant tendre ung paveillon ci devant. Et quant il
ot chanté son service et il fu yssu hors de la chappelle, si li dirent
qu'il estoit mort. *Et puis trairent leurs espees et le prirent.* Et quant
il li vouldrent coper la teste, (et) tantost *cil qui avoit servi Nostre
Seigneur* y demonstra si apertes miracles qu'*il ne pou[r]ent sur lui
ferir cop dont a li peussent mal faire.* Et si n'avoit vestus fors sa robe,
*ains reblouquoient leurs espees aussi comme s'il ferissent sur enclumes
d'acier.* Si y ferirent tant que leurs espees furent toutes despeciees,
et il furent touz lassez de coups qu'il i avoient donnés, ne il ne li
avoient encores tant de mal fait que sang fu issus de lui. Et quant
il virent ce, si furent touz dervés de yre et de mautalent, et il appor-
terent esche et fusil. *Si alumerent ung feu* ci devant qu'il l'ardroient,
car encontre feu ne dureroit il mie. *Si le despouillierent tout nu et
li osterent la haire* que vous veés illec. Et quant il se vist ainsi, si
en eust honte et vergoigne de soy meismes; si leur pria qu'il li
prestassent aucun aufubail, si qu'il ne se veist mie si villainement
comme il estoit. Et cil furent fel et crueulx; si dirent qu'il ne
vestiroit ja maiz de lin ne de lange, ains mourroit. Et quant il les
oÿ ainsi parler, si commença a sousrire. *Si respondi: 'Comment, fait
il, cuidiés vous que je puisse mourir par ce feu* que vous avés cy
appareillé pour moy ardoir?' — 'Vous n'en arés ja, font il, aultre
guerison.' — 'Certes, fait il, s'il plaist a Nostre Seigneur que je

[f. 541ʳ,
col. 2]

nor to perysshe me as moche as a threde, and there were ony on my body.'—'*Noo, sayd one of them, hit shalle be assayed.*' *And thenne* they *dispoylled hym, and putte upon hym this sherte, and cast hym in a fyre,* and there he laye all that nyght tyl hit was daye in that fyre, and was not dede. And soo in the morn I came *and fond hym dede. But* I fond *neyther threde nor skynne tamyd, and so tooke hym oute of the fyre with grete fere, and leyd hym here as ye may see. And now may ye suffer me to goo* may way, *for I have sayd yow* the sothe.' *And thenne he departed with a grete tempest. Thenne was the good man* and Syr Launcelot *more gladder than* they were *to fore.*

---

muyre, je le vueil bien. Mais se je muir, ce sera plus par la volenté Nostre Seigneur que par le feu, car cilz feu n'ara ja tant de force que poil de dessus moy en soit brullez. Ne il n'a ou monde si deliee chemise, se je l'avoie vestue et puis entrasse a tout ou feu, qui en fust mal mise ne empiree.' Et quant il oïrent ceste chose, si tindrent tout a fable quan qu'il disoit; et *nonpourquant li ung dist qu'il verroit par tans se ce porroit estre voir. Si osta sa chemise de son dos et li fist vestir, et tantost le getterent ou feu* qu'il avoient fait si grant que il dura dés hier matin jusques a hier soir bien tart. Et quant il fust estaint, *il trouverent* sans faille *le preudomme devié, mais il avoit la char* si *saine* et si *nette* comme vous povez encores veoir, *ne la chemise* qu'il avoit vestue *n'en fu oncques aultrement empiree* comme vous povés veoir. Et quant il virent ce, si en furent *moult espoventez. Il l'osterent de la et le porterent en ceste place ou vous le povez ores veoir,* et mirent sa haire delez lui et s'en alerent a tant. Et par cestui miracle que Cil qui il avoit tant servi [a fet], l'a Il ainsi fait (il) mourir en l'onneur de Lui ; or tu pues bien veoir qu'il n'est mie perilz mais sauvés. *Or m'en yray a tant,* fait l'ennemi, *car bien t'ay dist* ce dont tu estoies en doubtance.' Et si tost comme il eust ce dist, *si s'en ala* abatant lez arbres devant lui et *faisant la greigneur tempeste du monde,* si qu'il sembloit que tout le deable d'enfer s'en alassent par my la forest. *Et* quant *li preudoms* ot ceste merveille, *si est assés plus liés que devant;* et il met jus son livre et s'estolle, et vient au corps et le commence a baissier, et dist a Lancelot: 'Certes, sire, bel miracle a fait Nostre Sires pour cest hermitte. Car je cuidoie qu'il fust mors en aucun pechié mortel. Mais non est, Dieu mercy, ains est sauvés, si comme vous meismes povez avoir oÿ.' — 'Sire, fait Lancelot, car me dittes que cil est qui tant

And thenne Syr Launcelot dwelled with that good man that nyght.
*'Sire, said the good man, be ye not Sir Launcelot du Lake?'—'Ye,
sire,' said he. 'What seke ye* in this countrey?'—*'Syr, sayd Syr
Launcelot, I goo to seke* the adventures of *the Sancgreal.'—'Wel, sayd*

a huy parlé a vous? Son corps ne peu je veoir, mais sa parolle ay
je bien oÿ, qui estoit si laide et si hideuse qu'il n'estoit nuls homs
qui grant hideur n'en deust avoir.' — 'Sire, fait le preudoms, il
n'est homs terriens qui tant face a redoubter comme cil fait, car
c'est cil qui donne conseil a homme de perdre corps et ame.' Lors
sent bien Lancelot que ce est cil a qui il ot parlé. Et li preudoms li
prie qu'il li face huy mais compaignie a garder ce saint corps, et
demain li aist tant qu'il l'ait mis en terre. Et il dist que ce fera il
voulentiers, et moult liés [est] de ce que Dieux l'a amené en lieu
ou il puist faire service a si preudomme comme il est. Et il oste
maintenant ses armes et les met enmy la chappelle, et puis vi[e]nt
a son cheval et li oste le frain et la selle, et le laisse paistre. *Et puis
revient au proudomme faire compaignie.* Et quant il furent assis, *si* [f. 541ᵛ,
li commence li preudoms a demander: 'Sire* chevaillier, *donc n'estes* col.1]
vous Lancelot du Lac?' — 'Sire, fait il, oÿl.' — 'Et que querés vous?'
fait li preudoms. — *'Je vois, fait il, en la queste du Saint Graal.'* —
'Certes, fait li preudoms, querre le povez vous, mais au trouver avés
vous failli. Mais *se le Graal revenoit devant, je ne cuide mie que tu
le peusses veoir nient plus que ung avugle verroit une espee* qui devant
ses yeulx seroit. Et nonpourquant maint en ont demouré en tenebres
de pechié mortel long temps et en obscurité, que Nostre Sires re-
traioit puis a vraye lumiere si tost comme il veoit que lez cuers y
entendoient. Nostre Sires n'est mie lens de secourre lez pecheours.
Si tost comme il peut apparcevoir qu'il se trait devers Lui ou en
cuer ou en voulenté ou en aucune bonne oeuvre, il le vient visiter.
Et si tost comme cil a garni son hostel et nettoié de toutes ordures,
ainsi comme pechierres doit, Il descent et reposse en lui; nient plus
n'a li pecherres garde qu'Il s'en parte se il ne L'enchasse hors de
son hostel. Mais s'il y appelle aucun qui contraires Lui soit, Il
s'en part comme cil qui plus n'y peut demourer, puis que cil y est
acuillis qui touz jours Le guerroie. Lancelot, fait li preudoms, cest
exemple t'ay je monstré pour la vie que tu as longuement menee
puis que tu cheïs en pechié, ce est puis que tu receus l'ordre de
chevallerie. Car devant ce que tu fusses chevaillier, avoies tu

he, seke it ye may wel, but though it were here, ye shalle have noo

herbergié en toy toutes bonnes vertus si naturelment que je ne sçay nul jour homme qui peust estre ton pareil. Car tout premierement tu avoies virginité herbergié en toy si vraiment que oncques ne l'avoies enfrainte; car maintes foiz avint que quant tu pensoies a la coulpe ¹ charnel par quoy virginité est corrumpue, tu en escopoies en despit et disoies que ja en ceste ordure ne cherroies. Et lors affremoies tu qu'il n'estoit si haulte chose comme virginités et eschever luxure et garder son corps nettement. Et aprés ceste grant vertu qui tant est merveilleuse, avoies tu humilité. Humilité va doucement et souef, le chief enclin. Et ne fait mie aussi comme fait le pharisien qui disoit quant il ourroit au temple: 'Biau sire Dieux, je te rens graces et mercis de ce que je ne sui mie aussi desloiaux ne aussi mauvaiz comme sont mes voisins.' Et tieulx n'estoies tu mie, ains sembloies le pellicain qui n'osoit regarder l'ymage, tel paour avoit de ce que Dieux ne se courouçast de ce qu'il estoit li pecherres, ains estoit loings de l'autel et batoit son pis et disoit: 'Biaux sires Dieux, Pere poissans, ayez merci de cest pecheour!' En tel maniere se doit doulcement contenir qui veult acomplir lez oeuvres d'umilité. Ainsi faisoies tu quant tu estoies damoysiaux, car tu doubtoies et aimoies ton Creatour sur toutes choses, et disoies c'on ne devoit une choses terriennes doubter, mais on doit douter celui qui destruit ame et corps et peut conduire [en enfer]. Aprés ces deux vertus que je t'ay nommees, avoies tu une autre que on appelloit souffrance, qui est semblance a esmeraude qui est touz jours vert, car souffrance est ² si fort temptacions qu'elle ne peut estre vaincue, ains est touz jours verdoians et en une force, que ja nuls n'yra encontre que on ³ n'enporte touz jours
[f. 541ᵛ, col. 2] la victoire et l'onneur. Car nuls ne peut si bien vaincre son ennemy comme par souffrir. Et quel pechié que tu feisses aucune foiz par dehors, ce scés tu bien (aucune foiz) en ta pensee que ceste vertu avoies tu en toy herbergié trop naturelment. Et aprés ce avoies tu une aultre vertu herbergié en toy, si merveillieussement comme se elle te venist de nature: ce est droiture qui est vertus si haulte et si poissans que par lui sont toutes lez autres tenues en leur point, ne ja nulle foiz ne se changera, et a chascun rendra ce que il avra deservi et que le droit apportera. Droiture ne donne a nullui fors

---

¹ MS. *couple.*   ² Other MSS. *n'avra ja.*   ³ Other MSS. *qu'ele.*

power to see hit no more than a blynd man shold see a bryghte *suerd,*

---

ce qu'elle li doie donner, ne si ne tolt a nullui par hayne, ne ja n'espargnera amy ne parent, ains s'en yra touz jours selon la ligne de verité et de droit en tel maniere que ja ne chengera droite voie pour aventure qui aviengne. Aprés ce, en ton cuer et en ta voulenté avoies tu charité si haultement herbergié que ce estoit merveilles. Car se tu eusses toutes les richesses du monde entre tez mains, tu lez osasses bien donner pour l'amour de ton Creatour. Et lors estoit li feux du Saint Esperit en toy chault et ardant, et estoies voulentieulz et curieulz de tenir et d'amer en cuer ce que tes vertus t'avoient presté. Ainsi garnis de toutes bontés et de toutes vertus terriennes montas tu en hault degré et en hault ordre de chevaillerie. Mais quant l'ennemi, qui premiers fist homme pechier et le mena a dampnaçon, te vit si garni de toutes pars et si (des)couvert, si eust paour qu'il ne te peust sousprandre en nulle maniere. Si veoit appertement que trop exploitast bien a son oés se il te peust metre hors d'aucun de ces poins ou tu estoies ordenés a estre sergant Jhesucrist, et fu mis en si hault degré que ja maiz ne te deusses abaissier au service de l'ennemy. Si te doubta moult a assaillir pour ce que sa paine y cuidast avoir perdue. Lors se pourpensa en maintes manieres comment il te pourroit decevoir, tant que au darrain li fu advis que il te pourroit plus tost mener a mauvaise vie par femme. Et Salemons, li plus sages de touz hommes terriens; et Sanssés, le plus fort de touz hommes du monde; et Absalon, le filz David, le plus beau de tout le monde; et puis fist si que tout en out esté vaincu. Lors entra en la royne Genevre qui ne s'estoit mie vraiement faitte confesse puis qu'elle fut premierement venue en mariage, et l'esmut a ce qu'elle te regarda moult voulentiers tant comme tu demouras en son ¹ hostel. Et le jour que tu fus chevaillier, quant tu veis qu'elle te regardoit, si y pensas et en ce penser te feri l'ennemi si a descouvert, si durement, que il te fist (si) chanceler si qu'il te fist issir hors de droitte voie et entrer en celle que tu n'avoies oncques congneue: ce fut en la voie de luxure, en la voie qui degaste corps et ame si merveillieusement que nuls ne la peut bien savoir qui essaié ne l'a. Trés ce te tolli l'ennemy la veue. Car si tost comme tu eus lez yeulz eschauffés de luxure et espris de l'ardour, (et) enchassas humilité et entras en orgueil et voulsis aler teste levee

¹ MS. *ton.*

[P. 658]   and that is longe on your synne, and els ye were more abeler than

tout aussi comme ung lion, et deis en ton cuer que tu ne devoies
riens prisier, ne ne priseroies ja maiz, se tu n'avoies ta voulenté de
celle que tu veoies si belle. Et l'ennemy qui si tost ot la parolle que
langue lez a dittes, congnut que tu pecheroies mortelment et en
pensee et en voulanté. Si entra adonc moult tout dedens toy et en
[f. 542ʳ,   fist aler Cellui que tu avoies (oste) longuement ostellé et [qui
col. 1]   t'avoit] nourri et creu et (no) garni de toutes bonnes meurs. Si
t'avoit si hault monté que en son service t'avoit mis. Si que, quant
il cuida que tu feusses ses loiaux sergans, tu devins sergans a l'ennemi, et meis dedens ton corps autretant des vertus a l'ennemy
comme Nostre Sires y avoit mis de soies, car contre virginité et
chasteté herbergas tu luxure qui destruit et confont l'un et l'autre.
Et contre humilité receuz orgueil, comme cil qui ne prisoies nul
homme envers toy. Aprés ce enchaças toutes lez aultres vertuz que
je ay nommees, et recueillis les aultres qui contraires leur estoient.
Et nonpourquant Nostre Sires avoit mis en toy tant de bien que
de celle grant planté ne peut estre qu'il n'y eust aucune chose de
remenant. De ce remanant que Dieux te laissa as tu fait les merveillieusses prouesces par lez estranges terres et par les loingtains
païs, dont tout le monde parolle. Or pense que tu peusse puis avoir
fait, se tu eusses ces vertus sauvees en toy que Nostre Sires y avoit
mises trés ce que tu estoies en enfance: tu n'eusses mie failli a
achiever lez aventures du Saint Graal dont les aultres sont touz en
paine, ains eusses tant mis a fin comme nuls homs peust faire, fors
le Bon Chevaillier. Les yeulz ne te feussent mie avuglés devant la
presance ton Seigneur, ains le veisses tout appertement. Toutes
ces parolles et toutes ces choses t'ay je dittes pour ce que ci je suis
doulans que tu es si mal baillis et si honnis que ja maiz en lieu ou
tu viengnes n'aras honneur, ains te diront villenie touz cil qui
savront comment il t'est avenu en la Queste du Saint Graal. Et
nonpourquant tu n'as encores tant meserré que tu ne peusses encores trouver [pardon], se tu cries mercy vraiement a Celui qui
t'avoit si haultement garny et appellé a son service. Mais se tu ne
le veulz faire de bon cuer et de bonne voulenté, je ne te lo mie que
tu voises mie en ceste Queste plus. Car bien sachiés que nuls n'i
est entrés qui sen honte s'en puist repairer, s'il n'est vraiement
confés. Car la Queste n'est mie de terriennes choses, mais de celes-

ony man lyvynge.' *And thenne Sir Launcelot began to wepe. Thenne*

tiaulx, et qui ou ciel veult entrer ort et villain, il en est tresbuchiez
si felonnessement qu'il s'en sent a touz lez jours de sa vie. Ainsi
avenra a ceulz qui en ceste Queste sont entrés ort et entachié des
vices terrienes que il n'y saront tenir ne voie ne sentier, ains yront
foloiant par my les estranges contrees. Si est ore avenue la semblance
dont li Evangelistres parla la ou il dist: 'Il fu jadis ung preudomme
riches qui appareilla a faire noces. Si eust semont ses amis et ses
voisins. Et quant lez tables furent mises, si envoia ses sergans a ceulz
qu'il avoit semons qui devoient venir, et leur manda qu'il venissent et
que tout estoit appareillié. Et cil targierent et demourerent tant qu'il
annoia au riche homme. Et quant il vist qu'il n'en venoient mie,
si dist a ses sergans: "Alés de cy et courés par les rues et par les
quarrefours, et dittes aux privés et aux estranges, et aux povres
et aux riches, qui viengnent mengier, car lez tables sont mises et
que tout est prest." Et cil firent moult tout le commandement leur
seigneur et amenerent tant[1] avant eulz que toute la maison en fust
emplie. Et quant il furent touz assis, le sires lez regarda entre lez
aultres, si y vit ung homme qui n'estoit mie vestus de robe de noces. [f. 542r, col. 2]
Et il vint a lui, si li demanda: "Biaux amis, que quesistes vous
ceans?" — "Sire, fist li preudoms, je y ving aussi comme cil aultre."
— "Certainement, fait li sires, non estes, car il sont venu plain de
joie et de feste, et si sont venus vestus aussi comme on doit faire
aux noces. Mais vous qui n'avés aporté chose qui appartiengne a
feste, n'y devés mie venir." Et maintenant le fist oster hors de son
hostel et dist, voiant ceulz qui aux tables seoient, qu'il avoit semons
dix tant plus de gens qu'i n'estoient venus, dont on peut vraiement
dire que moult y a (peu) des appellés et pou des esleuz.' Ceste semblance dont li Evangelistres parle, povons nous veoir en ceste
Queste. Car par lez noces qu'il fist crier povons nous entendre [la
table du Saint Graal],[2] ou li preudomme mengierent, le vray chevaillier; et cil que Nostre Sires trouvera vestus de robes de noces,
c'es[t] de bonnes vertus et de bonnes graces que Dieu preste a
ceulz qui le servent. Mais a ceulz qu'Il trouvera desgarnis et desnués
de vraye confession et de vraye repentance et de bonnes oeuvres, ne
vouldra Il mie recevoir, ains les fera getter hors de la compaignie
aux aultres, si qu'il recevront autretant de honte et de vergogne

[1] MS. *tout.* [2] MS. *Jhesucrist.*

sayd the good man: 'Were ye confessid syth ye entryd in to the Quest of the Sancgreal?'—'*Ye, sir,*' sayd Syr Launcelot. *Thenne upon the morne, whanne the good man had* songe his masse, thenne they *buryed the dede man.* Thenne Syr Launcelot sayd: 'Fader, what shalle I do?'—'*Now, sayd the good man, I requyre yow take this hayre that was this holy mans and putte it nexte thy skynne, and it shalle prevaylle the gretely.*'—'Syr, and I wille doo hit,' sayd Sir Lancelot.—'*Also I charge you that ye ete no flesshe as long as ye be*

comme lez autres auront de honnour.' *A tant* se taist et regarde *Lancelot,* qui *plouroit* aussi durement comme se il veist morte la riens ou monde que il plus aimoit, comme cil qui tant est dolans qu'il ne scet qu'il doie faire ne dire. Et quant il a grant piece regardé, *si li demande s'il fu puis confés qu'il entra en la Queste. Et il respondit* a grant paine, si li dist *que oïl.* Si li conte toutes les parolles que cil li avoit dittes de trois choses.[1] Et quant il ot ce, si li dist: 'Lancelot, je te requier sur la crestienté que tu as, et sur l'ordre de chevaillerie que tu receuz, que tu me dies laquelle vie te plaist plus, ou celle que tu menas jadis ou celle ou tu es nouvellement entrés.' — 'Sire, fait il, je vous creant que nouvel estre me plaist a cent tans plus que li autres ne fist oncques, ne ja maiz tant comme je vive ne m'en quier partir pour chose qui aviengne.' — 'Or ne t'esmaies donc, fait li preudoms hermittes, car se Nostre Sires voit que tu li requieres secours de bon cuer, il t'envoiera tant de grace que tu li seras temples et ostelz, si qu'il se herbergera dedens toy.' En telles parolles trespasserent le jour. Et quant la nuit fut venue, si souperent pain et cervoise que il trouverent en l'ermitage, et puis s'en alerent couchier delez le corps. Si dormirent moult petit, car il pensoient ambedoy plus aux celestiaux choses que aux terriennes. *Au matin, quant li preudoms ot enfouï le* saint *corps* en la chappelle, droit devant l'autel, si entra en l'ermitage et dist qu'il ne s'en partiroit ja maiz en jour de sa vie, ains y serviroit son Seigneur tant comme il vivroit. Et quant il vit que Lancelot voult prendre ses armes, *si li dist: 'Lancelot, je vous commande* en non de penitance *que vous vestés la haire a cest saint homme* que nous avons afouÿ. *Et la vestés dès ore mais tout a pur vostre char.* Et je vous di que vous ne pecherés ja mais tant comme vous l'arés sur vous, *et ce vous doit*
moult bien asseurer. Et encores vous commant je que tant comme vous

[1] MS. *parollez.*

in the Quest of the Sancgreal, nor ye shalle drynke noo wyne, and that ye here masse dayly and ye may doo hit.' Soo he took the hayre and putte it upon hym, and soo departed at evensonge tyme. *And soo rode he in to a foreste, and there he mette with a gentylwoman rydynge upon a whyte palfrey, and thenne she asked hym: 'Syre knyght, whyder ryde ye?'—'Certes, damoysel, sayd Launcelot, I wote not* whyder I ryde *but as fortune ledeth me.'—*'A! Sire Launcelot, *said she, I wote what* adventure *ye seke, for ye were afore tyme nerer than ye be now, and yet shalle ye see hit more openly than ever ye dyd,* and that shalle ye understande in shorte tyme.' *Thenne syr Launcelot asked her where he myghte be herberowed that nyghte.* 'Ye shalle not fynde this

---

serés en ceste Queste, ne mengerés de char ne ne burés de vin. Et alés au moustier *chascun jour oïr la messe* et le service Nostre Seigneur, *se vous* estes en lieu que vous *le puissiés faire.' Et Lancelot* reçoit cest commandement en nom [1] de penitance, et se despouille devant le proudomme et reçoit la penitance de bonne voulenté. Et puis *prent la haire,* qui moult estoit aspre et poignant, *et la vest en son dos,* et depuis sa robe dessus. Et puis prent ses armes et monte sur son cheval et demande congié au preudomme. Et il li donne moult voulentiers et moult li prie de bien faire et le chastie quan qu'il puet et li dist qu'il ne laist en nulle maniere qu'il n'aille chascun jour a confesse s'il peut, ou au moins chascune sepmaine, si que l'ennemy n'ait povoir de lui empirer ne de traire soy a lui. Et il dist que si fera il. *Si s'en part a tant et chevauche par my la forest* toute jour a journee jusques a heure de vespres que oncques ne trouva aventure que a conter face.

Et aprés vespres *encontra une damoiselle qui chevauchoit ung blanc pallefroy* et venoit moult grant aleure. *Et* quant *elle* encontre Lancelot, si le salue et *li dist: 'Sire chevailler, ou alés vous?'* — 'Certes, damoiselle, *fait il, je ne say, fors la ou aventure me maine.* Car je ne sçay mie bien quelle part je puisse trouver ce que je quier.' — '*Je say bien, fait elle, que vous alés querant. Vous en fustes ja plus prés que vous n'estes ore, et* si en estes ores plus prés que vous n'en fustes onques mais, se vous vous tenés en ce ou vous estes entrés.' — 'Damoiselle, fait il, ces deux parolles que vous me dittes me semblent estre contraires.' — 'Ne vous chault, fait elle, car *vous le verrés encores plus appertement que vous ne le veés ore,*

[1] MS. *lieu.*

day nor nyghte, *but to morne ye shal fynde herberowe good, and ease of that ye be in doubte of.'* And thenne he commaunded her unto God. *Thenne he rode tyl that he cam to a Crosse and took that for his hoost as for that nyghte.* [Capitulum Tercium.] *And soo he putte his hors to pasture, and did of hys helme and his shelde, and made his prayers* unto the Crosse *that he never falle in dedely synne* ageyne. *And soo he leyd hym doune to slepe.*

And anone as he was on slepe hit befelle hym there an advysyon, that there came a man afore hym alle by compas of sterres, and that man had a crowne of gold on his hede, and that man ledde in his felaushyp seven kynges and two knyghtes. And alle these worshipped the Crosse, knelyng upon their knees, holdyng

---

ne je ne vous ay ore nulle chose ditte que vous ne veés encores bien.' Et quant la damoiselle li ot ce dist, si s'en voult aler, *et il li demande ou il pourroit hui mais herbergier.* 'Vous ne trouverrés, fait elle, *huy maiz l'ostel, mais demain* au soir *l'arés vous tel comme mestier vous sera, et si arés ce dont vous estes en doubtance.'* Et il la commande maintenant a Dieu et elle lui. Si s'en part a tant l'un de l'autre.

Et Lancelot chevaucha tout le jour entier le grant chemin par my le boys et tant qu'il lui anuita en l'entree de deux voies fourchiees *ou il avoit une croix* de fust. Et quant Lancelot voit la croix, si en fust moult liés *et dist que illeuc sera huy mais son hostel. Si* s'encline et puis descent, et oste *son cheval* le frain et la selle, et le *laisse paistre; et oste son escu* de son col *et* deslace *son heaume* et oste¹ de sa teste. Et quant il eut ce fait, si s'agenouille devant la croix *et dsit ses prieres* et ses (or)oroisons, et prie Celui qui en la Crois fut mis, pour qui honnour et en ramembrance ceste crois fut mises cy, qu'il le gart en tel maniere *qu'il [n']enchee en pechié mortel,* car il ne doute autant nulle chose comme a rencheoir. Et quant il ot faitte son oroison et prié Nostre Seigneur grant piece, *si s'acouste* dessus une pierre qui estoit devant la crois. Et il avoit moult grant talent de *dormir,* car il estoit las de chevauchier et de jeuner. Et pour ce li avint que il s'endormy maintenant qu'il fu acoustés sur la praerie et sur la pierre.

Et quant il fu endormis, si li avint que devant lui venoit uns homs touz avironnés d'estoilles; et cilz homs avoit une couronne d'or en sa teste et menoit en sa compaignie set² roys et deux chevailliers. Et [f. 542ᵛ, col. 2] quant il estoient venu devant Lancelot, si s'arestoient et *aouroient*

---

¹ MS. *deslace.*   ² MS. *vi.*

up their handes toward the heven; and alle they sayd: 'Fair swede *Fader* of heven, *come and vysyte us, and yelde unto us everyche as we* [P. 659] *have deserved!' Thenne loked Launcelot up to the heven, and hym semed the cloudes dyd open, and an old man came doun with a company of angels, and alyghte amonge them, and gafe unto everyche his blessynge, and called them his servauntes* and *good and true* knyghtes. *And whanne this old man had sayd thus, he came to* one *of tho knyghtes and sayd:* '*I have lost alle that I have sette in the, for thou hast rulyd the ageynste me as a warryour,* and used wrong werres with vayne glory, more for the pleasyr of the world than to please me. Therfor *thow shalt be confounded withoute thow yelde me my tresour.*'

---

toute la croix et faisoient devant leurs afflictions. *Et quant il avoient* grant piece *esté a genoulz, si* s'asseoient touz et *tendoient leurs mains vers le ciel et crioient touz* a haulte voix: '*Peres, vien nous visiter* et *veoir, et ren a chascun de nous ce qu'il a deservi,* et nous met en ton hostel, en la maison ou nous desirons a entrer!' Et quant il avoient ce dit, si se taisoient touz. *Et lors regardoit* [*Lancelot*] *vers le ciel et veoit les nues ouvrir. Si en issoit ungs homs a grant compaignie d'anges; et descendoit entre ceulz et donnoit a chascun la beneïçon et lez clamoit sergans bons et loiaux* et disoit: 'Mon ostel est appareillé a vous touz: alés en la joye qui ja ne faudra.' *Et quant il ot ce fait, si dist* a l'aisné *des deux chevaliers* [1]: (et dist) 'Fui de cy! *j'ay perdu quanques j'avoie mis en toy. Tu ne m'as* mie *esté* comme sergans, mais *comme guerroiers;* tu ne m'as mie esté comme fieulx, mais comme fillastre. Je te dy que *je te conforteray se tu me rens mon tresor.*' Et quant cil ot ceste parolle, si s'en fuioit d'entre lez autres et crioit mercy tant doulans que nuls plus. Et li home disoit: 'Se tu veulx, je t'aimeray: et se tu veulz, je te harray.' Et cil se departoit maintenant de toute la compaignie. Et li homs qui devers le ciel estoit descendus, venoit a l'autre chevalier joine; si le meuoit en semblance de lyon et li donnoit elles et disoit: 'Biaux filz, or pués voler par dessus toute chevaillierie.' Et cil commanchoit tantost a voler, et si devenoient ses elles si grans et si merveillieusses que tout le monde en estoit couvers. Et quant il ot tant volé que tout le monde le tenoit a merveille, si s'en aloit contremont vers les nues. Et maintenant ouvroit lez cieulz pour lui recevoir, et il entroit dedens sans plus demourer.

[1] MS. *vi rois.*

Alle this advysyon sawe Sir Launcelot at the crosse. *And on the morne he took his hors and rode tyl mydday, and there* by adventure *he mette with the same knyght that took his hors, helme and his suerd,* when he slepte whan the Sancgreal appiered afore the crosse. *Whanne Sire Launcelot sawe hym he salewed hym not fayre, but cryed* oñ hyghe: 'Knyghte, *kepe the, for* thou hast done to me grete unkyndenes.' *And thenne they put afore them their speres, and Sir Launcelot came soo fyersly upon hym that he smote hym and his hors*

Ainsi fu advis a Lancelot en son dormant. Et quant la nuit fut faillie et *le jour fu venus* et il fu esveilliez, si n'eut point oublié de celle avision qu'il eut veu en son dormant. Et quant il vit qu'il fut jour, si a levé sa main et fait signe de la croix enmy son front et se commande a Nostre Seignour et dist: 'Biaulz doulx peres Jhesus-crists, qui estes vrais conseillier et vray confort a touz ceulz qui de bon et de vray cuer vous reclaiment, Sire, toy aoure je et rent graces et mercy de ce que tu m'as garandi et delivré des grans mesaven-tures et des grans hontes qu'il me convenist souffrir, se ta grant debonnaireté ne fust. Sire, je suy ta creature que tu as demoustré si grant debonnaireté que quant l'ame de moy ert approuchié d'aler en enfer et en perdicion pardurable, tu par ta grant douçour l'en as retraitte et l'as rapellee de toy congnoistre et cremir. Sire, par ta grant misericorde, ne me laissiés ja maiz issir de ta voie, mais garde moy de si prés que l'ennemy, qui tous jours me gaitte, a recevoir ne me truist mie hors de tes mains!'

Et quant il ot ce dit, si se dresse en son estant et *vient a son cheval.* Si li met la selle et le frain, si lache son heaume et prent son escu, et puis monte et se remet enmy sa voie. Et chevauche comme il avoit fait le jour devant, et pense moult a ce qu'il avoit veu la nuit en son dormant, car il ne peut penser a quoy ce puist tourner, et si le vouldroit il moult savoir s'il pooit estre. *Et quant il a chevauchié jusques a heure de midi, il encontra* en une vallee *le chevaillier qui ses armes en avoit portees avant hier. Et quant cil le vit venir, si ne le salua point, ains dist: 'Lancelot! garde toy de moy,* car tu es mort se tu ne te pues de moy deffendre.' [MINIATURE AND
[f. 543ʳ, col. 1] RUBRIC: **Comment Lancelot abatist ung chevalier et lui ren-dist son cheval.**] *Si li vient le glaive alongié et le* fiert si durement qu'il li perce l'escu et le hauberc, mais en char ne l'a mie atouchié. Et *Lancelot, qui tout son pouvoir y met, le fiert si durement qu'il le*

doune to the erthe, that he had nyghe broken his neck. Thenne Sir Launcelot tooke the knyghtes hors that was his owne afore hand, and descended from the hors he sat upon, and mounted upon his own hors, *and teyed the knyghtes owne hors to a tree, that he myght fynde that hors whanne that he was arysen. Thenne Sir Launcelot rode tyl nyghte, and* by adventur *he met an heremyte, and eche of hem salewed other, and there he rested with that good man alle nyght and gaf his hors* suche as he myghte gete. *Thenne sayde the good man unto*

---

porte a terre, et li et le cheval, si felonnessement *qu'a pou qu'il n'a le col brisié.* Et il point oultre et puis revient arriere et voit le cheval qui ja estoit relevés. *Et il le prent* par le frain *et l'atache a ung arbre pour ce que, quant le chevaillier se relevera, qu'il le truist illec* tout prest pour monter. Et quant il a ce fait, *si se remet en sa voie. Si chevauche jusques au soir.* Et lors fu vains de jeuner, comme cil qui n'avoit mengié de tout le jour ne de l'autre jour devant. Et il eut chevauchié deus grans journees merveillieuses qui moult l'avoient travaillié.

Et quant il ot chevauchié jusques a heure de vespres, si gut la nuit devant ung hermitaige qui estoit en une montaigne. Et il regarde maintenant celle part *et voit* devant l'ui une chappelle seoir *ung hermitte* qui estoit vieulz et ancien et touz chanus. Si fust moult liez de ceste aventure; si s'adrece celle part *et le salue, et l'ermite li rent son salut* bel et moult courtoisement. 'Sire, fait Lancelot, pourriés vous huy mais herbergier ung chevaillier esrant?' — 'Biaux sire, fait le preudomme, s'il vous plaist a descendre, je vous herbergeray le mieulx que je pourray et vous donray a mengier de ce que je pourray et de ce que Dieux m'a presté.' Et Lancelot respont que il ne demande mieulx; si descent a tant et le preudoms maine le cheval en ung petit appentis qui estoit devant son hermitage, et li oste il mesmes le frain et la selle, et li donne de l'erbe dont il avoit assés a grant planté. Et puis prent l'escu et le glaive et le porte a l'ostel. Et Lancelot ot desja deslacé son heaume et sa ventaille abatue; si oste son hauberc de son dos, si se desarme et de lés porte en l'ermitage. Et quant il est tout desarmé, le preudhoms li demande s'il avoit anuit oÿ vespres. Et il dit qu'il ne vit huy mais ne maison ne rechest ne homme, fors ung qu'il encontra ore a midi. Lors entra le preudons en sa chappelle et appelle son clerc et commence moult tost vespres du jour et puis de la Mere

Launcelot: '*Of whens be ye?*'—'*Syr, sayd he*, I am of Arthur's courte, and my name is Sir Launcelot du Lake, that am in the Quest of the Sancgreal. And therfor *I pray yow to counceylle me of a vysyon*, the whiche I hadde at the crosse.' *And so he tolde hym*

[P. 660] *alle.* Capitulum quartum. '*Loo, Sir Launcelot, said the good man, there thou myghtest understande the hyghe lygnage that thou art comen of,* and thyne advysyon betokeneth: *After the passion of Jhesu*

Dieu. Et quant il ot ce fait qui au jour appartenoit, si s'en issi de la chappelle *et lors demande a Lancelot dont il estoit* et de quel païs. Et il li dist maintenant la verité de tout son estre ne il (se) ne se çoille mie vers lui de chose qui advenue lui soit ou Saint Graal.

[f. 543ʳ, col. 2] Et quant ly preudoms oÿ Lancelot, si li prent moult grant pitié de lui, car il voit qu'il commença a plourer trés donc qu'il commença a compter du Saint Graal. Lors li requiert ou nom de Dieu et de sainte Marie qu'il li die sa confession et trestout son estre. Et il dist que si fera il moult voulentiers, puis qu'il le veult. Si l'a maintenant ramené en sa chappelle et [Lancelot] li conte sa vie tout ainsi comme il l'avoit autre foiz contee, et puis li requiert pour Dieu qu'il le conseille, car il est ung des hommes du monde qui plus a grant mestier de conseil. Et quant le preudoms ot oÿ sa vie et sa repentance, si le reconforte moult et asseure, et li dist de bonnes parolles que Lancelot en est moult [plus] aise qu'il n'estoit devant, et lors li dist: '*Sire, pour Dieu, car me conseilliés de ce que* je vous demanderay se vous le savez.' — 'Or dites, fait (dont fait) le preudoms, et je vous conseillieray a mon povoir.' 'Sire, fait Lancelot, il *me fut* anuit *avis en mon dormant* que devant moy venoit uns homs tout avironné d'estoilles et amenoit avecques lui set¹ rois et deus chevailliers.' *Et lors li conte mot a mot la vision ainsi comme il l'avoit veue.* Et quant *li preudoms* ot ceste parolle, si *dist a Lancelot:* '*La peus tu veoir (a) la haultesce de ton lignage* et de *quels* gens *tu es descenduz*, et saches tu que ci a moult greigneur signifiance que moult de gent ne cuideroient. Or m'escoute se tu veule et ge te diray le commencement de ton parenté. Mais je le prandray de moult loings, car ainsi le me convient faire.

'Voirs fu que, *après la Passion Jhesucrist quarante deus ans, issi Joseph de Barismachie* de Jherusalem par le commandement Nostre Seigneur *pour preschier* et pour anoncer par tout la ou il verroit la

Criste fourty yere, Joseph of Armathye preched the vyctory of kynge
Evelake that he had in the batails the better of his enemyes. Of the
seven kynges and the two knyghtes: the first of hem is called Nappus,

verité et Nouvelle [Loi] et lez commendemens de Sainte Eglise. Quant il avint en la cité de Sarras, si trouva ung roy païen. Evalac avoit a nom. Et avoit guerre a ung sien voisin riche et poissant. Et quant il fut acointiez du roy, il le conseilla en telle maniere *qu'il eut la victoire de son ennemy et le vainqui en champ* par l'aide que Nostre Sires li envoia. Et maintenant qu'il fu repairiés a sa cité, receupt crestienté de la main Josephes le fil Joseph. Et quant li roys fu crestiennez et il ot sa loy guerpie, il crust si bien en Dieu et tant ama son Creatour que il fu aussi comme pilliers et fondemens de foy. Et bien fu apparans chose qu'il fu preudoms et vrays, la ou Nostre Sires li laissa veoir lez grans secrés et lez respoutailles du Saint Graal, dont oncquez chevaillier a celui temps n'eut (oncques) veu gaires se Joseph non, ne puis ne fu chevaillier qui riens en veist se ce fu aussi comme en dormant ou en songant.

'A celui temps vint en avision au roy Evalac que d'un sien nepveu qui estoit filz Nascien issoit ung grant lac de son ventre, et de lac issoient neuf flun moult bel et moult grant dont lez uit estoient moult grans et d'une parfondesse. Mais cil qui estoit le darrain estoit le greigneur de lé et de parfondesse que touz lez aultres ensemble. Et [1] estoient [si par]fonde et si bruians qu'il n'estoit riens qui lez peust souffrir. Et cils fluns estoit troubles ou commencement et espés comme boë, et ou milieu cler et nes, et en la fin d'autre maniere: car il estoit a cent doubles plus cler et plus biaux que ou milieu, et si doulz a boire que nuls ne s'en povoit saouler. Et tout tieulz estoit le darrains fluns. Et aprés regardoit Evalac et [f. 543ᵛ, veoit venir ung homme de vers le ciel, qui portoit le tesmoing et la col. 1] semblance de Nostre Seigneur. Et quant il estoit vers Evalac,[2] si lavoit ses piés et ses mains dedens, et tout son corps.

'Ce songe et ceste avision vit le roy Mordrains en son dormant. Si t'en moustr[er]ay ore la signifiance et que ce fu a dire. Le nepveu le roy Mordrain dont le lac issoit, ce fu Celuidoïnes, le filz Nascien, que Nostre Sires envoia en ceste terre pour abatre et pour confondre lez mescreans. Cil fu vraiement vray sergant a Dieu, cil fu des vrays chevaillier Jhesucrist, cil sceut du cours (et) des estoilles et

---

¹ MS. *en.*   ² Other MSS. *venuz au lac.*

an holy man; and the second hyghte Nacyen, in remembraunce of his graunte sire, and in hym dwelled oure Lord Jhesu Cryst; *and the thyrd was called Hellyas le Grose; and the fourth hyght Lysays; and the fyfthe hyghte Jonas; he departed out of* his *countrey and went into Walys, and toke there the doughter of Manuel, whereby he had the lond of Gaule; and he came to dwelle in this countrey, and of hym came kynge Launcelot, thy graunte syre, the whiche there wedded the kynges doughter of Irland, and he was as worthy a man as thow art;*

la maniere du firmament et des planettes autretant ou plus comme le philosophe en savoient. Et pour ce qu'il en fut aussi comme maistre en science et engin, vint il tout avironnés d'estoilles. Ce fu le premier roy crestien qui maintint le roiaume d'Escoce. Il fu vraiement 'lac', car il fut fontaine de science, et en lui peut on puisier touz lez poins et toute la force de virginité. Et de celui lac issirent neuf flun, ce sont neuf personnes de hommes qui sont descenduz de lui. Non mie ainsi qu'il soient touz ses filz, ains est descendus li uns de l'autre par droitte engendreure. *De ces neuf sont lez set roys et lez deus chevailliers. Le premier* chevaillier qui *issi de Celuidoïne, cilz a nom Vaspasiens,*[1] *et fut moult preudoms et moult ama son Creatour. Et l'autre ot nom Nasciens en ramembrance de son aÿeul; en celui se merveilla Nostre Sires* merveillieusement que on ne sceut a son temps nul si preudomme. *Et le tiers roy aprés ot a nom Heleyus le gros;* cil amast assés mieulz a estre detrenchiés d'espees qu'il feist riens contre son Creatour. *Et le quart a nom Ysaïs,* preus et loyaulx; ce fut cil qui oncques ne courrouça a escient Nostre Seigneur. *Li quins aprés ot a nom Jonaax,* bon chevaillier preux et loiaulx et hardis plus que nuls homs; cil essauça moult Sainte Eglise et esleva de tout son povoir; cil ne fist oncques a son escient chose dont il courouçast Nostre Seignour. *Cil issi de cest païs et s'en ala en Gaulle et prist la fille*[2] *Morneus dont il ot le roiaume de Gaulle. De celui issi le roy Lancelot ton aïeul, qui* se departi de Gaulle et *vint manoir en cest païs et eust a femme la fille du roy d'Irlande. Cil fut si preudoms comme tu seuls [estre] quant tu trouvas le corps en la fontaine boulant en la tombe que li homme gardoient. De celi issi le roy Bans ton pere* qui assez fu de plus haulte vie et de plus merveillieuse que moult de gens ne cuiderent;

[1] Probably a misreading of *Naspus,* due to analogy with a well-known name.
[2] MS. *le filz.*

and of hym cam kynge Ban thy fader, the which was the last of the seven kynges. And by the, Sir Launcelot, hit sygnefyeth that the Angels sayd thou were none of the seven felauships. And the laste was the IX knyght, *he was sygnefyed to a lyon, for he shold passe all*

en celui ot Dieu assés greigneur part qu'il ne fut advis au siecle, car il en y eust aucuns qui cuiderent que li deulz de la terre l'eust mort, mais non fist; ains avoit touz les jours de sa vie requis a Nostre Seignour qu'il le laissast trespasser de cest siecle de quelle heure qu'il le requerroit. Si moustra bien Nostre Sires qu'il avoit oÿ sa priere; car, si tost comme il demanda la mort du corps, il eut et trouva [1] la vie de l'ame.

'Les set personnes que je t'ay nommés, qui sont commencement de ton lignage, ce sont lez set roys qui apparurent en ton songe, qui vindrent devant toy [2]; ce sont set des fleuves qui issoient du lac que le roy Mordrains vit en son dormant, et en touz ces set a Nostre Sires lavé ses mains et ses piés. Or convient que je te die qui sont lez deux chevailliers qui estoient en leur compaignie. L'ainsné de ceulz, qui le[s] suivoit, c'est a dire qu'il estoit descendus d'eulz, ce es tu, car tu es descenduz du roy Ban qui estoit descenduz d'eulz; car il estoient assemblé devant toy, il desoient a haulte voiz: 'Peres, vien nous visiter!' Et pour ce t'acueilloient il en leur compaignie et prioient Nostre Seigneur qu'il venist querre eulz et toy, pour ce qu'il estoient commancement et racine de toy. Et pour ce disoient il: 'Ren a chascun ce qu'il a deservi.' Et par [3] ce dois tu entendre qu'il n'ot oncques entre eulz se [4] droitture non, que pour amour qu'il eussent a toy ne vouloient il prier Nostre Seignour se de ce qu'il devoient non,[5] c'est de rendre chascun son droit. Et quant il orent ce dist, il te fut avis que de vers le ciel venoit uns homs a grant compaignie d'anges et descendoit sur eulz et donnoit a chascun la beneïçon. Et ainsi comme tu le veiz en avision est il pieça avenu, car il n'y a nul d'eulz que nous ne cuidions qui soit en la compaignie des angles.

'Et quant il avoit parlé a l'aisné des deus chevailliers, et il li avoit dittes les [6] parolles dont tu te ramembres bien, — que tu doiz recongnoistre et prendre sur toy comme celles qui sont dittes pour toy et de toy, car tu es signifiés cil pour qui elles furent dittes; — il

[f. 543ᵛ, col. 2]

---

[1] MS. *tourva.* [2] MS. *le roy.* [3] MS. *pour.*
[4] MS. *sa.* [5] MS. *se de ce nom quil deuoient.* [6] MS. *ses.*

maner of erthely knyghtes; that is syre Galahad, the whiche thow gate on kynge Pelles doughter. And thou ought to thanke God more than ony other man lyvynge, for of a synner erthely thow hast no piere as in knyghthoode nor never shall be, but lytyl thanke hast thou gyven to God for al the grete vertues that God hath lent the.' *'Syr, said Launcelot, ye say that that good knyght is my sone?'*—'That oughtest thow to knowe and no man better, said the good man, for thou knewest the doughter of kyng Pelles flesshely, and on her thow begattest Galahad, and that was he that at the feest of Pentecost satte in the Sege Peryllous. *And therfor make thow hit knowen openly* that he is

venoit au joine chevaillier qui de toy est descenduz, car tu l'engendras en la fille au Roy Pescheor et ainsi descendi il de toy. *Si le muoit en figure de lion, c'est a dire qu'il le mettoit oultre toute maniere d'ome terrien,* si que nulz ne le ressemblast ne en fierté ne en povoir. Et si li donnoit elles pour ce que nulz ne fust si isniaux ne si vistes comme il est, ne que nulz ne peust aler si hault en prouesce ne en aultre chose, et li disoit: 'Biaux fieux, or pués voler par tout le monde et monter par dessus toute chevaillierie.' Et cil commançoit tantost a voler si durement qu'il devenoit si grans et si merveillieux si que tout le monde en estoit couvers. *Tout ce est avenu de Galaad, de ce chevaillier qui est ton filz.* Car il est de si haute vie que c'est merveille, ne de chevaillierie ne le peut nuls ressambler, ne toy ne autres. Et pour ce que il si hault alés en est que nuls n'y pou(u)rroit avenir, devons nous dire que Nostre Sires li a donné elles pour voler par dessus touz lez aultres. Par lui devons nous entendre l'uitisme flun que le roy Mordrains vit en son songe, qui plus estoit lez et parfons que tout lez aultres n'estoient ensemble. Or t'ay dist qui furent lez set roys que tu veis en ton songe et qui fu le chevaillier qui fu ostés de leur compaignie et qui est le darrain a qui Nostres Sires donnoit sa grace, si grant que il le faisoit voler par dessus touz lez aultres.'

—'Sire, fait Lancelot, ce que vous me dittes que le Bon Chevaillier est mon filz me fait tout esbahir.'

'Tu ne doiz mie estre esbahis, fait le preudons, ne esmerveillez. Car tu scez bien que *la fille au Roy Pescheour congneuz tu charnelment, et illec engendras tu Galaad,* ce t'a on ja mainte foiz dit. *Et cilz Galaad* que tu engendras en celle damoiselle, *est le chevaillier qui sist le jour de Penthencouste ou Siege Perillieux,* et c est ce che-

one of thy begetynge on kynge Pelles doughter, for that wyl be youre worship and honour and to alle thy kynred. *And I counceyle yow, in no place prece not upon hym to have adoo with hym.*'—'*Well, sayd Launcelot, me semeth that good knyghte shold praye for me unto the hyghe Fader that I falle not to synne ageyne.*'—'*Trust thow wel, sayd the good man,* thou faryst mykel the better for his prayer; *but the sone shall not bere the wyckednes of the fader, nor the fader shalle not bere the wyckednes of the sone, but everyche shalle bere his own burthen. And therfor beseke thow only God, and he wylle helpe the in alle thy nedes.*' *And thenne Syr Launcelot and he wente to souper, and soo leyd hym* to rest. *And the hayre prycked so Syr Launcelot's*

[P. 661]

---

vaillier que tu quiers. *Si le t'ay dist et fait congnoistre pour ce que je ne vouldroie mie que tu te preisses celui par bataille,* car tu le pourr[o]ies faire mortelment et toy mal baillir du corps. Car tu pues bien savoir [que], se tu assembloies a lui par bataille, ce seroit tantost alee chose de toy, puis que nulle prouesce ne se peut prandre a la soie.'

'— *Sire, fait Lancelot,* moult m'est grant confort de ceste chose que vous m'avés ditte, car *il me semble, puis que si hauls homs* est issus de moy et qui tant est preudoms, ne devroit mie souffrir que son pere, quel qu'il fust, venist a perdicion, ains *devroit prier,* ce m'est advis, *Nostre Seigneur* et jour et nuit que sa doulce pitié *me ostast de cest povre vie ou j'ay tant demouré.*'

'*Je te diray, fait li preudoms, comment il est.* Des pechiez mortelx porte le pere son faiz et le fiz le sien; *ne le filz ne partira mie a l'iniquité son pere, ne li peres a l'iniquité son fil, mais chascun, selon ce qu'il avra deservi, recevra son loier. Pour ce* ne *doiz tu* mie *avoir esperance* en ton fil, mais *seulement en Dieu. Car* se de lui requiers [1] aide, *il t'aidera et secourra a touz tes besoings.*'

'— Et puis qu'il est ainsi, fait Lancelot, que nuls ne me puet valoir ne aider fors Jhesucrist, Lui prie qu'Il me vaille et aist et ne me laist dés ore mais ca[oi]r es mains de l'ennemy, si que je Li puisse rendre celui tresor qu'Il me donna, c'est l'ame de moy, au grant jour espoventable que Il dira aux pecheurs: "Alés de cy, maleoites gens, ou feu pardurable!" Et Il dira aux autres la douce parolle: "Venez avant le benoit oir mon pere et son beneoit fil! Entrez en la joie qui ja ne fauldra!"'

[f. 544r, col. 1]

[1] MS. *ce celui requiert.*

skynne whiche greved hym ful sore, but he toke hit mekely and suffred the payne.

And soo on the morne he herd his masse, and took his armes, and soo toke his leve. Capítulum Quíntum. *And thenne mounted upon his hors and rode into a forest, and helde no hyhe waye. And as he loked afore hym, he sawe a fayre playne, and besyde that a fayre Castel, and afore the Castel were many pavelions of sylke and of*

Assés parlerent longuement entre Lancelot et le preudomme. *Et quant il fu heure de souper, il* issirent hors de la chappelle et s'assirent en la maisson au preudomme et *mengierent* pain et cervoise. Et quant il orent mengié, *le preudoms fist Lancelot couchier* sur l'erbe, comme cil qui autre lit n'avoit apparaillé. Et il s'i dormy assés bien, comme cil qui estoit vaincus de lasseté et de traveil et ne boit mie a la grant aiise du siecle comme il souloit. Car s'il y beast granment, il n'y dormist ja maiz, pour la terre qui estoit dure et pour *la haire* qui *estoit aspre et poingnant emprés sa char. Mais* il estoit ore a ce menés que *ceste mesaise* qu'il a conmencié *li plaist tant a souffrir* et embelist, qu'il n'essaia oncques mais riens qui tant li pleust, et pour ce ne li greve riens qu'il face. *Celle nuit dormi Lancelot et reposa en la maison au preudomme, et quant le jour apparut, si* se leva et *ala oïr le service* Nostre Seigneur. Et quant le preudoms ot chanté, *il reprist ses armes et monta sur son cheval et commanda son oste a Dieu.* Et le preudoms li pria moult qu'il en tenist en ce qu'il avoit conmencié nouvellement. Et il dist que si feroit il, se Nostre Sires li donnoit vie et santé.

Si se parti maintenant de laiens *et chevaucha par la forest* tout le jour *en telle maniere qu'il ne tenoit ne voie ne sentier.* Car il pensoit bien a sa voulenté a son estre et moult se repentoit des pechiez qu'il avoit faiz, pour quoy il estoit gettez de la compaignie qu'il avoit veu en son dormant. C'est une chose dont si grant douleur li estoit advenue au cuer qu'il avoit grant paour qu'il n'en cheïst en desesperance. Mais pour ce qu'il a mise du tout son esperance en Jhesucrist, cuide il encores estre venuz a ce lieu dont il est ostés, et faire compaignie a ceulx dont il est estrais (estraiz).

Et quant il a chevauchié jusques a heure de prime, *si vint en une moult grant place* qui estoit enmy la forest. *Et il voit devant lui ung chastel grant et fort,* avironné de murs et de fossés, *et la (ou) il avoit tendus paveillons de draps de soie et de diverses couleurs ournés* bien

dyverse hewe. And hym semed that he sawe there fyve hondred knyghtes rydynge on horsbak, and there were two partyes: *they that were of the Castel were all on blak horses, and their trappours blak. And they that were withoute were al on whyte horses and trappours, and* everyche hurteled to other *that it merveylled Syr Launcelot. And at the laste hym thoughte they of the castel were putte to the werse.* Thenne thoughte Sir Launcelot for to helpe there the weyker party in encrecynge of his chyvalry. *And soo Syr Launcelot threst in* among the party of the Castel, *and smote doune a knyghte, hors and man, to the erthe. And thenne he rasshed here and there* and dyd marveyllous dedes of armes. *And thenne he drewe oute his suerd and strake many knyghtes to the erthe,* so that alle tho that sawe hym merveylled that ever one knyghte myghte doo soo grete dedes of armes. *But alweyes the whyte knyghtes helde them nyghe aboute Syr Launcelot for to tyere hym and wynde hym.* But att the laste, as a man may not ever endure, *Syr Launcelot waxed so faynt of*

---

jusqu'a cent. *Et devant lez paveillons avoit monté bien jusqu'a cinc cent chevailliers* sur grans destriers, et avoient commencié ung grant tournoiement trop merveilleux, et estoient lez uns couvers de blanchez armeures et lez aultres de noirs, ne nulle autre diverseté d'armes il n'avoit entr'eulx touz. *Et cil qui avoient lez noires armeures se tenoient devers le chastel, et lez autres, qui avoient lez blanches, se tenoient devers la forest.* Si avoient commencié le tournoy trop merveillieux et trop grant, *et tant y avoit ja d'ommes abatus que ce estoit merveilles. Et il regarde* le tournoiement grant piece et *tant qu'il li est advenu que cil de devers le chastel en ont le pieur* et qu'il perdent place tournoy. [MINIATURE] *Et il laisse courrir le cheval et fiert le premier qu'il encontre si durement qu'il porte a terre lui et le cheval tout en ung mont.* Et il hurte maintenant a ung aultre; si brise[1] son glaive, mais toutes voies le porte a terre. *Et puis traist l'espee et commence a departir grans coups amont et aval, et point ça et la par my le tournoiement,* comme cil qui de grant prouesse estoit plains. Si fait tant en pou d'eure que touz cil qui(l) le veoient li donnoient le pris et le los de tout le tournoiement. Et nonpourquant il ne peut venir au dessus de ceulz qui contre lui sont, car tant sont souffrans et endurans qu'il s'en esbahit tout. Et il fiert sur eulz et maille aussi comme sur une piece de fust. *Mais cil* ne mon-

[f. 544r, col. 2]

---

[1] MS. *brisa.*

fyghtyng and *travaillyng, and was so wery* of his grete dedes, *but he myghte not lyfte up his armes* for to gyve one stroke, *so that he wende never to have borne armes. And thenne they alle took and ledde hym awèy into a forest*, and there made hym to alyghte and to reste hym. *And thenne all the felaushyp of the castel were overcome for the defaute of hym. Thenne they sayd* alle *unto Syr Launcelot*: 'Blessid be God that *ye be now of oure felaushyp, for we shalle holde yow in oure pryson.*' And soo they lefte hym with fewe wordes. *And thenne Syr Launcelot made grete sorowe:*—'*For never or now was I never at turnement* nor justes *but I had the best*, and now I am shamed.' *And thenne he sayd: 'Now I am sure that I am more synfuller than* ever I was.'

Thus he rode sorowynge, and half a day he was oute of despayre, tyl that he came into *a depe valey. And whanne Syr Launcelot sawe he myghte not ryde up in to the montayne, he there alyghte under an*

---

strent mie qu'il se sentent de coup qu'il leur donne, car nulle foiz ne recueillent, ains *prennent touz jours sur lui place. Si le lassent tant* par souffrir et *par endurer qu'il ne se puet mais aidier ne lever son espee, ains est si durement lassés et traveilliez qu'il cuide bien qu'il n'ait ja maiz povoir de porter armes. Et il le prennent* a force *et l'en mainnent devers la forest* et le mettent dedens ung paveillon. *Et touz lez compaignons furent maintenant vaincus qu'il leur failli, et cil* qui en menerent Lancelot *li dirent: 'Lancelot, nous avons tant fait que vous estes des nostres, et vous tenons en nostre prison.* Se vous en voulez issir, il convient que vous fianciés nostre voulenté.' Et il leur creante, et a tant s'en part maintenant et lez laisse en la forest.

Si s'en va en ung autre sentier que celui ou il avoit esté. Et quant il est grant piece eslongiés de ceulz qui pris l'avoient, (et) *il se pense qu'il a huy esté menés la ou oncques maiz ne peut estre menés, ce est (ce) que oncques mais ne vint en tournoiement qu'il ne venquist,* ne onques mais ne peut estre pris en tournoiement. Et quant il se pourpense, *si fait trop grant dueil et dist que or voit il bien qu'il est plus pecheur que* nuls aultres homs, car ses pechez et sa male aventure li a du tout tolu son povoir de tout son corps et la veue des yeulz; que de la veue des yeulz fut ce bien prouvee chose pour la veue du Saint Graal qu'il ne peut veoir; la force du corps a il [1] . . . [es]prouvee vraiement, car il ne fut onques mais entre si pou de

[1] End of line blank.

Appel tree *and there he lefte his helme and his shelde and put his hors
unto pasture. And then he leid hym doune to slepe. And thenne hym
thoughte there came an* old *man afore hym, the whiche sayd: 'A! Launcelot, of eville feythe and poure byleve, wherfor is thy wille tourned
so lyghtely toward thy dedely* synne *?' And whanne he had sayd thus
he vanysshed away, and Launcelot wyst not where he was become.*
  Thenne he took his hors and armed hym. *And as he rode by the
way he sawe a chappel where was a recluse, whiche hadde a* wyndowe
that she myghte see *up to the aulter. And* alle aloude *she called
Launcelot, for that he semed a knyghte erraunt. And thenne he came,*

---

gens comme il a esté a cest tournoiement qu'il li peust estre las ne
travailliez, ains le[s] faisoit au darrain voidier la place ou il voulsis-
sent ou non. *Ainsi dolans et courouciés comme il estoit, chevaucha tant
que* la nuit le sousprint *en une vallee grant et parfonde. Et quant il
vit qu'il ne pourroit mie venir a la montaigne, si descent dessoubz ung*
grant pueplier *et pense de son cheval: si li oste la selle et le frain, et
oste son escu de son col et son heaume* et abat la ventaille. Et s'assiet
maintenant dessoubz l'arbre *et puis s'en dort* assés legierement, car il
estoit traveilliez plus qu'il n'avoit esté pieça mais.
  Et quant il fu endormis, *si li fu advis que devant lui venoit uns
homs* qui moult bien sembloit estre preudoms, et venoit vers lui
aussi comme courouciez, et lui disoit: '*Hé! homs de pute foy et de
male creance, pour quoy est ce que ta voulenté est si legierement tournee
vers ton* ennemy *mortel?* Et se tu ne t'y gardes, il te fera cheoir
ens ou parfont puis dont nuls ne resourt.' *Et tantost qu'il ot ce dit,
si s'esvanüist en telle maniere que Lancelot ne savoit qu'il estoit
devenus.* Si estoit mout durement a malaise de ceste parolle; mais
pour ce ne s'esveilla il mie, ains se dormy jusques a l'endemain que
le jour fut apparut cler et biaux. Et il se lieve et fait le signe de la
croix enmy son front. Et il regarde maintenant tout entour luy,
mais il ne voit mie son cheval. Et nonpourquant tant le quiert
amont et aval qu'il l'a trouvé. Si y met maintenant la selle; si
monte si tost comme il est armés.
  Et quant il s'en voult aler, il regarde a destre du chemin et *voit*
prés de lui a une archié *une chappelle ou il avoit une recluse* que on
tenoit a une des bonnes dames du monde. Et quant Lancelot voit
la chappelle, si dist que voirement il est meschant et que ses pechiez
le destournent de touz biens: car la ou il est ore, vint il (est) de

and she asked hym what he was, *and of what place, and where aboute he wente to seke.* **Capitulum Sertum.** *And thenne he told her alle togyder word by word, and* the trouthe how *it befelle hym at the turnement.*

And after told her his advysyon, that he had had that nyghte, *in his slepe, and prayd her to telle hym what hit myght mene,* for he was [P. 663] not wel contente with hit. '*A! Launcelot, sayd she, as longe as ye were knyghte of erthely knyghthode, ye were the moost merveillous man of the world, and moost adventurous.* Now, said the lady, *sythen ye be sette amonge the knyghtes of hevenly adventures, yf adventure felle the contrary* at that turnement, *have thou no merveille, for that turnement yesterdaye was but a tokenynge of oure Lord. And not for*

---

telle heure que bien peust estre alés a la chappelle touz le jours et demande[r] conseil de son estre. Et il tourne celle part et descent et atache son cheval a ung arbre, et oste son heaume et son escu et son espee, et met tout devant l'uys de la chappelle. Et quant il est entrés dedens, si voit que touz les garnemens estoient sur l'autel touz prests pour revestir, et devant l'autel estoit le chappellain vieulz et chanuz aux coustes et aux genoulz, et desoit son confiteor. Et ne demoura gaires qu'il se revesti des armes Nostre Seigneur et commença la messe de la Mere Dieu. Et quant il ot chanté et il se fu devestuz, la rencluse *qui avoit une petite* p[orte] *par ou elle* vaoit *a l'autel, (et elle) appelle maintenant Lancelot pour ce que chevailliers esrans li sembloit* et bien cuidoit que de conseil eust mestier. *Et il vint a lui et elle (et elle) lui demanda dont il estoit et qu'il aloit querant. Et si li dist tout mot a mot* quanqu'elle lui avoit demandé. *Et* quant il li a tout dit, *il li conte l'aventure du tournoiement* ou il avoit hier esté, et comment ceulz aux armes blanches le prinrent et la parolle qu'il leur avoit ditte,[1] *et amprés li conte toute l'avision qu'il avoit veue en son dormant.*

Et quant il li a tout conté son estre, *si li prie que elle le conseille a son povoir, et elle li dist* maintenant: '*Lancelot, tant comme vous fustes* [f. 544v, col. 2] *chevaillier des chevailliers terriens fust vous le plus merveillieux homs du monde et le plus aventureulz. Ore quant vous estes entremis de chevailliers celestiaux, se aventures merveilleuses vous aviennent, ce n'est mie merveilles.* Et nonpourquant de ce tournoiement que vous veistes hier vous diray je le senefiance. *Car quanques vous veistes*

[1] Other MSS. *qui li avoit esté dite.*

thenne there was none enchauntment, for they at the turnement were erthely knyghtes. The turnement *was a token to see who shold have most knyghtes, outher Clyazar, the son of kynge Pelles, or Argustus, the sone of kynge Harlon.* But Clyazar *was alle clothed in whyte,* and Argustus was coverd in blak, the whiche were comen. *Alle what this betokeneth I shalle telle yow.* The daye of Pentecost, whan kynge Arthur helde his court, it befelle that *erthely kynges and knyghtes toke a turnement to gyders, that is to say* the Quest of the Sancgreal. *The erthely knyghtes were they the whiche were clothed al in black; and the coverynge betokeneth the synnes* wherof they be not confessid. *And they with the coverynge of whyte betokeneth vyrgynyte, and* they that chosen *chastyte. And thus was the* Quest *begonne in them.* Thenne thow behelde the synners and the good men, and when thow sawest the synners overcomen, thow enclynest to that party *for

---

ne fut fors aussi comme une demonstrance de Nostre Seignour. Et non-pourquant sans faille nulle et sans decevement, estoit cil tournoiemens de chevailliers terriens, mais assés y avoit (assés) greigneur senefiance que moult de gent ne cuideroient. Tout avant vous diray pour quoy li tournoys fut empris: *pour veoir lequel aroit plus de chevailliers, ou Elyzer, le filz au roy Pellé[s], ou Argustes, le filz au roy Herlant.* Et pour ce que on peust congnoistre les uns des autres, *fist Elizer couvrir lez siens de blanches [1] couvertures.* Et quant il furent a jouste, si furent lez noirs vaincus, encores leur aidissiez vous, et encores eussent il greigneur gent que lez autres.

'*Or vous diray la signifiance de ceste chose.* Avant hier, *le jour de Penthencouste, prirent lez chevailliers terriens et li celestial ung tournoiement ensemble, c'est a dire* qu'il commençoient ensemble chevaillerie: car lez chevailliers qui sont en pechié mortel, ce sont lez chevaillers terriens, et li celestial — ce sont lez vrais chevailliers et lez preudommes qui n'estoient mie en ordure de pechié, — commencierent la Queste du Saint Graal. Ce fu li tournoiement qu'il enprinrent. *Les terriens,* qu'il avoient la terre [2] es yeulz et ou cuer, *prindrent noires couvertures, comme cil qui estoient couvers de pechiez* noirs et horribles; *et lez autres, qui estoient celestiel, se couvrirent des couvertures blanches, ce est de virginité et de chasteté* ou il n'avoit noire tache. Et *quant* li tournoiemens fut commencié, c'est a dire quant *la* Queste *fu commenciee, tu regardas lez pecheours et lez preu-*

bobaunce and pryde of the world, and alle that must be lefte in that Quest. For in this Quest thow shalte have many felawes and thy betters, for thow arte soo feble of evylle truste and good byleve. This made hit whan thou were there where *they took the and ledde the in to the forest. And anone there appiered the Sancgreal* unto the whyte knyghtes, but thow was soo feble of good byleve and feyth that thou myghtest not abyde hit for alle the techynge of the good man. But anone thou tornest to the synners, and that caused thy mysaventure, that thou sholdest knowe good from evylle and *vayne glory of the world,* the whiche is not worth a pere. *And for grete pryde thou madest grete sorow that thou haddest not overcome alle* the whyte knyghtes with the keveryng of whyte, by whome was betokeneth vyrgynyte and chastyte. *And therfor God was wroth with* [P. 664] *yow,* for God loveth no suche dedes in this Quest. *And this advision signefyeth that thou were of evil feythe and of poure byleve,* the whiche *wille make the to falle in to the depe pytte of helle, yf thow kepe the not.*

---

dommes. Si te fu advis que lez pescheours estoient vaincus, et pour ce que tu estoies de la partie aux pecheours, cheïz tu en pechié mortel: *si te tournas devers eulz* et si te mellas aux proudommes. Bien t'i mellas tu, quant tu Galaad ton filz voulsis jouster a celle heure qu'il abati ton cheval, et le Perceval ensemble. Et quant tu eus esté grant piece ou tournoiement et tu fus si lassés que tu ne povoies mais en avant, *li preudomme te prinrent et te mirent en la forest,* et oÿs qu'il te requeroient. Et quant tu fus avant hier entrés en la Queste du Saint Graal *et il s'apparut a toy,* lors te trouva il si vil et si ort et si entachié de pechiez que tu ne cuidoies mie que Nostre Sires feist ja maiz de toy son chevallier ne son sergant. Mais maintenant te prindrent li hermitte, li proudomme et lez religieusses personnes qui te mirent en la voie Nostre Seigneur, qui est plaine de vie et verdour aussi comme la forest estoit. Si te conseillierent ce qui estoit prouffitable a l'ame. Et quant tu te fuz partis d'eulz, tu ne retournas mie a la voie ou tu avoies esté devant, ce est a dire que tu ne reveins mie a pechié si mortelment comme tu faisoies devant. Et nonpourquant, *puis qu'il te souvient de la vaine gloire de cest siecle et ton orgueil* que tu souloies mener, *tu commenças a faire ton dueil de ce que tu n'avoies tout vaincu, dont Nostre Sires se deust avoir cour-* [f. 545ʳ, *roucié a toy. Et bien le te monstra en ton dormant, quant il te dist que* col. 1] *tu estoies de povr(r)e foy et de male creance, et* te remantut que

Now have I warned the of thy vayne glory and of thy pryde, that thow hast many tymes erryd ageynst thy Maker. Beware *of everlastynge payne,* for of alle erthely knyghtes I have moost pyte of the, for I knowe wel thow hast not thy pyere of ony erthely synful man.' And soo she commaunded Syr Launcelot to dyner. *And after dyner he toke his hors and commaunded her to God, and soo rode in to a depe*

l'ennemy *te feroit cheoir ou plus parfont puis d'enfer se tu ne t'i gardoies.*

'*Or t'ay devisé* la signifiance du tournoiement et de ton songe, *pour ce que tu te gardes* que tu ne te departes de la voie de verité, *ne par vaine gloire ne par mauvaise racine. Car a ce que tu as meserré maintes foiz vers ton Creatour saches vraiement que* se tu faiz vers lui chose que tu ne doies, il te laira tant fourvoier et trebuscher de pechié en pechié que *tu cherras du tout en pardurable paine,* c'est en enfer.'

Et a tant se taist maintenant la dame et il respont: 'Dame, vous en avés tant dist, et vous et li preudomme a qui je en ay parlé, que se ja maiz cheoie en pechié mortel, on me deveroit plus blasmer que autre pecheour.' — 'Diex vous ottroit, fait elle, par sa doulce pitié que vous n'y renchéés!' Et lors li redist: 'Lancelot, ceste forest est moult grant et moult desvoiable. Si y puet bien ung chevaillier esrer a journee que ja n'y trouvera maison ne recest. Et pour ce vous pri je que vous me dïés se vous mengastes huy ne hier, car se vous n'avés mengié, nous vous donrons de tel charité que Dieux nous a prestee.' Et il dist qu'il en a bien mestier. Et elle li fait apporter pain et yaue, et il entre en la maison au chappelain; si prent tel charité que Dieux li a envoyé. *Et si tost comme il a mengié, si se part de laiens et commande la recluse a Dieu. Et chevaucha* tout le jour a journee, et gut la nuit en une roche haulte et merveilleusse sans compaignie de nullui fors que de Dieu. Et il fu grant partie de la nuit en prieres et en oroisons, et si dormy grant piece.

Et a l'endemain, quant il vit le jour apparoir, il fist le signe de la croix enmy son vis, et puis se mist a coutes et a genoulz contre oriant et fist sa priere telle comme il la savoit. Et maintenant vint a son cheval. Si monta, quant il eust mis le frain et la selle, et puis racuilli son chemin si comme il avoit fait autre foiz. Si chevauche jusques a heure de nonne *tant qu'il vint en une valee moult parfonde* et a veoir belle et delitable, entre trois roches grans et merveil-

*valeye, and there he sawe a ryver and an hyhe montayn. And thorou
the water he must nedes passe, the whiche was hydous; and thenne in
the name of God he took hit with good herte.* And when he came over,
*he sawe an armed knyghte, hors and man black as ony beare. Without
ony word he smote Syr Launcelots hors to the erthe, and soo he passed
on, he wyst not where he was become. And thenne he took his helme
and his shelde,* and thanked God of his adventure. 𝔥𝔢𝔯𝔢 𝔩𝔢𝔟𝔢𝔱𝔥
𝔬𝔣 𝔱𝔥𝔢 𝔰𝔱𝔬𝔯𝔶 𝔬𝔣 𝔖𝔶𝔯 𝔏𝔞𝔲𝔫𝔠𝔢𝔩𝔬𝔱. 𝔄𝔫𝔡 𝔰𝔭𝔢𝔨𝔢 𝔴𝔢 𝔬𝔣 𝔖𝔶𝔯
𝔊𝔞𝔴𝔞𝔶𝔫𝔢, 𝔱𝔥𝔢 𝔴𝔥𝔦𝔠𝔥𝔢 𝔦𝔰 𝔱𝔥𝔢 𝔛𝔙𝔍 𝔅𝔬𝔬𝔨.[1]

lieusses. Et quant il vint en la valee, si commença a penser trop
durement. *Et lors regarda devant lui et voit l'iaue* grant que on
apeloit Marcoise, qui la forest departoit en deus parties. Et quant
il voit ce, si ne scet que faire, car il voit que *par my l'eaue, qui tant
est rade et perilleuse, le conviendra passer,* et ce est une chose qui
moult l'esmaie. *Et nonpourquant il met si du tout son esperance en
Nostre Seigneur, car il s'en gette tout hors du penser* et pensse qu'il le
passera bien a l'aide de Dieu.

En tandis qu'il estoit en ce pensser, li avint une aventure moult
merveilleuse. Car *il vit* devant issir *ung chevaillier armé d'unes
armes plus noires que meure, et seoit sur un grant cheval noir. Et la
ou il vit Lancelot, si li a drecé le glaive alongié sans nul mot dire, et
fiert le cheval Lancelot si durement qu'il occist,* mais lui ne toucha il.
*Si s'en va si grant aleure qu'il est en moult pou d'eure eslongiés, si
que Lancelot ne le peut maiz veoir. Et* quant il voit son cheval devant
lui occis, *il se relieve* et si n'en est mie moult doulans puis qu'il
[f. 545ʳ col. 2] plaist a Nostre Seigneur. Si ne le regarda oncques, ains s'en va a
pié *si armés comme il estoit.* Et quant il est venuz jusques a l'iaue, si
ne voit mie conment il puist oultre passer. Si s'areste et oste son
heaume et son espee et son glaive, et se chouche tout delés une
roche, et dist qu'il attendra illuecques tant que Nostre Sires li
envoiera secours.

[1] Malory, as well as the French *Queste*, passes here to the adventures of
Gawain. The continuation of the episode of the 'Eau Marcoise' (*Mortoyse*
in Malory) is found in book XVII, ch. xiii (p. 707).

BIBLIOGRAPHY

I. EDITIONS

Black-Letter

I

The noble and Joyous book entytled le morte Darthur | Notwyth- **1485**
stondyng it treateth of the byrth | lyf | and actes of the sayd kyng
Arthur | of his noble knyghtes of the rounde table | theyr meruayl-
lous enquestes and aduentures | thachyeuyng of the sangreal | & in
thende the dolorous deth & departyng out of thys world of them al |
whiche book was reduced in to englysshe by syr Thomas Malory
knyght as afore is sayd | and by me deuyded in to XXI bookes
chaptyred and enprynted | and fynnysshed in thabbey westmestre
he last day of Juyl the yere of our lord | M | CCCC | LXXXV |
Caxton me fieri fecit

This is the colophon of the first edition of the *Morte Darthur* printed by
Caxton in 1485. Like all his books, this edition has no title. In this respect
Caxton followed the usage of the scribes, for 'with one exception only,[1]
and at the very end of his career, where the title of the book is printed
alone in the centre of the first page, his books appear without any title
page whatever' (William Blades, *Biography and Typography of William
Caxton, England's first printer*, 1877, p. 45).

The type, according to Blades, is No. 4. The book contains 431 leaves
($11\frac{3}{8} \times 8$). The lines are $4\frac{5}{8}$ inches long and the average number of lines
on a page is 38. The Preface finishes on sig. iiii. The table of 'rubrysshe'
runs through 34 pages, and the book itself begins on sig. a. There are two
complete alphabets: a to z, and A to Z; these are followed by aa, bb, cc,
dd, ee. The book finishes on the verso of ee 6 so that ee has only six leaves
instead of the usual eight.[2]

Two copies of this edition are known. One was sold with the Harleian
Library to Osborne the bookseller and bought of him for £5 5s. by Bryan
Fairfax, who sold it eventually to Child, an ancestor of the Earl of Jersey.[3]
At the sale of the Osterley library in 1885 it was bought for £1,950 by
Mrs. Abby E. Pope, of Brooklyn, N.Y., and left the British Isles. On the
death of Mrs. Pope, it was purchased by Mr. Robert Hoe, and in 1911
acquired by J. Pierpont Morgan for $42,800.[4] It is now in the Pierpont
Morgan Library in New York. This copy is perfect throughout and in
good condition.

---

[1] *The Chastising of God's Children.*
[2] Sommer notes (*op. cit.*, ii. 4) that 'R iii is misprinted for sig. S iii, and S ii for
T ii'.   [3] Cf. Dibdin's *Typographical Antiquities*, 1810, vol. i, pp. 242, 254.
[4] Cf. Hicks, *Sir Thomas Malory*, p. 5.

190   BIBLIOGRAPHY

The other copy was bought by Mrs. John Rylands at the sale of Earl Spencer's library in 1892, and is now in the John Rylands library. It wants eleven leaves which have been supplied by Whittaker in facsimile from the Morgan (then Osterley) copy.[1] The John Rylands copy was used by Sommer for his reprint of the *Morte Darthur*. The second leaf of the table of contents of a third copy has also been preserved (cf. Bagford, *Fragments*, vol. viii, No. 58).

2

1498 *The* booke of the noble kyng. Kyng Arthur sometyme kynge of Englonde of his noble actes and feates of armes of chyualrye. his noble knyghtes & table round and is devyded in to. XXI. bookes.

This is the beginning of Wynkyn de Worde's edition which appeared in 1498. The only extant copy of it is in the John Rylands library, and two leaves of a second copy (sig. t ij and t iij) are preserved in the Bodleian (Douce Fragments, No. 10). The John Rylands (Althorp) copy wants eleven leaves (the first leaf of the table of contents and signatures a 3, r 2, 𝕰 3, 𝕰 4, 𝕿 5, 𝖀 3, B 1, C 6, D 1, E 2). The colophon, which is partly damaged, reads as follows:

'Thus endyth this noble & Ioyous boke entytled le morte dathur. Not wythstonding it treateth of the sayd kynge Arthur of his noble knyghts of the round table. theyr merueyllous enquestes & aduentures. thachyeuynge of the Sancgreall. And in the ende of the dolorous deth. & departynge out of this worlde of them al. Whyche boke was reduced into Englysshe by the well dysposyd knyghte afore namyd. And deuyde. in to. XXI. bokes .chapitred. & enprynt . . . fyrst by Wylliam Caxton | on wh . . . soule god haue mercy. A newel . . . prynted. and chapitres of the sam . . . brisshed at Westmestre by Wynk . . . Worde yᵉ yere of our lord M.C. . . . LXXXXVIII. and ended the XXV . . . Marche. the same yere.'

The text is practically the same as Caxton's. Caxton's Preface is reproduced, though it here follows instead of preceding the 'Table of Rubrysshe'. There are, besides, differences of spelling and emendations in detail. In Chapter XII of Book XXI Wynkyn de Worde interpolates a passage which is not in Caxton but which has been reproduced in all later editions.[2]

3

1529 *The* booke of the moost noble and worthy prince kyng. Kyng Arthur sometyme kynge of grete Brytayne now called Englonde whiche treateth of his noble actes and feates of armes and of chyualrye. of. his noble knyghtes of the table round and this volume is devyded in to. XXI. bookes.

This is the second edition of Wynkyn de Worde. The only extant copy

---

[1] On these facsimiles see Sommer, *op. cit.*, ii. 3.
[2] Cf. Strachey's edition, pp. xxxii and 488.

is now in the British Museum. It once belonged to Grenville but eventually passed into the library of Archdeacon Wrangham, whose manuscript notes are found on the fly-leaf. It lacks the title-page and seven leaves of the table of contents, of which only sig. aaa 8 bbb 1–8 are preserved. The text is not quite identical with that of 1498, as may be seen from the opening lines quoted above.

4

The story of the most noble and worthy Kynge Arthur, the *1557* whiche was one of the worthyes chrysten, and also of his noble and valiaūte knyghtes of the rounde Table. Newly imprynted and corrected. MCCCCCLVII.
Imprynted at London by Wyllyam Copland.

Copland's edition exists in three copies in the British Museum, of which one is perfect (formerly in the Huth Library). The second copy (c. 11. b. 12) is complete except for the title-page, and the third (634. k. 4) lacks several leaves, which have been replaced partly by facsimiles, partly by reprints. The signatures run a to d in eights; e has nine leaves; f to z and A to O in eights. The text is based on Wynkyn de Worde's edition.

5

The storye of the most noble and worthy Kynge Arthur, the which *c.* 1585 was the fyrst of the worthyes Chrysten, and also of hys noble and valyaunt knyghtes of the rounde Table. Newly imprynted and corrected, betweene Paules wharfe and Baynardes Castell by Thomas East.

This edition was printed twice, once in folio and once in quarto. The British Museum possesses a folio copy which is complete throughout. The text is drawn from Wynkyn de Worde and Copland.[1]

6

The most ancient and famovs history of the renowned prince *1634* Arthur, King of Britaine. Wherein is declared his Life and Death, with all his glorious Battailes against the Saxons, Saracens, and Pagans, which (for the honour of his Country) he most worthily atchieued. As also, all the Noble Acts, and Heroicke Deeds of his Valiant Knights of the Rovnd Table. Newly refined and published for the delight, and profit of the Reader. London. Printed by William Stansby for Jacob Bloome. 1634.

There are two copies of this edition in the British Museum, one perfect and the other lacking several leaves (the title-page, the preface, and two leaves of the first section). The book is divided into three parts, each of

[1] On the date of this edition see Sommer, *op. cit.*, p. 8, note 2.

which has the title separately. The first part has sig. A–Z and Aa–Ii 4, the second A–Z and Aa–Rr, and the third A–Z and Aa–Pp 4. Each signature is in fours. There is no division into books as in Caxton, and in each of the three parts the chapters are numbered from I to the end. There are in all five hundred chapters (151, 173, and 176). The text is derived from Thomas East's edition, as may be seen from an omission which exactly corresponds to a complete leaf in East's folio.[1] This edition was reprinted by Wright in 1856 (*v. infra*, No. 10).

Roman Type [2]

7

1816 [3] La Mort D'Arthur, The most ancient and famous historye of the renowned Prince Arthur and the Knights of the Round Table by Sir T. Malory. London. 1816.

> This edition was published by J. Haslewood in three 24mo volumes. The text is based on Stansby, but is full of errors and misprints.

8

1816 The History of the renowned Prince Arthur, kyng of Britain with his life and death and all his glorious Battles, likewise the noble acts and heroic deeds of his valiant knights of the round table. London. 1816. (*Walker's British Classics.*)

> This edition is in two 24mo volumes. It is based on Stansby, but the reprint is by no means exact. Errors and misprints are as frequent as in the previous edition.

9

1817 The byrth, lyf and actes of kyng Arthur; of his noble knyghtes of the Rounde Table ther merueyllous enquestes and aduentures thachyeuyng of the sanc greal, and in the end le morte Darthur with the dolorous deth and departyng out of this world of them al. With an introduction and notes by R. Southey. Printed from Caxton's edition, 1485. London, 1817.

> This edition was published by Longmans & Co. in two volumes 4to. Southey wrote the introduction and notes but had nothing to do with the

[1] Cf. Strachey, *op. cit.*, p. xxxii.
[2] This list includes complete editions only. Selections and popular adaptations have been left out of account.
[3] That there was no reprint of the *Morte Darthur* in the eighteenth century is ascertained by Thomas Warton. In his *Observations on the Faerie Queene* (first edition, 1754, p. 15) he states that '*the last edition* [of the *Morte Darthur*] *is dated* 1634'. The statement is repeated in a later reprint of the *Observations* dated 1807 (vol. i, p. 28).

seeing it through the press, which was entrusted to Upcott. Southey states in the introduction that this edition 'is a reprint with scrupulous exactness from the first edition by Caxton, in Earl Spencer's library' (p. xxviii). But such is not the case. There are several departures from Caxton's edition, and among these we may note the interpolation of seventeen pages (167_{18}–169_{17}; 276–279; vol. ii, 202_{13}–204_{14}, 446–455) which were intended as a substitute for the missing leaves in Earl Spencer's copy. This interpolation, as Strachey has established,[1] was supplied from the first edition of Wynkyn de Worde, 'but with the spelling occasionally altered, and here and there a small word put in, left out, or changed'.[2]

Southey's introduction marks an important date in the history of Malory research, though his information is frequently inaccurate. It certainly falls short of his original plan—to give 'the whole bibliology of the Round Table in the preliminaries and indicate the source of every chapter in the notes '.[3]

10

La Mort d'Arthure. The History of King Arthur and of his Knights of the Round Table compiled by Sir Thomas Malory, Knt. edited from the text of the edition of 1634 with introduction and notes by Th. Wright. London 1858. 8°.   1858, 1866

This is a most accurate reprint of Stansby's edition of 1634, which Th. Wright judged preferable to that of Caxton, as it was the latest of the old editions and also because its orthography and phraseology, 'with the sprinkling of obsolete words, not sufficiently numerous to be embarrassing, preserves a certain clothing of mediaeval character'. To this Strachey rightly objects (*op. cit.*, p. xxxiv) that 'nothing can justify the reprinting the most corrupt of all the old editions when the first and best was within reach'. The book contains an interesting introduction and some useful notes.

11

Morte Darthur, Sir Thomas Malory's Book of King Arthur and of his Noble Knights of the Round Table. The original edition of Caxton revised for modern use with an Introduction by Edward Strachey. London and New York. 1868. 8°. Globe edition.   1868

This edition is a reprint of the original Caxton with the spelling modernized, and 'those few words which are unintelligibly obsolete replaced by others which, though not necessarily unknown to Caxton, are still in use' (*Introd.*, p. xxxv). The Introduction contains a study of the *Authorship and Matter of the Book*, a bibliographical account of the previous editions, and an *Essay on Chivalry*.

[1] *Op. cit.*, pp. xxxiii–xxxiv.
[2] On the origin of the colophon in this edition see *ibid.*, pp. xxxiv and 487–91.
[3] *The Life and Correspondence of R. Southey*, ed. by his son, the Rev. C. C. Southey, London, 1805, vol. iii, p. 125. On Southey's contribution to the study of Malory's sources see above, p. 128.

It was first published in March 1868 and reprinted at various dates. An Index was added in 1869 and the Introduction rewritten in 1891.

12

1889– Le Morte Darthur by Syr Thomas Malory, the original edition of
91   William Caxton now reprinted and edited with an introduction and glossary by H. Oskar Sommer, Ph.D., with an essay on Malory's prose style by Andrew Lang, M.A. Vol. I—Text. London: Published by David Nutt, in the Strand, 1889. Vol. II— Introduction. *Ibid.*, 1890. Vol. III—Studies on the Sources with an introductory essay by Andrew Lang, M.A. *Ibid.*, 1891. 4°.

This edition is a faithful reprint of the original Caxton from the copy which is now in the John Rylands library, save that Roman type has been substituted for Black-letter. It follows Caxton's print word for word, line for line, and page for page. The spelling has been faithfully preserved, and even the misprints which occur in Caxton have been reproduced.

Vol. ii contains: a bibliographical account of the various editions of the *Morte Darthur* and of their relation to one another; a list of errors, omissions, and other irregularities in Caxton's impression; a collation of Whittaker's facsimiles (*v. supra*, No. 1) with the original pages; a study of the language of the *Morte Darthur* (incomplete and much inferior to C. S. Baldwin's work, *v. infra*, No. 17); a collation of Caxton's and Wynkyn de Worde's editions; a list of names and places; and finally, a glossary.

Vol. iii opens with an essay by Andrew Lang entitled 'Le Morte Darthur'. It deals with Malory's treatment of the 'Celtic myths', but what is said here about Malory is more true of his French predecessors than of his actual work. The remarks on Malory's style (pp. xx–xxi), and the survey of modern Arthurian literature (pp. xxi–xxv) which conclude the essay well deserve attention. Andrew Lang's essay is followed by Sommer's 'Studies on the sources of "Le Morte Darthur"' (pp. 1–294). On these studies see *supra*, pp. 128–9, 132 note 2, 150, 153, and 154. The *Appendix* (pp. 295–333) contains extracts from MSS. Add. 25434 and Harl. 1629 ('The Adventures of Alysaunder Le Orphelyn' and 'The Great Tournament of Galahalt of Surluse') printed without punctuation. The volume is concluded by a Supplement (pp. 335–8) containing various Addenda and a list of misprints.

13

1893–4 The birth, life and acts of King Arthur, of his noble Knights of the round table, their marvellous enquests and adventures, the achieving of the San Greal, and in the end le morte d'Arthur, with the dolorous death and departing out of this world of them all.— The text as written by Sir Thomas Malory and imprinted by Wm. Caxton at Westminster the year 1485 and now spelled in modern

style. With an introduction by Prof. J. Rhŷs and embellished with
many original designs by A. Beardsley, Edinburgh 1893. Dent. 4°.

The text of this edition is a fairly faithful copy of Caxton's in modern
spelling. The Introduction deals with the question of Malory's birthplace,
which Professor Rhŷs assigns to Wales (*v. supra*, pp. 125–6), and with the
Celtic elements in Arthurian Romance. Vol. ii contains a Glossary of
obsolete words.

In 1906 this edition was reprinted for Everyman's Library (2 vols.),
and was reissued in the same form in 1908, 1910, 1912, 1916, 1919, and
1923. In 1927 it appeared again in the original form (one volume) with
a note on Aubrey Beardsley by Aymer Vallance (pp. v–x), a 'Note on the
designs omitted from the First Edition' by R. A. Walker (p. xi), and a
note on the methods of transcription by F. J. Simmons.

14

Le Morte Darthur by Sir Thomas Malory, MDCCCXCVII,   1897
published by J. M. Dent and Sons, London. In 4 volumes 16mo.
(The Temple Classics, edited by I. Gollancz.)

The text of this edition is based on Caxton, but a considerable number
of Caxton's misprints and errors have been removed, and the spelling and
punctuation have been thoroughly modernized. Vol. iv is concluded by a
Bibliographical Note (pp. 313–17) and a Glossary (pp. 319–24).

15

Le Morte Darthur, Sir Thomas Malory's Book of King Arthur   1900
and of his Noble Knights of the Round Table. In two vols.
London, Macmillan and Co., 1900. 8°. (Library of English
Classics.)

The text of this edition is 'in accurate accordance with Caxton's text,
as represented by Dr. Sommer's reprint' (p. viii). The spelling has been
modernized, obvious misprints have been corrected, and in a few cases
emendations have been introduced from Wynkyn de Worde—'not that
Wynkyn had any more right to emend Caxton than we, but because even
a printer's conjecture gains a little sanctity after four centuries'. The
edition is prefaced by a useful 'Bibliographical Note' by A. W. Pollard.
On his discussion of Malory's identity *v. supra*, p. 124. The text of the
Morte Darthur is concluded by a Glossary including proper names. In the
subsequent issues the index of names was separated from the glossary.
This edition was reprinted in 1903 and in 1927.

16

Le Morte Darthur. The Book of King Arthur and of His Noble   1921
Knights of the Round Table. By Sir Thomas Malory, Knt.

London: Philip Lee Warner, publisher to the Medici Society, Ltd. MDCCCCXXI. 4 vols. Small 4°.

This edition is a reprint of A. W. Pollard's text (see No. 15). It contains forty-eight illustrations by W. Russell Flint. The lettering of the title-page is engraved after the design by M. Engall. Vol. iv is concluded by a Glossary (pp. 202–12).

II. CRITICAL WORKS[1]

17. Baldwin, C. S., *The Inflections and the Syntax of the Morte d'Arthur of Sir Thomas Malory*, Boston 1894, 156 pp. [Systematic account of Malory's handling of morphology and syntax.]

18. Bruce, J. D., *The Middle English Metrical Romance 'Le Morte Arthur'* (*Harleian MS*. 2252): its Sources and its Relation to Sir Thomas Malory's 'Morte Darthur' (Anglia, xxiii (1901), pp. 67–100). [Study of Malory's relation to the French *Mort Artu* and the English stanzaic *Le Morte Arthur*. J. D. B. restated his conclusions in his edition of 'Le Morte Arthur' (E.E.T.S., Extra series, No. 88, Introduction). For H. O. Sommer's criticisms see *Anglia*, xxix. 529–38.]

19. Chambers, E. K., *Sir Thomas Malory* (English Association, Pamphlet No. 51), 1922, 16 pp. [Essay on the *Morte Darthur* containing a valuable study of its genesis and structure.]

20. Hibbard, L. A., *Malory's Book of Balin*, in *Mediaeval Studies in Memory of G. Schoepperle Loomis*, Paris and New York 1927, pp. 175–95. [Comparison of Malory's Book II with its French source.]

21. Hicks, Edward, *Sir Thomas Malory, his turbulent career, a biography*. Cambridge, Harvard University Press, 1928. 118 pp. [Sketch of Malory's life based on some hitherto unpublished documents, *v. supra*, pp. 4–6 and 122.]

22. Kittredge, G. L., *Who Was Sir Thomas Malory?* Boston 1897. (Reprint from vol. v. of *Studies and Notes in Philology and Literature*). Pp. 85–106. [Identification of Sir Thomas Malory, *v. supra*, pp. 9, 116, 119, 120, 125. Kittredge's discovery was first announced in Johnson's *Universal Cyclopaedia* in March 1894.]

23. Kittredge, G. L., *Sir Thomas Malory*. Barnstable (privately printed). 1925, 12 pp. [50 copies only. Additional notes on Malory's identity.]

24. Löseth, E., *Le Roman en prose de Tristan, le roman de Palamède et la compilation de Rusticien de Pise, analyse critique d'après les manu-*

---

[1] In this list completeness is not aimed at. General manuals, casual notes and reviews, as well as works on Malory's influence, have been omitted. The works are quoted in alphabetical order. Their chronological order is as follows: 33, 30, 26, 25, 24, 17, 35, 22, 34, 18, 27, 29, 31, 28, 19, 23, 32, 20, 21.

scrits de Paris, Paris 1890, pp. xxii–xxiii. [Note on the sources of Malory's *Tristan*.]

25. Paris, Gaston, [Introduction to] *Merlin, roman en prose du XIIIᵉ siècle* (*Société des anciens textes français*), Paris 1886, pp. lxx–lxxii. [Discussion of Malory's Books I—IV and their sources. The theory here advanced has retained its force in spite of all subsequent researches on the subject.]

26. Paris, Gaston, *Le sujet du poème de Chrétien* (Romania XII, pp. 498–508). [Study of Malory's version of the story of the cart (Book XIX of the *Morte Darthur*).]

27. Schofield, W. H., *Chivalry in English Literature: Chaucer, Malory, Spenser, Shakespeare*, Cambridge, 1912, pp. 75–123, 262–3, 284.

28. Scudder, Vida D., *Le Morte Darthur of Sir Thomas Malory, A Study of the Book and its Sources*, London and New York 1921, 430 pp. [General account of the French and English Arthurian tradition before Malory followed by an appreciation of the *Morte Darthur*.]

29. Sommer, H. O., *Die Abenteuer Gawains, Ywains und Le Morholts mit den drei Jungfrauen* (*Beihefte zur Zeitschrift für romanische Philologie*, xlvii), Halle 1913, p. xxvii. [Brief comparison of Malory's pp. 140–51 with the corresponding section in MS. B.N. fr. 112.]

30. Trautman, Moritz, *Der Dichter Huchown und seine Werke* (Anglia, i, pp. 145–6). [Note on the source of Malory's Book V and on its relation to the alliterative *Morte Arthure*. Cf. *supra*, pp. 128 and 136.]

31. Vettermann, E., *Die Balen Dichtungen und ihre Quellen* (*Beihefte zur Zeitschrift für romanische Philologie*, lx), Halle, a. S., 1918, pp. 52–84 (*Malory's Book of Balyn the noble Knyght*). [Detailed account of the relation of Malory's Book II to its source with an interesting collation of parallel passages (pp. 67–70). Pp. 52–61 contain a résumé of various biographical data.]

32. Vinaver, E., *Le Roman de Tristan et Iseut dans l'œuvre de Thomas Malory*, Paris 1925, 244 pp. [Study of Malory's *Tristan* (Books VIII—XII) in relation to its French source.]

33. Warton, Thomas, *Observations on the Faerie Queene of Spenser*. London 1754, pp. 15–31. [Warton states that the *Morte Darthur* was 'translated into English from the French, by one Sir Thomas Maleory, Knight, and printed by W. Caxton, 1484' (*sic*), and proceeds to discuss Spenser's indebtedness to Malory. This is one of the first definite references to Malory's work in the eighteenth century.[1] In a footnote Warton adds: 'This Book was

---

[1] Caxton's Malory is described in Ames's *Typographical Antiquities* (1749), but it is only in Warton's book that the *Morte Darthur* enters into criticism.

reprinted twice or thrice. The last Edition is dated 1634.' On this remark *v. supra*, p. 192 note 3.]

34. Wechssler, Ed., *Ueber die verschiedene Redaktionen des Robert de Boron zugeschriebenen Graal-Lancelot Cyklus*, 1897, pp. 22–37. [Study of the origins of Malory's *Merlin* and *Lancelot*. Cf. *supra*, pp. 129, 149, and 153.]

35. Williams, T. W., Letter to the *Athenaeum*, No. 3585, pp. 64–5 (11 July 1896). [Note on a document which excluded 'Thomas Malorie, *miles*' from a general pardon in 1468. *V. supra*, p. 123.]

INDEX

208 INDEX

Vincent, Richard, 117.
— Robert, 117, 121.
— William, 121.
Virgin Birth, 79.
Vulson, see Colombière.
Vyrgyn Mary, Sainte Vierge, Sainte-Marie, 102, 174.

Wace, 16–17, 19, 85, 87, 88–90, 93.
Wales, Walys, Gal(l)es, 59, 125–7, 131, 143, 144, 176, 195.
Walker, R. H., 195.
Walker's English Classics, 192.
Wallensköld, Axel, 19.
Walter, Archdeacon of Oxford, 14, 15.
Walther, Marie, 56.
Warton, Thomas, 55, 113, 192, 197.
Warwick, 6, 120, 122; county of W., see Warwickshire.
Warwick, Richard Beauchamp Earl of, 2–4, 55, 116, 121, 138.
Warwick, Richard Neville Beauchamp Earl of, (the 'King-maker'), 4, 122.
Warwickshire, county of Warwick, comitatus Warwici, 1, 2, 7, 9, 116, 117, 120, 121, 123.
Wechssler, E., 129, 134, 148, 149, 153, 198.
Wells Cathedral, 123; see also Historical MSS. Commission.

Westminster, 6, 10, 13, 121, 189, 190, 194.
Weston, J. L., 26.
Whalley, Rev. P., 119.
Whittaker, 190, 194.
Wichemale, Sir John, 120.
Wilkinson, Thomas, 116, 117–18.
William of Malmesbury, 16.
Williams, T. W., 116, 123, 198.
Winchester, 13, 14.
Winwick(e), 117, 118, 120, 121.
Wlson (Vulson), see Colombière.
Wolfram von Eschenbach, 15.
Wrangham, Archdeacon, 191.
Wright, Thomas, 192, 193.
Wynkyn de Worde, 190–1, 193, 195.

Yorkists, 90.
Yorkshire, 116, 126.
Ysaïs, see Lysays.
Yseult, see Iseult.
Yvain (poem by Chrestien de Troyes), 20, 23, 43, 45.
Yvayns aus Blanches Meins, 36.
Yvayns li Granz, 36.
Ywain, 63, 132, 133, 134, 197.
Ywain and Gawain, 43.

Zeitschrift für französische Sprache und Literatur, 23, 31.
Zeitschrift für romanische Philologie, 23, 134, 197.